Airpower in Afghanistan 2005–10
The Air Commanders' Perspectives

Edited by

DAG HENRIKSEN

Lieutenant Colonel, Royal Norwegian Air Force
Royal Norwegian Air Force Academy

Foreword by

JAAP DE HOOP SCHEFFER

11th Secretary General of NATO, 2004–09

Air University Press
Air Force Research Institute
Maxwell Air Force Base, Alabama

Project Editor
Jerry L. Gantt

Copy Editor
Tammi K. Dacus

Cover Art, Book Design, and Illustrations
Daniel Armstrong

Composition and Prepress Production
Michele D. Harrell

Print Preparation and Distribution
Diane Clark

AIR FORCE RESEARCH INSTITUTE

AIR UNIVERSITY PRESS

Director and Publisher
Allen G. Peck

Editor in Chief
Oreste M. Johnson

Managing Editor
Demorah Hayes

Design and Production Manager
Cheryl King

Air University Press
155 N. Twining St., Bldg. 693
Maxwell AFB, AL 36112-6026
afri.aupress@us.af.mil

http://aupress.au.af.mil/
http://afri.au.af.mil/

Library of Congress Cataloging-in-Publication Data

Henriksen, Dag.
   Airpower in Afghanistan 2005-10 : the air commanders' perspectives / edited by Dag Henriksen, Lieutenant Colonel, Royal Norwegian Air Force, Royal Norwegian Air Force Academy ; foreword by Jaap De Hoop Scheffer, 11th Secretary General of NATO, 2004-09.
       pages cm
   Includes bibliographical references.
   ISBN 978-1-58566-235-7
   1. Afghan War, 2001—Aerial operations 2. Air power—Afghanistan—History—20th century. 3. Norway. Luftforsvaret—Foreign service—Afghanistan. 4. United States. Air Force—Foreign service—Afghanistan 5. Canada. Royal Canadian Air Force—Foreign service—Afghanistan 6. Afghan War, 2001—Participation, Norwegian. 7. Afghan War, 2001—Participation, Canadian. 8. Afghan War, 2001—Personal narratives. 9. Combined operations (Military science)—Afghanistan. I. Title.
   DS371.412.H46 2014
   958.104'748--dc23
                                                     2014038665

Published by Air University Press in November 2014

Disclaimer

AIR FORCE RESEARCH INSTITUTE

Contents

PART III

THE COUNTERINSURGENCY DEBATE

List of Figures

Figures

Foreword

Afghanistan has been a rewarding, complex, and challenging mission for all nations involved, not least for Afghanistan itself. Few, if any, anticipated that the initial attacks on the Taliban regime in Afghanistan in fall 2001 would become the longest war in the history of NATO and the United States of America. Today, more than 12 years later, it is still too early to conclude the successes and failures of this campaign or predict how Afghanistan will evolve once the majority of international military forces leave the country in 2014. In the end, it will be up to the Afghans themselves to make their own decisions, destiny, and future.

When I took office as the 11th secretary general of NATO in early 2004, the transatlantic wounds from the US invasion in Iraq in spring 2003 were still fresh. Many European nations rigorously opposed that war and felt the United States had manufactured the rational for the invasion. But the wounds healed sooner than I thought. In summer 2003, NATO assumed responsibility for the ISAF mission in Afghanistan, and I saw how NATO, through its commitments in Iraq and Afghanistan, gradually brought the allies together. Looking back at the Iraq war, I learned two important lessons: (1) whenever Europe presents itself as a counterweight for the United States, the result is a divided Europe, which saddens me as a European; and (2) a United States that thinks it can do it all alone is also doomed to fail. To a certain extent, these lessons guided my approach to Afghanistan in my numerous discussions and meetings with alliance members and representatives from the wider international community. Afghanistan was always going to be a team effort if we were to succeed.

If anything, the international effort in Afghanistan has required patience. Patience with the political process of NATO and its member nations; patience with the government in Afghanistan and its capability to address the many challenges of its nation; patience in transforming our mentality, structures, and organizations to adhere to the comprehensive approach we all knew was a prerequisite for success; patience with the political dynamics of Western governments seeking quick and identifiable results, as opposed to the conventional wisdom of counterinsurgencies that prolonged time is often required and results seem to have a pace and presentation style of their own; patience from our domestic constituencies, which year after year saw an ever increasing accumulated number of their service men and women sacrificing their lives and limbs without a clear end state or exit strategy in sight.

The handling of Afghanistan should be seen as a process. In the early twenty-first century, NATO forces were not adequately prepared, trained, educated, and equipped to fight a counterinsurgency in mountainous Afghanistan. International and security politics literally changed overnight after 9/11. It had taken years to change our mentality and international structures after the Cold War a decade earlier, and in many ways we were still in that transformational mode when the airplanes hit the Twin Towers and Pentagon. Adapting to the new situation and the war in Afghanistan (and Iraq) needed time. I sometimes felt the often harsh criticism of our efforts in Afghanistan did not reflect that reality.

When evaluating our efforts, there are positives and negatives that need to be addressed. Surely a commonly agreed upon and cohesive strategy of how to handle Afghanistan took too long to develop. With Iraq draining much of the US resources, Afghanistan for years did not receive the resources and political attention this difficult operation needed to make the progress we all wanted for this nation. For years the operation was an allied patchwork of individual nations being responsible for PRTs and provinces without a sufficient overarching allied cohesive effort. It proved difficult to implement the theoretical construct of a comprehensive approach to real-life challenges in theater. The Afghan ability to deal with corruption, narcotics, and governmental competencies has proved less efficient and more challenging than first expected. Although these efforts have had dedicated operational lines since 2006, achieving the level of "security," "governance and reconstruction," and "development" we all strived for has proved very difficult. None of these issues had its origins in ill will, lack of empathy with the Afghans, or lack of dedication. Sometimes it is just hard to succeed.

Conversely, there is no doubt that progress has been made. The influence of al-Qaeda in the theater has diminished significantly. Democratic elections have been held, a government elected, a parliament formed, and a constitution adopted. Infrastructure has been strengthened, and the Afghan economy is much stronger today than before the international involvement. Basic health care in Afghanistan has improved dramatically, and education is now a norm for millions of Afghan children. Women's status has improved in Afghanistan, and the millions of young girls attending school compared to the pre–9/11 situation is perhaps the most heartening success of all progress made in this country. The number and competence of the Afghan National Security Forces (ANSF) are increased to a level that hopefully soon enables them to provide basic security and stability for Afghanistan. This is a fundamental for any nation. It is a basic foundation to ensure the long-term economic and political investments necessary to meet the expectations of most Afghans and enable Afghanistan to face the challenges of a volatile and increasingly economic competitive region. Educating, mentoring, and growing its military and police forces to be better positioned to provide basic security and the rule of law will perhaps be our most significant contribution and legacy.

As the ISAF and OEF mission comes to an end in 2014, it is time to identify the lessons we have learned after more than a decade of war. Airpower has been a necessary but controversial military tool in this war. The general proficiency of US and NATO airpower is outstanding, as proven in the 1991 Gulf War, the Balkans, Iraq, Afghanistan, and Libya. In Afghanistan it played a pivotal role in protecting our own forces and shaping the battlefield. No doubt insurgent forces learned a lesson in fall 2001 and found it tactically unsustainable to mass large forces to effectively attack allied ground forces—they knew massing forces would provide an easy target for attack helicopters, drones, fighters, and bombers. By influencing the opponent and protecting our own forces, airpower became a protector of our own center of gravity: the will by individual nations to sustain troop contributions in Afghanistan.

Still, it is no secret that the high number of civilian casualties generated a perception in Afghanistan and elsewhere that airpower was a particularly indiscriminate military tool, which threatened allied cohesion as well as the counterinsurgency credo of "winning hearts and minds." In reality, the civilian casualties attributed to airpower were likely unfair, as both artillery shells and insurgent propaganda inflated the claim of airpower's collateral damage effects. And I know from countless briefings in theater what extraordinary measures were taken to avoid civilian casualties. Still, the perception of airpower as a threat to Afghan civilians has remained a political and military challenge for NATO and the United States.

Thus, I welcome a book that invites a deeper reflection on this technologically advanced, diverse, lethal, and influential military capability. I am particularly pleased that this is not merely a tactical evaluation, but rather sees airpower in the context of broader political goals, military strategy, and operational planning. The employment of modern military force must be seen in light of the broader context of politics (legitimacy), international law (legality), and strategy as being but one of many sources of power to influence the situation at hand. This is perhaps particularly important in a counterinsurgency operation like Afghanistan.

The international effort in Afghanistan is not yet over. Although the main efforts of the ISAF nations are coming to an end, the journey of the modern Afghan nation has barely begun. A lot of sacrifices have been made on behalf of the Afghan people the past decade, and more sacrifices will be made in the years to come. I pay tribute to the men and women who have served in Afghanistan and their families. For all of us who have been deeply involved in this war, I trust we can look back on this colossal effort one day and agree it was worth it. A part of that premise is that we should learn as much as possible from our efforts, continue to refine what worked, and ensure we do not make the same mistakes in future conflicts. I hope this book can contribute to this end.

Jaap de Hoop Scheffer
Minister of Foreign Affairs,
The Netherlands, 2002–03
11th Secretary General of NATO, 2004–09

Author Biographies

Major General Jaap Willemse

Maj Gen Jaap Willemse graduated in 1979 from the Netherlands Royal Military Academy, majoring in business economics. He received his flying training at Sheppard AFB, Texas, and became an operational NF-5 pilot with the 316th Squadron at Gilze-Rijen Air Base and 314th Squadron at Eindhoven Air Base. Following his transition to the F-104G in 1983 he was posted to Volkel Air Base. After converting to the F-16 in 1984 he became a weapons instructor and flight commander. From 1989 till 1992 he was stationed at Sheppard  AFB, Texas. After a tour in 1992 at the Fighter Branch at the Royal Netherlands Air Force (RNLAF) Headquarters, he was appointed commander of the 306th Reconnaissance Squadron and was involved in its deployment as part of the RNLAF detachment at Villafranca Air Base, Italy, during Operation Deny Flight. He attended the Advanced Staff Officers' Course at the Netherlands Defence College in 1995. He was appointed commander of the 312th Fighter-Bomber Strike Squadron in 1997 and was tasked with the command of the combined Dutch/Belgium Deployable Air Task Force operating from Villafranca, where the unit was joined by Norwegian and Danish F-16s for Operation Determined Falcon. In August 1998 Major General Willemse was appointed commanding officer at Leeuwarden Air Base and was responsible for the deployment of the Leeuwarden F-16-AM detachment for Operation Allied Force. He became deputy director of material for projects and weapon systems at the RNLAF Headquarters in 2001. In June 2004 he was appointed deputy commander of the Combined Air Operations Center 2 Germany. From August 2005 till February 2006 he was deployed to Kabul, Afghanistan, as the deputy commander of the NATO-led ISAF mission. In September 2006, he assumed the position of vice chairman to the NATO Air Defence Committee and the NACMO Board of Directors, responsible for the oversight of NATO air defense policy and the execution of the NATO air command and control system program. In July 2009, Major General Willemse was assigned as assistant chief of staff for command, control, communications, computers, and intelligence (ACOS C4I) at Allied Command Transformation, Norfolk, Virginia. Maj Gen Jaap "Grey" Willemse retired from the RNLAF in August 2012 as a command pilot with more than 2,500 flying hours in T-38, NF-5, F-104G, and F-16AM aircraft. Today he is an independent consultant specializing in aviation and interim management.

Lieutenant General Allen G. Peck

Lt Gen Allen G. Peck earned his commission upon graduation from the US Air Force Academy in 1975. He served as an F-15 aircraft commander, instructor pilot, and standardization and evaluation flight examiner. General Peck completed two tours on the Air Staff at the Pentagon and a joint assignment as chief of current operations at US Central Command and was a national security fellow at Harvard. The general commanded an air operations group in Germany, an air expeditionary wing in Saudi Arabia, and the Air and Space Expeditionary Force Center. General Peck was a key planner for the Kosovo air operation and served in the Vicenza combined air operations center as the chief of combat plans during the subsequent NATO-led campaign. He later served with the commander of Air Force forces at the USCENTCOM combined air operations center during the opening phase of Operation Iraqi Freedom. As USCENTCOM's deputy combined force air component commander 2005–06, he oversaw planning, tasking, execution, and assessment of coalition air operations for Operations Iraqi Freedom and Enduring Freedom. The general is a command pilot with more than 2,700 hours in the F-15, including more than 300 combat hours. His last assignment, prior to retiring in October 2011, was as commander of Air University, Maxwell AFB, Alabama. General Peck served as a senior mentor in the USAF Operational Command Training Program, participating in joint war games, exercises, and general/flag officer–level war-fighting courses. He currently serves as civilian director of the Air Force Research Institute at Maxwell AFB.

Major General Charles S. "Duff" Sullivan

Major General Sullivan enrolled in the Canadian Forces in 1979 and received his pilot wings in 1981. His first assignment as a military pilot was to instruct on jet aircraft. On completion of his fighter pilot training on the CF-5 and F-18 Hornet in 1986, he was posted to Baden-Sollingen, Germany, as a combat-ready multirole fighter pilot. During his air force career, he accumulated more than 3,500 flying hours in jet aircraft, 1,600 of which were flown in the CF-18 Hornet in the ground attack and air superiority role. He has flown operational missions over Europe, the Persian Gulf, Bosnia, Croatia, Kosovo, Canada's high Arctic, and the North Atlantic, and served as a forward air controller in support of the United Nation's protection force in the Balkans in 1994–95. He has commanded a Tactical Air Control Party, a CF-18 fighter squadron, an air force fighter wing and main operating base, and NATO's air component during combat operations in Afghanistan. Duff has also served in several senior executive and high-profile leadership positions throughout his career, most notably as Director-General of Capability Development at National Defence Headquarters in Ottawa, Senior Defence Advisor in the Prime Minister of Canada's Privy Council Office, and Director of Operations for the Canadian NORAD Region during 9/11 and the G8 Summit in Kananaskis, Alberta. In 2009 Duff served at the rank of major general on a 12-month tour of duty in Afghanistan in three high-profile leadership positions: Commander of NATO's Air Component, Director of ISAF's Air Component Element, and Deputy Chief of ISAF joint operations. On completion of his assignment in Afghanistan, Duff elected to take an early retirement from the military to focus on being a better husband and father to his young and active family. Retiring at the height of his career was made more difficult when Canada's Chief of Defence offered him a promotion and the opportunity to command

Canada's air force. On returning from Afghanistan, Duff joined Canada's Air Navigation Service Provider as the Chief of Operational Safety Oversight. Outside of normal working hours, he is an active hockey and soccer dad for his three children and is involved in public speaking and mentoring on leadership and ethics, command safety oversight and risk management methodologies, command, and coalition and full-spectrum joint operations.

Major General William L. Holland

Maj Gen William L. Holland entered the Air Force in 1976 after receiving his commission through the ROTC program at East Carolina University. He became an A-10 pilot in 1981. He was the chief, standardization and evaluation; chief, weapons and tactics; and flight commander, 25th Fighter Squadron, Suwon Air Base, South Korea (1984–86); commander, A-10 Division, Air Force Fighter Weapons School, Nellis AFB, Nevada (1991–93); commander, 4406th Operations Group, Southwest Asia (1996–97); director, plans and operations, and deputy director, combined air operations center, Vicenza, Italy (1997–99); commander, 51st Fighter Wing, Osan AB, South Korea (2002–03); and director, air and space expeditionary force matters, and deputy chief of staff for air and space operations, Headquarters US Air Force, Washington, DC (2003–06). He was USCENTCOM's deputy combined force air component commander from 2006 to 2007. In 2007 he became the vice commander, Ninth Air Force, and deputy commander, US Air Forces Central, Shaw AFB, South Carolina. He became the commander, Ninth Air Force, Air Combat Command, Shaw AFB, in 2009 and held this position until he retired 1 December 2010 after 34 years of service. Major General Holland is a command pilot with 2,500 flying hours. He is currently employed by the city and county of Sumter, South Carolina, as the executive director of the Shaw-Sumter Partnership for Progress. He is also the executive coordinator for the Military Base Task Force chartered by the governor of

South Carolina. He serves on several boards in Sumter, throughout the state, and at his alma mater, East Carolina University.

Lieutenant General Frederik H. Meulman

Lt Gen Frederik H. Meulman completed his training at the Royal Military Academy in Breda, the Netherlands, in 1975, after which he held a number of positions with the Fifth Guided Missile Group in Germany. From 1988 to 1990, he attended the Advanced Staff Course at the Royal Netherlands Air Force Staff College. He was then posted to the Airpower Research Institute in the College for Aerospace Doctrine, Research and Education at Air University, Maxwell AFB, in the United States. He was subsequently posted to the RNLAF Staff College at the Netherlands Defence College as a lecturer in airpower. From 1993 to 1995, Meulman was assigned to the defense concepts division of the Netherlands Ministry of Defence, followed by the appointment as head of the operational plans and requirements of the Directorate of Operations, Tactical Air Force. From 1998 to 2000, then-Colonel Meulman was commander of the Guided Missile Group at De Peel Air Base. In 2000, he was posted to the Defence Staff as head of the Military-Strategic Affairs Division. One year later, in 2001, he moved to the position of deputy director of the Military Intelligence and Security Service and was promoted to the rank of air commodore. In 2003, then–Major General Meulman became deputy commander of the Combined Air Operations Centre in Kalkar (CAOC 2). From June 2004 to the end of 2006, he was the deputy commander of the Royal Netherlands Air Force. From January 2007 until February 2008, Meulman held the position of deputy commander–Air at the ISAF headquarters in Kabul, Afghanistan. On 3 March 2008, he was appointed deputy chief of defense and was promoted to lieutenant general. As of 15 April 2010, he was the Netherlands' permanent military representative to NATO and the EU Military Committee in Brussels. Lieutenant General Meulman retired from the RNLAF on 1 June 2013.

Major General Maurice H. "Maury" Forsyth

Maj Gen Maury Forsyth was commissioned in 1978 through the Air Force ROTC at South Dakota State University where he earned a bachelor of science degree in microbiology. The general completed undergraduate navigator training in 1979 (F-4 weapons systems officer) and undergraduate pilot training in 1984. He was an F-15 instructor pilot/mission commander from December 1984 until December 1987, serving as chief of squadron scheduling and flight commander, 12th TFS, Kadena AB, Japan. He was commander, Combined Force Air Component, Combined Task Force, Operation Northern Watch, Incirlik AB, Turkey (1999–2001); commander, USAFE Theater Air and Space Operations Center, Headquarters USAFE, Ramstein AB, Germany (2001–03); commander, 51st Fighter Wing, Osan AB, Republic of Korea (2003–05); and deputy director for Global Operations (J39), Operations Directorate, the Joint Staff, Washington, DC (2005–07). From June 2007 until June 2008 he was USCENTCOM's deputy combined force air component commander. With more than 3,500 total flight hours and 730 combat hours, General Forsyth has served in Operations Desert Storm, Southern Watch, Northern Watch, Enduring Freedom, and Iraqi Freedom. He has commanded two squadrons, a combined force air component, two centers, and a fighter wing. Additionally, he has served on the headquarters staffs of Tactical Air Command, Air Combat Command, Allied Air Forces North, NATO, US Air Forces in Europe, and the Joint Staff. In 2008 he became commandant of the Air War College at Maxwell AFB, and in 2010, commander of the Curtis E. LeMay Center for Doctrine Development and Education and vice commander, Air University, Maxwell AFB. Major General Forsyth retired from the US Air Force on 1 October 2010. He is currently the 10th president of Randolph-Macon Academy in Front Royal, Virginia.

Lieutenant General Jouke L. H. Eikelboom

Lt Gen Jouke L. H. Eikelboom started his military career as an officer cadet at the Dutch Royal Military Academy in Breda in 1975. Upon graduation, he went to Canada for his military pilot training and continued in the NF-5 at Twenthe Air Base in the Netherlands. In 1981 he transferred to Leeuwarden Air Base to fly the F-16. He is a fighter weapons school graduate and a flying instructor and has worked on improvements for pilot training and exercises for F-16 pilots over a number of years. As commanding officer of 323 Squadron, he was closely involved in the establishment of the Dutch Fighter Weapons School. In 1992 Lieutenant General Eikelboom attended the Advanced Staff Course at the Netherlands Defence College. From July 1993 to February 1995 he was based at the Royal Netherlands Air Force Headquarters in The Hague, first at the Operational Plans Directorate and subsequently as the chief of operations and training within the Fighter Branch. In January 1995 he was posted to Leeuwarden Air Base as wing commander. During this posting he was deployed to Italy, in April 1995, as the detachment commander of an F-16 unit at Villafranca Air Base, as part of Operation Deny Flight. In summer of 1995 he and his pilots flew many combat missions in the air campaign Deliberate Force over Bosnia. In September 1996 Lieutenant General Eikelboom was posted to Italy again at Vicenza as battle staff director at the NATO air force headquarters for the Bosnia operations. In March 1997 he was stationed in Washington, DC, as the first representative of the Netherlands at the Joint Strike Fighter Program Office. Lieutenant General Eikelboom was posted to Volkel Air Base as the commander (1999–2002); in November 2001 he was a member of the CENTCOM international airfield survey team in Tajikistan, Kazakhstan, and Kyrgyzstan in support of Operation Enduring Freedom. He was stationed at CENTCOM as a senior national representative of the Netherlands for Operation Enduring Freedom (2002), and upon his return to the Netherlands in 2002, he took the position of deputy chief of staff for operational requirements at the Air Force Headquarters in The Hague. In January 2004 he was appointed deputy chief of staff for plans and policy for the RNLAF, and in mid-2005 he deployed to Afghanistan as contingent commander for the Netherlands armed forces in Afghanistan. He was appointed director of operations for the chief of defense responsible for the strategy and planning of operations (2005–07), and in 2008 he took the position as director for air operations at Headquarters ISAF in Kabul. General Eikelboom assumed his NATO appointment as chief of staff, Allied Joint Force Command Headquarters Brunssum on 2 September 2009. After 36 years of service, he retired from the Royal Netherlands Air Force in March 2012. Today he is CEO of the European Network for Cyber Security.

Major General Douglas L. Raaberg

Maj Gen Douglas L. Raaberg is a 1978 honor graduate of the US Air Force Academy. He has held numerous operational, command, and staff positions. He was a KC-135A copilot and aircraft commander (1979–83) and then flew the FB-111A (1983–87). He later became a B-1B aircraft commander, instructor pilot, and operations officer, 9th Bomb Squadron, Dyess AFB, Texas (1991–93), and then the commander, 9th Bomb Squadron (1993–95). Other positions include political-military plan-  ner, Middle East/Africa Division, Directorate of Strategic Plans and Policy (J5), Joint Staff, the Pentagon, Washington, DC (1996–98); commander, 509th Bomb Wing, Whiteman AFB, Montana (2002–04); deputy director of operations, US Central Command, MacDill AFB, Florida (2004–06); and director of air and space operations, Headquarters Air Combat Command, Langley AFB, Virginia (2006–08). He was USCENTCOM's deputy combined force air component commander in 2008–09. General Raaberg was responsible for humanitarian assistance and disaster relief operations for the 2005 earthquake victims in Pakistan. While commanding the Air Force's only B-2 stealth bomber wing during Operation Iraqi Freedom, he executed the first overseas forward deployment of the B-2 and then sustained combat missions from two locations. He commanded the 7th

Operations Group when the B-1B employed in combat for the first time in Iraq. The general holds the world record for the fastest non-stop flight around the globe with refueling in the B-1. He is a command pilot with more than 4,700 flying hours, primarily in the FB-111, B-1, and B-2. He flew 35 combat missions in support of Operation Enduring Freedom and ISAF in Afghanistan. Major General Douglas L. Raaberg retired from the Air Force on 1 January 2010. Today he is an executive in the aerospace industry.

Lieutenant General Stephen L. Hoog

Lt Gen Stephen L. Hoog is a 1979 distinguished graduate of the US Air Force Academy. He has served as an F-16 aircraft commander, instructor pilot, and weapons chief, as well as F-16 instructor and academic department head for the Fighter Weapons Instructor Course, Nellis AFB, Nevada. He has been a student at the Marine Corps Command and General Staff College (1990–91); commander, 555th Fighter Squadron, Aviano AB, Italy (1994–96); student at the Air War College, Maxwell AFB, Alabama (1996–97); chief, weapons division, Secretary of the Air Force Office of International Affairs, Washington, DC (1997–99); commander, 388th Fighter Wing, Hill AFB, Utah (2001–03); commander, Air and Space Expeditionary Force Center, Air Combat Command, Langley AFB, Virginia (2004–06); director, Air Component Coordination Element, Multinational Force–Iraq (2006–07); commander, 57th Wing, Nellis AFB (2007–08); commander, US Air Force Warfare Center, Nellis AFB (2008–09); deputy commander, US Air Forces Central Command; deputy combined force air component commander, US Central Command; vice commander, 9th Air Expeditionary Task Force, Air Combat Command, Southwest Asia (2009–10); and commander, Ninth Air Force, Air Combat Command, Shaw AFB (2010–11). General Hoog is a command pilot with more than 3,000 flying hours, including 181 combat hours over Bosnia and Iraq. He was commander, Alaskan Command, US Pacific Command; commander, Eleventh Air

Force, Pacific Air Forces; and commander, Alaskan North American Aerospace Defense Command Region, Joint Base Elmendorf-Richardson, Alaska, prior to assuming his current duties as assistant vice chief of staff and director, Air Staff, Headquarters US Air Force, Washington, DC.

Lieutenant Colonel Dag Henriksen

Lt Col Dag Henriksen enlisted in the Royal Norwegian Air Force (RNoAF) at the age of 19 in 1991. He specialized in air battle management (fighter controller, fighter/SAM allocator, weapons allocator) and served at Control and Reporting Centre (CRC) Reitan (1996–99) and Sørreisa (2001–03). He served in NATO operations in the Baltics (Baltic Accession) in 2005 and in Afghanistan (airspace manager, combined joint operations center, ISAF HQ) in 2007. He graduated from the RNoAF Academy in 2001 and is a graduate of the Norwegian Defence Command and Staff College in Oslo (2009–10). He served almost a year as an exchange officer to the US Air Force Research Institute (AFRI), Maxwell AFB, in 2012. He has studied political science and history at the Norwegian University of Science and Technology (NTNU) in Trondheim, Norway, and has a PhD in military studies from the University of Glasgow, United Kingdom. He has been a senior lecturer in airpower at the RNoAF Academy from 2003 onward. In January 2013 he became the head of the Department of Airpower and Technology at the RNoAF Academy. Henriksen published the book, *NATO's Gamble: Combining Diplomacy and Airpower in the Kosovo Crisis, 1998–1999*, in 2007 and has written a number of articles on the cohesion between political goals, military strategy, operational planning, and the tactical use of airpower in Kosovo, Afghanistan, Israel, and Libya. He lives with his family in Trondheim, Norway.

Acknowledgments

This book would not have been published had it not been for the trust and confidence invested in me by the contributing generals. They had no official duty or requirement to provide their experiences, insight, thoughts, and perspectives on the use of airpower in Afghanistan, but opted to do so. For that I will always be grateful. I hope the end result does them as much credit as they deserve.

Neither would this book have been published had it not been for the "silent backing" of the Royal Norwegian Air Force (RNoAF) leadership in general and the intellectual tradition of the RNoAF Academy in particular. For the past 20 years, the leadership of the RNoAF has provided resources to build a small but very competent airpower community. They have done so without putting any intellectual restrictions on the analytical work performed by the men and women at the RNoAF Academy and have regularly praised the often critical books and articles stemming from this institution. Largely due to this framework of resources and analytical leverage, the culture within the RNoAF Academy has stimulated academic research and development and explicitly articulated the ambition of providing publications for a wider international audience. As such, this book stands on the shoulders of the tradition, discussions, and work originating from my friends and colleagues at this institution the past two decades.

This book was largely written and edited during my stay at the US Air Force Research Institute (AFRI) at Maxwell AFB, Alabama, in 2012. I would like to thank the people at AFRI, the Air University Press, and the wider Air University community for their hospitality and inclusiveness. I will always remember my year in Montgomery with great affection.

Conversely, I would like to thank the RNoAF and the RNoAF Academy for identifying the value of a stronger academic relationship with the US Air Force and providing the time and resources for me and my family to have a year to focus on research, development, and academic cooperation. It has not only provided the opportunity to get better acquainted with the predominant academic institution of the US Air Force, Air University, but also the internal dynamics of the United States as a nation. It has been a truly unique experience I will always treasure.

Sincere gratitude goes to my friend and then dean of the US Air Force Research Institute, Dr. Dan Mortensen, for providing

ACKNOWLEDGEMENTS

much-needed comments, thoughts, and insights to this manuscript. The book is better for his contribution.

I would like to thank my colleagues Ole Jørgen Maaø and Nils E. Naastad for providing thoughtful comments to my epilogue chapter. A particular thanks goes to Øistein Espenes, who despite his busy schedule agreed to contribute his perspectives and analysis of this manuscript. As the manuscript started to materialize, he was diagnosed with a serious illness. Despite my insistence that he focus all his energy on getting well, he pledged that he would contribute as much as his strength allowed him to do in between hospital surgery and treatment. I am honored for all his contributions and hope I can one day return the favor.

Finally, and most importantly, my most profound gratitude goes to my family: Anne Katrine, Maren, and August. You provide the love, meaning, and direction I need to live a full life. I can merely hope I manage to convey my love, warmth, and gratitude back to you in a manner that allows you to understand how fundamental and important you all are in my life.

Lt Col Dag Henriksen, RNoAF
US Air Force Research Institute
Maxwell AFB, Alabama
15 December 2012

Introduction

Although there will be a US/NATO presence in Afghanistan for years to come, the International Security Assistance Force (ISAF) is history. On 1 January 2015, the ISAF mission ended and transitioned to the significantly more limited NATO-led Resolute Support Mission. It has been the longest war in the history of both NATO and the United States. It has been the most challenging political and military effort in the history of NATO. The operation has challenged structures, doctrines, and perceptions on every level of war. Immense sacrifices have been made in treasure and casualties. Although both the United States and NATO will leave military advisors and a certain capability intact in Afghanistan and within the larger theater of operations, it is clear that the thrust of the international community's military effort is over. The time has come for addressing the larger lessons of this war.

A growing body of literature is dedicated to the task of understanding the reason or rationale for the United States' and the international community's involvement in Afghanistan. This includes important books and articles that analyze the international context and political processes creating the conditions for the use of force in Afghanistan and debate the political dynamics and decisions of this endeavor. This book, however, is not focusing on the "whys and hows" of entering this war, or any normative evaluation of the wisdom behind the decision to go to war, or the strategy chosen. Rather it seeks to describe and explain the actual use of military force in Afghanistan and the context and dynamics that influenced and governed this use of force once the decision was made to engage there militarily. It seeks to provide insight and understanding of the processes influencing the cohesion between political goals, military strategy, operational planning, and the actual tactical execution of force as perceived and implemented in theater at the time. While the international effort has increasingly entailed a comprehensive approach with a clear civilian (involving various instruments of power) and military component, the military component—the actual use of force—within a landlocked country like Afghanistan has mainly consisted of land forces (including special operations) and airpower (including carrier-based aircraft). This book seeks to address the latter military component and bring forward the larger lessons, challenges, and dynamics related to the use of airpower.

The reader should not consider this book merely a narrow insight into the peculiarities of airpower, as most of the content addresses issues at the strategic and operational level of war with roots and ramifications far outside the airpower community. This book is arguably equally important as a testimony of NATO/ISAF's and the United States' approach to war and the broader challenges of alliance/coalition warfare.

Critical analyses of the broader features of airpower are, unfortunately, few and far between. The airpower community has traditionally overfocused on its tactical execution and had less robust intellectual roots in the operational and strategic levels of war. This has influenced the literature provided by airmen, who tend to lean largely toward technology, platforms, and a more tactical outlook. Thus, one can perhaps argue that the greatest strength of the airpower community is also its greatest weakness: its cultural emphasis on tactical execution of air operations has produced a very high level of professionalism at the tactical level. Conversely, it has not been able to establish a similarly robust culture for addressing the strategic and operational challenges of war. This has precluded some important debates and lessons of a more overarching and strategic nature that would have proved beneficial to the men and women sent to lead our effort in Afghanistan. Airpower should be debated, it should be critically analyzed, and the lessons should be brought forward to help us better prepare for war in the future. If anything, this book is a somewhat sad commentary on the air, land, and joint communities' lack of intellectual and organizational ability to identify and implement basic airpower lessons from the past.

Airpower has arguably been the key asymmetric strength for NATO/ISAF and the United States in theater but also a source of friction for the local population, the Karzai government, and, increasingly, the domestic civilian population in many countries engaged in Afghanistan. It appears to have been the number one killer of insurgents but also caused collateral damage and civilian casualties to an extent that influenced the "center of gravity" defined as the Afghan people by a number of commanders in Afghanistan, thereby influencing the political dynamics of this operation. Airpower has significantly contributed to reducing the loss of our own soldiers in combat and thus protecting NATO/ISAF and the US center of gravity: the political will to continue its engagement in Afghanistan. So, when ISAFs deputy commander–Air in 2007–08, Gen Frederik H. Meulman, argues that "without airpower in Afghanistan—the mission is doomed to fail," he is arguably as correct as the commander, ISAF (COMISAF) 2009–10, Gen Stanley McChrystal, who argued that due to civilian casualties and its political implications, "air power contains the seeds of our own destruction if we do not use it responsibly."

Many airmen perceive airpower as having been reduced to an inflexible close air support "911 emergency call" for troops in contact with the enemy in a very land-centric military environment. Some informally argue that the airpower community, as well as the political and military establishments of most countries involved, was caught off guard with the engagement in a rural country with limited resources and infrastructure while too focused on and accustomed to the advantages many perceived airpower provided in the 1990s. As a consequence, we entered this war without adequate equipment, training, education, or doctrines to fight an asymmetric threat in what increasingly became a difficult counterinsurgency campaign. Others claim the use of airpower—and indeed the use of military force more generally—has suffered from the lack of a clear political and military overarching strategy for Afghanistan. There seems, however, to be a reasonable consensus that airpower has been a very important military tool in this conflict, that this military tool has not been exploited to its full potential, and that there has been too limited a focus on how airpower more broadly can contribute to a counterinsurgency operation of this nature.

An important foundation for this analysis is that this book is not limited to airpower alone. It would be a mistake to separate the use of airpower from the overarching political ambition and military strategy of this war, or the combination of other sources of power, if the most important lessons regarding the use of airpower in Afghanistan are to be identified and brought forward. As noted, the intent is rather explicitly to seek to evaluate and explain to what degree there has been adequate cohesion among political goals, military strategy, operational planning, and the tactical use of airpower; to focus on what airpower has influenced in Afghanistan; and—perhaps more important in this particular war—to examine what has influenced the use of airpower. I argue that only by including the context, dynamics, and processes influencing its use will it be possible to analyze and explain the role of airpower in a constructive and informative manner.

I asked the former air commanders in Afghanistan to provide their perspectives to let those responsible for utilizing airpower in this war describe what they experienced every day in theater regarding the overall cohesion—to let them bring forward the most important lessons they have identified. This is the strength of the book but also its weakness. The strength relates to the fact that these few individuals had the greatest oversight of the use of airpower in Afghanistan. They were involved in the debates, processes, and decisions at the time, and are better positioned than anyone else to explain the dynamics influencing the use of airpower. With one exception, they have all retired from the military and are thus less restricted by protocol or other considerations affecting a serving officer. The weakness stems from the fact that their views will be more similar to that of a memoir than an academic analysis. This book is the product of air commanders debating the issues from personal angles and perspectives, and what you see is largely dependent on where you stand. It has a more subjective nature than the ideal objective textbook approach. Memory is often selective, and recollections risk influence by vanity and the desire to project one's own influence and perspectives at the time as better or more informed than it actually was. Sometimes, it is just difficult to remember what actually happened five, six, seven, or more years ago. As one air commander pointed out regarding his own ability to contribute to this project, smiling, "If I knew there was going to be a test, I would have taken notes."

The book limits itself to the time period 2005–10. I could have included other parts of this war. The use of airpower in fall 2001 is of great significance to the political and military progress made in Afghanistan at the time. Its role in Operation Anaconda in 2002 easily could have deserved an entire chapter. The constant, tireless effort of air transport has been a precondition for the war effort for years. Still, the greatest political and military change in the international community's approach to Afghanistan after the operation commenced was NATO/ISAF taking over responsibility of Regional Commands South and East in summer/fall 2006. From then on, and as the Iraq War winded down, troop numbers in Afghanistan grew significantly—as did the political and military importance and prestige of this war. Afghanistan gradually became the most significant military engagement for both NATO and the United States.

This takeover is a logical starting point for the book. I chose, however, to start one year prior, in 2005, to include the lead up to this takeover. The resources, focus, and outlook in 2005 signify in many ways the level of effort that had motored on for years in Afghanistan and a point of departure for a situation that would rapidly change. This was the year that more detailed planning started for ISAF to assume responsibility for the entirety of Afghanistan. NATO/ISAF and the United States went from a limited approach and relatively slow pace in Afghanistan to a steep increase in air and ground activity in the subsequent years. As depicted by the statistics in the appendix, the use of airpower dramatically increased from 2006 onward. I argue that it is important to include the year preceding the takeover to fully understand the structures, level of resources, and mentality of both NATO/ISAF and the United States that would mark the strengths and weaknesses of this transition in the ensuing years.

The scope of the book ends in summer 2010. On 1 December 2009, Pres. Barack Obama delivered a speech at the US Military Academy at West Point which in effect signified the beginning of the end to NATO's and the US military's engagement in Afghanistan. The subsequent year, during its 2010 summit in Lisbon, NATO formally adopted the timeline to hand over the responsibility for security to the Afghan National Security Forces (ANSF). By continuing through 2010, the book covers the initial "surge," the role and influence of Gen Stanley McChrystal as COMISAF, and the beginning of Gen David Petraeus's tenure in that role. It gives insight into the counterinsurgency debate that had influenced the use of force in Afghanistan for years and the role of airpower in this regard. The last air commander of ISAF represented in this book is Lt Gen "Duff" Sullivan. When he left office in November 2009, the ISAF Joint Command (IJC) was established. With the war in Iraq winding down, the subsequent US force buildup and increased influence in Afghanistan, the Obama administration coming into office, and the establishment of the IJC, a new chapter in the saga of airpower in Afghanistan was in the making from 2010 onward. Combined with the need to stop at a healthy distance from ongoing operations, this proved to be a logical time frame to end this project.

Another argument for choosing the period 2005–10 is because, I would propose, these were the formative years of airpower in Afghanistan as we know it today. This period entails a dramatic and unparalleled increase in air operations. During this period, the insurgents moved back in theater and challenged NATO/ISAF and US forces to the degree that eventually a surge was necessary to avoid losing even more ground and to enable a better transition of responsibility to the Afghans. It is the period with the greatest political and military uncertainties and challenges for the NATO alliance—an alliance which suddenly found itself in a counterinsurgency it was largely unprepared to fight and without a clear military strategy, end state, or defined date for withdrawal. It is the period that shapes the broader structures and application of airpower in Afghanistan. Without in any way diminishing the challenges in Afghanistan before 2005 and/ or from 2010 onward, and acknowledging that there have been important organizational and procedural changes in this latter period, I would argue that the main overarching structures and guidance for the application of airpower—the larger issues of air infrastructure, procedures, and command and control in theater—largely had been argued, devised, tested, evaluated, and put in place by summer 2010. This book seeks to portray the processes, dynamics, and decisions of this formative period.

The use of airpower in Afghanistan has always been dominated by the United States. The overwhelming resources of the US Central Command Air Forces (CENTAF), their experience and competence, their command and control infrastructure, and their combined air operations center (CAOC) at Al Udeid, Qatar, have exerted immense influence on this operation. But the role and influence of the air organization at ISAF headquarters in Kabul, Afghanistan, has increased significantly over the years. While it has sometimes been difficult to distinguish the use of airpower within the ISAF framework from efforts in the US Operation Enduring Freedom construct, the perspectives from both actors are important to have the full picture of airpower's role in theater. This has proven to be a useful dynamic for this book. The air commander of ISAF and the in-theater air commander from CENTCOM were asked to review the same time period, with all its events, contexts, dynamics, and debates. Having both sides present their lessons and perspectives offers the reader two distinct views on the often difficult processes and dynamics. By following the evolution of both CENTAF and ISAF in Afghanistan and how various air commanders view the rationale, foundation, and lessons from these changes, the reader has the opportunity to see the longer lines on the use of airpower in this conflict and to view these lines of thought as they were perceived at the time.

I have divided the book into three parts. Part I, "The Status of the International Community's Military Engagement in Afghanistan, 2005–06," seeks to establish a certain point of departure for the use of airpower. It provides the outlook from ISAF Air and CENTAF in a period of relative calm and before ISAF takes over the largely more challenging regions in the South and East. It describes the situation when ISAF starts planning for the takeover and what its emphasis was at the time. It similarly provides the perspective of CENTAF, for which Afghanistan was a limited conflict subordinate to the war in Iraq and ISAF a relatively minor player with regard to airpower. While it may be easy to criticize in retrospect the lack of progress in Afghanistan, these chapters give insight into the focus, processes, priorities, and military leverage as they were perceived at the time.

Part II, "ISAF Assumes Responsibility for Afghanistan," focuses on the period when ISAF takes its first steps in addressing the challenges in all of Afghanistan. It starts with the first significant NATO/ISAF operation commenced in Regional Command South (RC-S) in August–September 2006, Operation Medusa. This operation proved to be a very difficult start for NATO/ISAF and an operation that would influence the relationship between NATO/ISAF and the United States for years. The chapter on Operation Medusa is the only one not based on the tenure and experiences of the incumbent air commander. Instead, it was written by the officer in charge of the investigation team after the operation. I opted to include this chapter due to the exceptional story of this operation and the impact it had on US-ISAF relations, as well as the broader air infrastructure and the use of airpower in theater. For the rest of Part II, air commanders from both organizations provide their experiences and lessons from their tenures.

The third and last part is titled "The Counterinsurgency Debate." By late 2008, the COMISAF at the time, Gen David D. McKiernan, was moving the organization more into the counterinsurgency modus operandi. Although many tend to view Gen Stanley A. McChrystal as the champion of counterinsurgency in Afghanistan, contributors to this book challenge this perspective and place greater emphasis on the foundation established by General McKiernan. In this period (2008–10), the role of airpower in Afghanistan was challenged and addressed publicly—particularly during General McChrystal's tenure. The ambition is to capture this period, debate, and lessons as seen from the air commanders' perspectives.

Finally, a few notes for the reader: The US generals contributing to this book were the deputy combined force air component commanders (DCFACC). As such, they were not the air commander during their tenure. The contributing DCFACCs have been explicit that they do not in any manner try to posture themselves as the air commander.

The CENTCOM CFACC was dual-hatted until 2009 as commander of the US Ninth Air Force, located at Shaw AFB, South Carolina. My reason for choosing the deputy CFACCs is that they were the extension of the CFACC in the theater. They were stationed at the CAOC at Al Udeid; they were the ones supervising the activity in theater; they were the ones in daily communication with ISAF; and they were the ones making the day-to-day decisions. The five DCFACCs are clear that the CFACC was often in theater and had access to information that they did not necessarily receive; thus, my decision might preclude some lessons from surfacing. Still, it is my view that those leaders involved in the day-to-day dynamics, processes, dialogue, and decisions are better positioned to provide the firsthand primary-source lessons of airpower in theater.

Secondly, while all US DCFACCs in this time frame contributed, that was not the case for ISAF air commanders, two of whom opted not to tell their story. This is a weakness of the book, particularly because the only two air commanders declining to contribute were those serving immediately before, during, and after Operation Medusa (March 2006–January 2007). As the reader will understand, Operation Medusa plays a very significant role in terms of understanding the internal processes of ISAF leading to this disheartening operation, the subsequent relationship between ISAF Air and the CAOC at Al Udeid, the subsequent process of enabling ISAF Air to exert more influence on air operations, and the perception of general incompetence in handling the lessons from this operation. Operation Medusa plays an important role in understanding the dynamics of airpower in theater long after it ended, and to have the perspective of those two individuals involved in the planning, execution, and evaluation of that operation would have been hugely beneficial. Still, the book includes the US DCFACC's view of the operation, as well as that of the Canadian general who was co-president of the combined investigation board convened by commander US CENTAF to investigate the operation.

This book relies on the memory of the contributing air commanders. It is their story. For better or for worse, they portray the people, meetings, events, and processes as they perceive them. When they mention individuals in their story, I have opted to refer to positions rather than names in many cases, because the lessons are less about the actual individual. Still, those who want to know the names of these individuals can relatively easily search the Internet. These individuals have no way of offering their view in this analysis. They likely have their own interpretations of events that may differ from those presented herein. The format of this book—having each air commander provide a chapter—precludes these perspectives from being included, and the reader should acknowledge this limitation.

Three of the air commanders provided their own text, which I then edited as, I presume, any editor more or less would normally do. These are Lt Gen Frederik Meulman, Maj Gen Charles S. Sullivan, and Maj Gen Jouke Eikelboom. (I met each of them personally, some more than once.) The other six contributors were clear that a precondition for their participation was that I draft the chapter for them due to a very busy schedule. So the process entailed my interviewing Lt Gen Allen G. Peck and Maj Gen Jaap Willemse personally, while conducting telephone interviews of Maj Gen William L. Holland, Maj Gen Maurice H. Forsyth, Maj Gen Douglas Raaberg, and Lt Gen Stephen L. Hoog. After transcribing the interview, I then sent a proposed initial draft to each general. They had total freedom to reject, approve, adjust, and reorganize everything. Their mandate was to ensure that this became their chapter and that everything in their chapter was their meaning, their emphasis, their perspectives, and their story. Once their feedback was implemented, it was reviewed by two trusted academic colleagues who provided comments on each chapter as well as the cohesion of the book. Those comments were injected when feasible and subsequently fed back to the generals for a last approval before publication. My final draft was further edited by Air University Press to conform to its publication style and to seek conciseness and clarity. This process may have influenced this book to a larger degree than normal. My writing the first draft of five chapters certainly provided an opportunity to bring more cohesive language and structure to the book; however my suggested choice of structure and emphasis might have influenced the text in a different way than if the generals had written it initially themselves. I do not believe this has changed the lessons provided in any significant manner, as the text was based on the interviews of each general, but I mention this because the reader should be aware of this potential influence.

While the lessons from Afghanistan by no means are a recipe for how our next war should be fought, it is my hope that officers (and politicians, scholars, journalists, and others) of all nationalities, services, and ranks will find some important lessons in this book and that these at least spur debates, dialogues, and creativity that better prepare us for what lies ahead. Contrary to many observers over the past decade, I am not sure the wars of Afghanistan and Iraq will be the future norm. While our technology often has the capacity to adapt to various scenarios—this time a counterinsurgency and a counterterrorism effort—I would argue that our very human intellectual capacity has proven to be less flexible. Just as the US Army and Marine Corps in their 2006 counterinsurgency Field Manual 3-24 acknowledge that "counterinsurgency operations generally have been neglected in broader American military doctrine and national security policies since the end of the Vietnam War over 30 years ago," the airpower community should acknowledge that we, too, have a huge job before us to generate and improve the intellectual strength, flexibility, and culture for approaching future wars. The wars of the future will have their own unique features and should be approached accordingly.

Lt Col Dag Henriksen, PhD
Royal Norwegian Air Force

Notes

1. "NATO and Afghanistan," NATO homepage, http://www.nato.int/cps/en /natolive/topics_69349.htm?; and Elise Labott and Mike Mount, "NATO Accepts Obama Timetable to End War in Afghanistan by 2014," *CNN.com*, 22 May 2012, http://www.cnn.com/2012/05/21/us/nato-summit/index.html.

2. See former COMISAF Gen Stanley A. McChrystal's "Tactical Directive" from 2009: "Like any insurgency, there is a struggle for the support and will of the population. Gaining and maintaining that support must be our overriding operational imperative—and the ultimate objective of every action we take. . . . We must avoid the trap of winning tactical victories—but suffering strategic defeats—by causing civilian casualties or excessive damage and thus alienating the people." McChrystal, "Tactical Directive," Headquarters International Security Assistance Force, Kabul, Afghanistan, 6 July 2009. See also former COMISAF Gen David A. Petraeus's updated tactical directive from 2010: "We must continue—indeed, redouble—our efforts to reduce the loss of innocent civilian life to an absolute minimum. Every Afghan civilian death diminishes our cause. If we use excessive force or operate contrary to our counterinsurgency principles, tactical victories may prove to be strategic setbacks. We must never forget that the center of gravity in this struggle is the Afghan people; it is they who will ultimately determine the future of Afghanistan." Petraeus, "Tactical Directive," ISAF HQ, Kabul, Afghanistan, 2010-08-CA-0046.

3. Frederick Meulman, interview by author, 24 November 2007, ISAF Headquarters, Kabul, Afghanistan.

4. Dexter Filkins, "U.S. Tightens Airstrike Policy in Afghanistan," *New York Times*, 21 June 2009, http://www.nytimes.com/2009/06/22/world/asia/22airstrikes.html?_r=1.

5. President Obama stated,

The 30,000 additional troops that I am announcing tonight will deploy in the first part of 2010—the fastest pace possible—so that they can target the insurgency and secure key population centers. . . . Taken together, these additional American and international troops will allow us to accelerate handing over responsibility to Afghan forces, and allow us to begin the transfer of our forces out of Afghanistan in July of 2011. Just as we have done in Iraq, we will execute this transition responsibly, taking into account conditions on the ground. We will continue to advise and assist Afghanistan's Security Forces to ensure that they can succeed over the long haul. But it will be clear to the Afghan government—and, more importantly, to the Afghan people—that they will ultimately be responsible for their own country.

"Remarks of President Barack Obama—As Prepared for Delivery: The Way Forward in Afghanistan and Pakistan," 1 December 2009, US Military Academy at West Point, http://www.politicsdaily.com/2009/12/01/i-do-not-make-this-decision-lightly-obama-afghanistan-troop-s/.

6. When Lieutenant General Hostage became CFACC and USAFCENT commander in 2009, the position was divested of its 9AF responsibilities, and he was forward-based at Al Udeid rather than being stationed at Shaw, as his predecessors had been. Lt Gen Allen G. Peck, e-mail to author, 12 March 2013.

7. US Army and US Marine Corps Field Manual 3-24 (Marine Corps Warfighting Publication No. 3-33.5), *Counterinsurgency*, 15 December 2006, vii, http://army-pubs.army.mil/doctrine/DR_pubs/DR_a/pdf/fm3_24.pdf.

Abbreviations

ACCE	air component coordination element
ACE	air coordination element/air component element
ACO	airspace control order
ALO	air liaison officer
AOC	air operations center
AOR	area of responsibility
ASOC	air support operations center
ASOG	air support operations group
ATC	air traffic control
ATO	air tasking order
AWACS	airborne warning and control system
BDA	battle damage assessment
CAOC	combined air operations center
CAP	combat air patrol
CAS	close air support
CDDOC	CENTCOM Deployment Distribution Operations Center
CENTAF	US Air Forces Central Command
CENTCOM	US Central Command
CFACC	combined force air component commander
CIVCAS	civilian casualties
CJOC	combined joint operation center
COA	course of action
COIN	counterinsurgency
COMISAF	Commander ISAF
CRC	control and reporting center
CSAR	combat search and rescue
CT	counterterrorism
DCFACC	deputy combined force air component commander
DCOM	deputy commander
DOD	Department of Defense
DT	dynamic targeting
DTOC	Direct Targeting Operations Centre
EW	electronic warfare
FAC	forward air controller
FMV	full motion video
FOB	forward operating base
GIRoA	government of The Islamic Republic of Afghanistan

IJC	ISAF Joint Command
ISAF	International Security Assistance Force
ISR	intelligence, surveillance, and reconnaissance
JDAM	joint direct attack munition
JPEL	joint prioritized effects list
JTAC	joint terminal attack controller
JUON	joint urgent operational needs
KAF	Kandahar Airfield
KAIA	Kabul International Airport
LNO	liaison officer
MAAP	master air attack plan
MDP	military decision process
MEDEVAC	medical evacuation
MNFI	Multinational Force Iraq
MQ-1	Predator (RPA)
MQ-9	Reaper (RPA)
NTISR	nontraditional ISR
OEF	Operation Enduring Freedom
OIF	Operation Iraqi Freedom
OPCOM	operational command
OPCON	operational control
PGM	precision guided missile
PRT	provincial reconstruction team
PSAB	Prince Sultan Air Base
RAOC	regional air operations center
RC	regional command
RPA	remotely piloted aircraft
TACOM	tactical command
TACON	tactical control
TACP	tactical air control party
TCN	troop-contributing nations
TIC	troops in contact
TST	time-sensitive targeting
TTP	tactics, techniques, and procedures
UAV	unmanned aerial vehicle
USAF	US Air Force

Part I

The Status of the International Community's Military Engagement in Afghanistan, 2005–06

Chapter 1

Silence before the Storm

Maj Gen Jaap Willemse, RNLAF, Retired

Deputy Commander International Security Assistance Force
Kabul, Afghanistan
August 2005–February 2006

Since I am privileged to provide the opening chapter of this book, I believe it is important as an analytical starting point to take the reader back to the situation in Afghanistan in 2005–06. Then, the evolvement of strategy, the operational context, and force structure—the overall approach to Afghanistan, if you will—was quite different than what we have observed the past few years. The International Security Assistance Force (ISAF) was in its infancy but preparing to take more responsibility. I believe the best way to illustrate this is to tell the story—in terms of airpower—of a significant incident that occurred during my seven-month tenure as deputy commander of ISAF.

The Attack on PRT Meymaneh

This was the time of the Danish cartoons of the Prophet Mohammad and subsequent attack on the Norwegian-led provincial reconstruction team (PRT) Meymaneh in the Faryab Province in northwestern Afghanistan.[1] On this particular day—Tuesday, 7 February 2006—we had several incidents related to the cartoons in our area of operations (AOR). Among them was a fairly aggressive demonstration just outside the gates of ISAF headquarters (HQ) in Kabul. Rocks were thrown into our compound, some shots were fired outside the gate, and we subsequently had to close the headquarters. Commander ISAF (COMISAF) was at Kabul International Airport (KAIA) at the time and could not get back into the headquarters due to the demonstrations.[2] This meant that I was in charge and must handle the onset of the largely unforeseen events that unfolded at PRT Meymaneh.

We received initial reports that a big crowd was gathering in Meymaneh, and the demonstration soon got out of hand. Several circumstances, in my view, complicated the situation: Today the PRT is relocated to the city's outskirts, but in 2006 it was located right in the middle of the city. That made it very difficult to defend for both the personnel on the ground as well as from the air. The Norwegian commander was not there at the time, so the deputy was leading what escalated, for all practical terms, into a fight to defend the integrity and life of the PRT and its personnel. The only adequate communication ISAF had with the PRT that morning was through a satellite phone with the PRT's joint terminal attack controller (JTAC), the officer responsible for directing combat aircraft in close air support or other offensive air operations. In effect, the JTAC is the individual who is trained and equipped to talk directly to the pilots delivering munitions in situations demanding close coordination with our own forces to enhance effectiveness and avoid fratricide (blue-on-blue). The satellite communication with the JTAC was the only means to develop situational awareness (SA) for me and my team at ISAF HQ. So the actual real-time SA on what was happening on the ground at PRT Meymaneh was not always clear to us, to put it mildly. The situation was dynamic and changed rapidly, as tactical situations often do. We understood that attackers were throwing rocks and Molotov cocktails, exchanging shots with PRT defenders, and firing rocket-propelled grenades (RPG) into the PRT. It was getting out of control.

We decided to launch the two Dutch F-16 alert aircraft at our disposal. They were overhead Meymaneh fairly quickly. Soon thereafter, the JTAC requested "weapons release approval." This represented a command-and-control issue that must be addressed at once. Remember, this was in 2006 within a relatively quiet and peaceful northern region that had provided very few situations to practice delicate command-and-control issues of this nature. The dilemma and subsequent thought process governing our response was related to (1) limited situational awareness, (2) the inherent right to self-defense, and (3) the potential strategic effects of a too heavy-handed response. The right to self-defense has become a universal right for troops as well as private citizens of most nations. In Afghanistan we also had the term *extended self-defense*, which in practical terms meant that if a coalition partner got into a situation where the lives of its troops were endangered, we had the right to defend them as well. As I saw it, that was the situation in Meymaneh.

So we immediately had a few problems. First of all we had very limited communications. We actually had relatively good communications with the JTAC through the satellite phone but not with the PRT commander or acting commander. That raised the question of *if* and *how* coordination was organized between the JTAC and the acting commander. This was not always entirely clear. When the JTAC asked for weapons release approval, we had a discussion internally at the HQ but also with the JTAC. Our position was that with almost no communications with the acting commander at the PRT and a generally low SA of a tactical, fluid, and rapidly changing situation occurring hundreds of miles from the HQ, it was very difficult to authorize any weapons release from the air. We told the JTAC that under current ISAF rules of engagement (ROE) he had the inherent right of self-defense, he had the best situational awareness, and he should be able to handle the situation together with the Dutch F-16s overhead. I do understand that the situation was not particularly easy for the JTAC, who found himself in the middle of a town amid innocent civilians mixed with aggressive demonstrators who most likely had planned the attack for some time.

Can you actually release a weapon under those circumstances? I must say, I really did not think so. Therefore, we asked the JTAC to take into account *distinction* not to harm innocent civilians and *proportionality* if he found that the situation did warrant a release of weapons from the F-16s. As JTAC, he had to take into account the various measures at his disposal: We had obviously moved beyond the point when talking to the demonstrators could assist the effort. As for the F-16s, they could fly low over the crowd, fire a "warning burst" from their cannons, or drop a bomb outside of town—still near enough for the blast to be seen and felt—to let the demonstrators know they were within reach and try to scare them off. These are tactical decisions well within the ROEs that warrant eyes on the ground to have the SA to make the timely and adequate decision when and where to hit. We discussed this with the JTAC and made it clear that in the end, he, *together with the F-16 crews*, had to make the call.

Not everyone in the HQ necessarily agreed with this point of view. There were those who would like to stick to the procedure requiring COMISAF to approve the release of weapons, even in a case of (extended) self-defense. I had to point out that every soldier and unit has the inherent right of self-defense and that trying to impose a limitation to this right to seek approval from the top military echelons is contrary to the needs of soldiers on the ground seeking air support in rapidly changing tactical situations threatening their lives.

Still, I could understand some staff officers' concerns. A small tactical situation can have severely negative strategic effects, and the situation at Meymaneh could become a classic example. It is slightly embarrassing to admit that we spent a lot of time and energy on these internal discussions, but it goes to show the very limited level of violence, the procedural training, and the mind-set in our AOR at the time. Today we are used to the activity in Regional Command South (RC-S) and East (RC-E), and even the level of violence in the north (RC-N) has increased significantly, but in 2005 and early 2006 the context was very, very different. Given our relatively calm AOR and the low level of enemy activity in Kabul, in the north, and in the west, for us to go right away with a weapons release from an F-16 would have been an enormous escalation.

So together with the Dutch senior national representative (SNR) and the JTAC, we decided to go for an increase in the use of force. The F-16s made a low-level pass over the crowd, but no bombs were dropped. To what extent the F-16s helped the situation, I am not sure, but they probably had some effect as a "show of force." We became aware that there happened to be a police unit from Kabul in Meymaneh, so I was asked by COMISAF to contact the Afghan minister of interior. After I explained the issue at hand, the police force did intervene to some extent. To what extent the whole situation was orchestrated by various actors in the region is not for me to conclude, but I think it is fair to say we had indications that not everything that happened that day was sparked spontaneously. In the end PRT personnel fought off the attackers together with a British "quick reaction force" that entered the premises later that day. The situation calmed down, and life in Meymaneh resumed its regular pace and activity. When the dust settled, a number of Afghans had been killed, a few Norwegian soldiers had been wounded, and the damage to the PRT and its equipment was severe.[3] We subsequently decided to move the PRT to the outskirts of town to make it more defendable and less vulnerable.

The point of telling this story is not simply to provide a full account of events, enhance my role, or downplay that of others. There are many more nuances to this story than portrayed here, and the discussion of self-defense and who should have ordered what is of less relevance in this particular piece. What is important for the reader is to understand the point at which NATO and ISAF—and in a sense, even the United States and the international community— embarked on a journey to place troops on the ground in large numbers a few months later. To understand why the attack on PRT Meymaneh put such strain on ISAF HQ and the PRT itself must be seen through the lens of the ISAF mind-set in that period of time. It was a totally different situation. The northern and western provinces represented, relatively speaking, a very calm operational environment.

With regard to the use of airpower, the situation at Meymaneh was by far the most critical incident in fall 2005 to winter 2006. One may perhaps smile at that today, but the reality at the time was that having eight F-16s as our total combat power—of which two were on alert—was considered to be enough. And it was. I am not criticizing the way we operated or conducted our mission—quite the contrary. I believe we did a good job. But it shows the culture and the level of training and refinement within the chain of command to handle high-intensity warfare. It shows our limitations in communications; our limitations in providing situational awareness and intelligence, surveillance, and reconnaissance (ISR); our limitations in terms of exercising command and control in our AOR—and that our entire modus operandi as of February/March 2006 was far from the realities we would encounter merely six months later when ISAF assumed responsibility for RC-S and, a few months later, RC-E.[4]

Strategy

In terms of strategy and a broader, more long-term focus on Afghanistan, I must admit all this was in its infancy in ISAF HQ at the time. We discussed it a lot, of course, as officers involved in an operation always do, but we simply did not have a pointed, commonly agreed upon, strategic document or outlook. In a sense that is understandable, since development of an overarching strategy was also part of the process of expanding the ISAF mission to include the south and east AORs. Still, I would argue that a clearer overall objective of the engagement in Afghanistan would have been beneficial. In reality, most of our airpower operations were reactive and ad hoc—we tried to handle problems as they arose. The headquarters' general planning horizon was one to two years ahead and focused almost entirely on two concrete issues: the 2005 parliamentary elections in Afghanistan and the transition to broaden ISAF's area of operations to include the southern and eastern regions, thus the whole of Afghanistan.

Also, ISAF consisted of a number of PRTs that, more often than not, were controlled and driven by their respective nations rather than ISAF HQ, thus operating autonomously instead of as part of a cohesive, long-term effort. Our mission could hardly be qualified as "counterterrorism" or "counterinsurgency (COIN)." ISAF was there to assist the government of the Islamic Republic of Afghanistan (GIRoA) with security and reconstruction, but there was far too little coordination and integration of other means of power to deserve a label anything close to COIN. And our focus and resources were certainly not designed to single out and chase al-Qaeda or other terrorists in a coordinated counterterrorism endeavor. In reality, the role of ISAF airpower was limited to support of the PRTs when they asked for assistance.

I think it is fair to say that coordination between the PRTs gradually improved. We held conferences where the PRT commanders came to ISAF HQ to share and discuss experiences, lessons, and the way forward. It was more a question of trying to coordinate some of the PRT activities to gradually and increasingly pull in the same direction. I believe COMISAFs from 2005 onward focused on improving the collective effort of the PRTs and succeeded to some extent. Still, it was far from a cohesive force that operated under the same strategy, mandate, or direction. Although we coordinated and cooperated as much as possible with the Afghan government, efforts within ISAF to stand up the Afghan security forces were limited. Such efforts were primarily undertaken by US forces but certainly not within the framework of ISAF. As noted, the focus of ISAF HQ was far from dealing with an exit strategy of that nature.

My description might sound a bit somber, but in reality ISAF did what was expected of it. The force structure and posture reflected the contributing nations' political will and objectives in Afghanistan. The ISAF involvement in Afghanistan should be seen as a continuously developing political process paralleling our military evolvement. Without a well-developed, politically agreed upon strategy, we exercised the mandate vested in us by the nations involved. Within those strategic limitations, I would argue that we did a good job. In retrospect one can of course argue that four or five years into the Afghan operation, we should have had a bit more clarity of what we wanted to achieve, but that process is a political one. Few nations wanted to cede control of their PRTs entirely to COMISAF and were relatively comfortable with the existing situation. It appeared that the internal debates over whom and how to handle the southern and eastern provinces demanded enough political debate and hard decisions at the time.

Airpower in a Land-Oriented Environment

One of the goals of this book is to take a closer look at the link between the strategic level and the subordinate levels, how the operational level converted the strategic guidance to air operations, and to what degree there was cohesion between the strategic direction of the war and the tactical application of airpower. For a number of reasons, this cohesion largely did not exist in fall 2005–winter 2006. I have already touched upon the lack of a well-developed strategy and the more general ad hoc approach to air operations. The challenge of utilizing airpower, however, ran much deeper. The integration of air and land forces—often referred to as "air-land integration"—was a huge challenge, as it had been for years, and I believe continued to be an issue long after I left Afghanistan.

In this land-oriented and land-driven operation, the airpower community was rarely asked how to contribute to the overall mission for Afghanistan. Rather, the dynamic involved reactive requests for support by individual land commanders within the various PRTs due to confrontation with the enemy on the ground (troops in contact). There seemed to be a professional culture or mind-set within the PRTs and ISAF HQ that rarely asked what—except maybe airlift—airpower might contribute to this operation other than rapid kinetic attacks (e.g., dropping bombs) on insurgents challenging our ground forces. There was less integration and dialogue on how to exploit the diverse military tool of airpower and more "you must be there when we need you"—a sort of one-way, one-dimensional, kinetic "emergency call" for commanders on the ground which lacked the fundamentals for a truly *joint* effort. Perhaps we could have expressed *how* we could assist the ground commander *and* the overall mission better, but the ISAF leadership, me included, did not manage to create a climate which facilitated such discussions.

Soon after we entered ISAF HQ and started to address the expansion of the ISAF mission, we—inside and outside ISAF HQ—immediately had a debate on what it meant, in practical terms, for the air component to be tasked to support the land component. Should ground force commanders within each regional command have their own air assets for planning and operations? It really came to discussions that I never thought we would revisit. It was like turning the clock back to the interwar period before World War II and considering whether we should reestablish an "Army Air Corps/Force" for handling the situation in Afghanistan. To me it was clear that with the limited resources we had in ISAF at the time, we could not realistically dedicate assets to regional commanders. What we could do was apportion missions before large ground operations, but that is a fundamentally different approach. In my view the whole debate was a step back. Ground commanders should not be interested in owning aircraft. We had to keep telling some of our colleagues from the ground forces that there was no need for them to own the "hardware," but it continued to be an issue. In my view these discussions were marked by the perspectives of individuals, their character, and their trust. "Can we trust you to show up when we need you?" was an often-heard remark. The general response was, "Well, show us when we did not show up when you needed us." In a sense this goes to the fundamentals of the application of force. There was a certain lack of overarching perspective, of trust, and of *joint* perspective or what each service could bring to the table to make the overall mission succeed.

This problem would become much more evident once ISAF assumed responsibility for the southern and eastern regions, RC-S and RC-E. At the time, we did not have many resources to integrate with the land component. Upon my arrival in Afghanistan, we had an air organization consisting of COMISAF at the top, me as the deputy commander focused on the air dimension of our mission, and a brigadier general as the commander of our small air task force (ATF). Besides the eight Dutch F-16s,[5] the ATF had some limited airlift capacity. Airlift was really important, and although we had limited numbers—you never feel you have enough airlift capacity—it was adequate for the limited demands at the time. So that was basically our air task force—a few F-16s and a few transport aircraft. Adding to this limited force was the lack of means to provide adequate command and control. We did not have the C2 structure to control aircraft or provide adequate SA within ISAF HQ. Airspace management and coordination was largely done through standard procedures ("procedural control") because we often did not have radar or radio contact with the aircraft due to the topography of the Hindu Kush Mountains and the lack of equipment. We tried to get the NATO airborne warning and control system (AWACS) for communication and airspace control but did not succeed. So it would be wrong to claim that airpower could have brought much more to the table in early 2006. This was due in part to the small piece of the airpower inventory or capability we controlled. But it is noteworthy to identify the structural approach to Afghanistan that was evident at the time. The operation was seen through the lenses of ground warfare and ground security for ISAF and Afghan personnel. There was little overarching debate or creative thinking with regard to the use of airpower in the theater or how it all fit into rebuilding Afghanistan. So when the situation changed and significantly more airpower capability became available in the years to come, the military structural approach to Afghanistan did not change. There did not seem to be any awareness of this being a problem or an issue that needed to be addressed. This would later become a problem both at the strategic level and at the tactical level.

The Relationship between ISAF and Operation Enduring Freedom

Describing ISAF's limited air resources does not provide all the nuances of the available assets, the command relationships involved, and the flexibility in these structures. Although not considered a problem at the time, there was a constant "change of hats" for air assets in the theater. Each resource could have a "national" hat, a "NATO/ISAF" hat, and/or an "Operation Enduring Freedom (OEF)" hat based on missions and national transfer of authority (ToA). For instance, we often asked Germany for transport assistance when needed. The Germans had helicopters and C-160s in their national chain of command stationed in northern Afghanistan, which they could make available to us if requested. These often represented a tremendous asset and gave a degree of flexibility that we greatly appreciated. It shows the dynamics between the contributing nations and what was formally assigned to NATO/ISAF.

This was also true for ISAF cooperation with the US-led Operation Enduring Freedom. Both the Dutch F-16s and other allied fighters deployed to Afghanistan were frequently tasked for OEF missions. There was not always a clear-cut or seamless distinction between ISAF and OEF missions. Nations could opt to make their resources available to the United States or other allies, and did.[6] The important thing for us was to draw a line and stay out of the operational coordination when that happened. It was a unilateral decision for each nation, and I certainly understand the importance of such flexibility. I guess we all knew that it also represented a security investment; if any of our troops were in danger and we needed more resources to avoid a serious blow to our collective war effort, we knew we could ask the US forces to assist. The downside, of course, was that it was difficult for all observers—Afghans, the media, and ourselves at times—to clearly distinguish the daily use of airpower in the theater. If you participate in OEF before lunch and ISAF in the afternoon, it reduces the distinction between the operations—a distinction of significant political importance within many NATO countries.

The relationship with the US forces is worth noting. The US chain of command ran through the US Central Command (CENTCOM), which directed operations in both Iraq and Afghanistan simultaneously as well as other operations within its AOR. The C2 of the air effort in Iraq and Afghanistan was done at the combined air operations center (CAOC) in Al Udeid, Qatar. Due to the overwhelming US resources and very limited resources of ISAF at the time, it was difficult to be treated as an equal partner. In reality, all tasking of ISAF air assets—whether initiated by ISAF or OEF—came from the US CAOC at Al Udeid. In reality, the majority of air operations in Afghanistan were led from/by the CAOC at Al Udeid. ISAF's ability to communicate or influence decisions was limited. CENTCOM, understandably, appeared focused on Iraq, where it experienced some very real hardships at the time. ISAF was not the major player and was treated accordingly. We ended up having a British representative take care of ISAF coordination, and that worked fairly well. Surely we were kept out of the loop when assets were reallocated to OEF missions, and communication between ISAF HQ and CAOC Al Udeid did not appear to have the utmost priority.

The air resources and operational experience of our US colleagues are often so overwhelming compared to other allied partners that over the years we have come to rely on them as a basis for almost any NATO military operation. In the case of Afghanistan, the chain of command became somewhat blurry, because the tasking of air assets was done through a US-only air operations center and not through the NATO chain of command. It was a "marriage of necessity" or of "realpolitik" rather than an optimal command relationship for NATO. The relationship started out as that of a "mosquito and an elephant," but both ISAF and the CENTCOM had to adapt to the increasingly significant role of ISAF. NATO's institutionalized integrity had to be balanced against the enormous unilateral US strength in the theater and the need to retain full operational control of US assets in this particular war. I feared the transition to RC-S and RC-E in the fall of 2006 would experience significant friction in this regard.

Assisting the Government of Afghanistan

In February/March 2006, ISAF HQ had no defined exit strategy by which to navigate or to provide direction for its work. To be direct, ISAF HQ was very far from dealing with any form of overarching exit strategy at that time and had enough on its plate in terms of dealing with daily operations and the planning for/assisting with the elections and the upcoming takeover of RC-S and RC-E.

Discussions took place on whether or not one should focus on the Afghans taking over the responsibility of security at some point, but at that time these were loosely framed elaborations more than concrete guidance. As far as I remember—quite some time has passed since then—we were, on a small scale, engaging in activity similar to what we today call "operational mentor and liaison teams (OMLT)," but this was mainly a US endeavor with US officers in charge of training some Afghan National Police (ANP) and Afghan National Army (ANA) personnel. We had little interaction with Afghan air force authorities at that time. Their resources were very, very limited, and we had problems identifying how to proceed.

Let me illustrate our relationship and challenges with Afghan authorities at the time. We (NATO) became involved in developing Kabul International Airport into a civil airport again, which could generate much-needed legitimate income. Our role was advisory, with GIRoA agencies in charge of the program. The capability of Afghan government institutions at the time represented a huge challenge. It became clear that, with the exception of the Ministry of Defense and maybe parts of the Ministry of Justice, the bureaucratic skills and general competence and knowledge of these agencies were limited. It was very difficult for us to cooperate with the Ministry of Transportation and other agencies while limiting ourselves to an advisory role. We quickly understood that we were the ones who must produce initiatives and get the process moving forward. We started a number of initiatives, such as meeting the fundamental need for an instrument landing system (ILS) and an air traffic control (ATC) structure to handle air traffic in and out of the airport. We soon realized that providing these resources and starting training is one thing, but there were no structures in which these initiatives would fit. Who was to do the maintenance, and which institutions were to ensure national oversight for the broad array of personnel, material, and institutions that make up a functional international airport? We had individual Afghans who did very well in training and courses, but because the pay was not particularly good, we lost quite a few of those participating in these courses—they just quit. In a sense, it showed the dilemmas we were facing. There were few limits as to what individual Afghans could manage if provided training and education; the problems were tied to more structural issues of the society and the lack of administrative skills and institutions. Our aim was always to have Afghans lead these projects, but that often proved difficult in real life.

Summary and Conclusions

For me personally it was a great experience to be the deputy commander of ISAF as an airman in a land-heavy headquarters in a land-heavy operation. With scarce resources, we flew ballots and security personnel all around Afghanistan and managed to secure the 2005 elections, which led to the first Afghan Parliament to be forged and implemented since the early 1970s. It mattered. With limited fighter resources, we contributed to the training of forward air controllers, supported the PRTs, and provided adequate security from the air in our AOR. We assisted the Afghan government in building its international airport in Kabul and other projects. Gradually, we managed to facilitate better coordination between the PRTs to learn from each other and pull more in the same direction. We started the planning to assume responsibility of RC-S and RC-E and had laid a good foundation for that upon our departure. These were all significant achievements.

I guess evaluating our performance as an alliance, and Afghanistan as a nation, to a large degree depends on your perspectives. As much as I point out our achievements, it was equally clear we had a very pragmatic, day-to-day approach to Afghanistan. We knew, of course, there was a political process paralleling ours and that we could only perform within the limits of our political mandate. That meant we did not operate with any exit strategy guiding our effort—indeed, with any particular strategy at all. Airpower focused on solving ad hoc problems for the largely nationally driven and autonomous PRTs when they needed assistance. And we did not have enough good, qualitative, overarching discussions between ground and air officers in terms of how we could use our collective resources to achieve better overall results.

One significant problem was the process of accumulating and transferring knowledge within our own organization. When you rotate every six months, the new headquarters set to take over your job starts sending people two to three months before the turnover to be prepared. The problem is, of course, that those you are set to replace have only been in the job for three to four months themselves and have hardly built any in-depth situational awareness on operations, Afghanistan, or the theater as a whole. It was very difficult to invest in relations and build adequate teams when you were about to be replaced as soon as you started to feel comfortable with your job portfolio. The Allied Rapid Reaction Corps (ARRC) from the UK was replacing us, and NATO decided to go to at least a nine-month rotation cycle. This was later set to one year for senior personnel, but in 2005–06 this was a problem. It was a problem for the Afghans, too, who had to build relations with a new crew every six months.

This book has an overarching goal of analyzing the cohesion between strategy, how this strategy is transformed to military operations at the operational level, and the tactical execution of air operations. The short answer would be that in my term as deputy COMISAF, there was no such cohesion. The first two levels simply were not well developed, and we had such limited resources that we could achieve only ad hoc tactical execution of air-to-ground operations in support of PRTs. Furthermore, the Americans were the ones with adequate resources and were the real airpower factor in the theater. Thus, the air leadership from the CAOC at Al Udeid is probably better positioned to talk about the larger airpower lessons from that period. This is important for what would happen later in 2006. We had some ideas for the transition—for instance, that each regional command should have its own regional air coordination center. We ended up debating what the role of this center would be—whether it should have tasking authority and/or coordination authority or should be just a liaison team. These factors became important once ISAF assumed responsibility for the whole of Afghanistan, but they had not been worked through when I left Afghanistan.

During my tenure, ISAF was hardly in the loop when it came to planning the air structure and air dimension after the transition. This was mainly a US-led endeavor, not surprising considering that the United States had almost all the air assets. But from a NATO perspective, this was not entirely according to protocol. Formally, it would be logical that ISAF HQ be involved to a larger extent in planning the air portion of taking over RC-S and RC-E. In retrospect, the land-dominated focus of ISAF HQ and the air dominance of CENTCOM in Afghanistan through its CAOC at Al Udeid would influence our approach to Afghanistan in the years to come.

Notes

1. The "Danish cartoon controversy" refers to a situation that occurred shortly before the attack on PRT Meymaneh:

> After a Danish newspaper [*Jyllands-Posten*] and other European publications displayed 12 cartoons caricaturing the Prophet Muhammad in 2005 and early 2006, violent protests erupted around the world. Muslims throughout the Middle East and Africa rioted. They burned embassies and churches and fought with police; at least 200 died and many more were injured. The incident highlighted some of the issues raised by Europe's growing Muslim minority: How do you draw the line between free expression and respect for religion?

"Danish Cartoon Controversy," *New York Times*, 12 August 2009.

2. The COMISAF from August 2005 until May 2006 was Italian army general Mauro Del Vecchio.

3. In his address to the Norwegian Parliament on 8 February 2006, the Norwegian foreign minister, Jonas Gahr Støre, pointed out that the PRT consisted of 54 personnel, of which 33 were Norwegians. Six Norwegian soldiers had suffered injuries, and two of them had been evacuated to a hospital. Jonas Gahr Støre, "Utenrikspolitisk Redegjørelse for Stortinget 8. Februar 2006" [Foreign policy exposition for the parliament, 8 February 2006], http://www.regjeringen.no/nb/dep/ud/aktuelt/taler_artikler/utenriksministeren/2006/utenriksministerens-utenrikspolitiske-re.html?id=273242.

4. ISAF would assume responsibility for RC-S on 31 July 2006 and RC-E some two months later on 5 October 2006. "About ISAF: History," http://www.isaf.nato.int/history.html.

5. In July 2005, Belgium sent four F-16s to partner with the Dutch force contribution. The Belgian contribution was replaced by four Norwegian F-16s stationed in Kabul for a three-month period. The total number of aircraft was still 6–8 fighters in this period. Bjorn Claes, "Belgian F-16s Head to Afghanistan," *F-16.Net*, 6 July 2005,

http://www.f-16.net/news_article1409.html; and Royal Norwegian Ministry of Defence, "F-16s for ISAF in Afghanistan," press release no. 40/2005, 9 November 2005, http://www.regjeringen.no/en/dep/fd/press-centre/Press-releases/2005?F-16s-for-ISAF-in-Afghanistan.html?id=419729.

6. For instance, when Norway decided to send four F-16s to assist ISAF in spring 2006, the government wrote: "The purpose is to ensure that ISAF has access to combat aircraft capable of demonstrating a presence and, if necessary, of providing close air support to units on the ground if critical situations should arise. In emergency situations, aircraft under ISAF's command will also be able to assist ground forces engaged in the United States led operation 'Enduring Freedom.' " Royal Norwegian Ministry of Defence, "F-16s for ISAF in Afghanistan."

Chapter 2

Airpower: The Theater Perspective

Lt Gen Allen G. Peck, USAF, Retired

*US Central Command Deputy Combined
Force Air Component Commander
June 2005–June 2006*

Predictions are hard to make . . . especially about the future.

—Lawrence P. "Yogi" Berra

I was privileged to be assigned as deputy combined force air component commander (DCFACC) from June of 2005 to June of 2006, serving under two highly regarded CFACCs: Lt Gen Buck Buchanan and Lt Gen Gary North, who assumed the duties in February 2006. These officers wore three major hats: commander of Ninth Air Force, overseeing five wings and four direct-reporting units in the eastern United States; commander of US Air Forces Central Command (CENTAF), deployed to CENTCOM's area of responsibility; and theater CFACC, exercising tactical control (TACON) of air forces from other services and from coalition partners made available for tasking. The CFACC was also designated by the CENTCOM commander to serve as airspace control authority for Iraq and Afghanistan, personnel recovery coordinator, space coordinating authority, area air defense commander, and theater electronic warfare coordinator. As the senior full-time Airman assigned in theater, I exercised these responsibilities on a daily basis on behalf of the CFACC.

There has been much discussion, both in the United States and worldwide, on why the wars in Afghanistan and Iraq became so difficult, why we did not anticipate so many of the problems that arose, and why we apparently entered the wars in Afghanistan and Iraq—in general terms—unprepared for what turned out to be a decade of counterinsurgency warfare. I would like to touch upon this issue in my introduction, before going into the more detailed analysis of my tenure as deputy CFACC.

During the mid 1980s, well prior to my tour as deputy CFACC, I was assigned to the Air Staff at the Pentagon. I recall participating in a total force capabilities assessment war game, during which an argument broke out on where future conflicts would likely occur. There were of course a variety of opinions: North Korea attacks its neighbor to the south, the Soviet Union drives to the Arabian Gulf via Iran, Israel becomes embroiled in another fight in the Mideast, and so on. One of the attendees stood up, strode confidently to a world map pinned to the wall, and asserted, "Well at least I know one place we are not going to send ground forces, and that is right here," pointing to Afghanistan. I mention this incident because it taught me a lesson on the lack of predictability of world affairs and, perhaps of particular importance for officers preparing for war, how difficult it is to predict the location or nature of future conflicts. Our failure to predict the fall of the Berlin Wall and the attacks of 9/11 are, of course, other examples that illustrate the dangers of using extrapolation to prepare our security posture for the future.

That does not mean we can ignore the lessons of previous wars. Some have argued, and rightfully to some extent, that we forgot the lessons of Vietnam and irregular warfare (IW) when approaching Afghanistan and Iraq. In hindsight it is easy to acknowledge that we perhaps should have incorporated more of those lessons when planning for Operation Iraqi Freedom (OIF) and Operation Enduring Freedom (OEF). But conversely, it will be interesting to watch the lessons of *these* wars on *future* conflicts. I would not be surprised if 30 years from now people will say, "Oh, we have neglected the lessons from Iraq and Afghanistan." I think we are already seeing a certain dynamic, or shift if you will, in the way we perceive these two conflicts. Just as General Bradley and President Kennedy warned of getting involved in "the wrong war, at the wrong place, at the wrong time, and with the wrong enemy," this phrase has since been intimately connected to US evaluations of various military enterprises of the past—and has been used to describe the war effort in Iraq as well. When you look at the results after 10 years in Afghanistan and Iraq, in land-dominated wars with hundreds of thousands of boots on the ground, it is hard not to acknowledge that this did not turn out exactly as we expected. Inevitably people are challenging the notion that the best course of action was to invest heavily in our ability to get in there on the ground, adopt a COIN doctrine of mingling with the people, and gradually help reshape their society into one with good governance, rule of law, and economic prosperity. Perhaps an outcome will be a general (if not universal) consensus that to posture for future conflicts we will need to put more investment in strategically vital air, naval, and special operations forces (SOF) and let domestic surrogates fight the ground war in their own countries. We cannot avoid the hard discussions regarding the lessons of Afghanistan and Iraq, just as the lessons from Vietnam escaped our focus in the decades preceding these wars.

Strategy

From my perspective, it was difficult to discern a commonly agreed upon strategy for approaching Afghanistan. Instead, it seemed we had two competing strategies or narratives at work. The first focused on a relatively small footprint on the ground in Afghanistan, with the objective of eliminating the threat that al-Qaeda poses to Western interests.[1] By systematically rooting out the main force behind the 9/11 attacks, we could argue that to go for the root cause of the problem would be more cost-effective in terms of economy, personnel, and equipment. Airpower, special forces, remotely piloted aircraft (RPA), and ISR would be key ingredients in this strategy. The ambition of this strategy was not to stabilize or conduct a nation-building of Afghanistan but rather kill or capture those individuals who were threatening the United States whenever we could reasonably identify and locate them. This strategy acknowledges that we need to have a certain presence in Afghanistan but just a fraction of those needed to conduct a full-fledged counterinsurgency. In fall 2001, we had some significant success using, particularly, SOF on the ground with state-of-the-art equipment to communicate with highly capable and lethal airpower. Cooperating with the Northern Alliance initially proved very effective in attacking enemy forces, and even today many believe that *that* was what we should have continued to do.

The second competing strategy was driven by the notion that killing terrorists would not fix the deeper problem of a failed state. Only by assisting Afghanistan to become a functioning state at least capable enough to provide for its own security would we eliminate the danger of it once again becoming a training base for terrorists. This would be the counterinsurgency approach, perhaps most publicly argued by Gen David Petraeus.

From a strategy standpoint, the real issue was the generation of worldwide terror. Without entering the discussion of whether it was wise to engage both Afghanistan and Iraq, in terms of strategy or military plans for approaching Afghanistan, we started almost from scratch. There was very little intelligence, targeting analysis, or anything else done prior to 9/11 that we could use for handling Afghanistan. Thus, the development of strategy became important. Somewhat unfortunately, we ended up having the competing narratives that, in many ways, we still have today. In practical terms it meant that we—over time—had to focus on both.

Putting the Square Conventional-Warfare Peg into the Round Irregular-Warfare Hole

The dominance of US airpower in traditional wars has not been lost on those who threaten our national interests. The conflicts in Iraq and Afghanistan illustrate how US military power has adapted and transformed to meet new challenges presented by enemies who, recognizing our conventional dominance, attempt to find and exploit seams in our capabilities. This dynamic challenged our approach to war as well.

We can logically expect enemies overwhelmed by US conventional military strength to turn increasingly to irregular warfare. That challenged us when approaching Afghanistan and Iraq in 2001 because, in my view, we arrived in theater with a conventional-warfare culture, whereas COIN is a very difficult type of warfare requiring a totally different strategy and mind-set. Counterinsurgency theorist Bernard B. Fall argued that "the straight military aspects, or the conventional military aspects of insurgency, are not the most important. . . . I would like to put it in even a simpler way: *When a country is being subverted it is not being outfought; it is being out-administered.*"[2] In other words, a government which is losing to an insurgency is not necessarily being defeated in armed conflict, but rather is losing the battle for control of the populace. It really speaks to the fact that the military has a role in a counterinsurgency, but there are many other nonmilitary variables that have to be addressed. One significant factor is to evaluate the status, or level, of governmental and administrative sophistication of the nation you are trying to assist. I think that was an issue in Afghanistan that we should have considered more carefully. If you compared Afghanistan with Iraq—as we had to do, fighting both wars—the differences between the two nations were stark: Iraq had a governing infrastructure and an ability to control populous supplies and basic needs. While certainly not up to *our* standards, there was a distinct capability there. The level of education was far higher and the communications and infrastructure largely more evolved. In short, there were structures there that could be built upon that made its potential for success significantly higher than Afghanistan. Afghanistan did not have the same governing structures or level of education, and never has—it is a landlocked country with enormous infrastructure challenges due to its topography, a high level of illiteracy, deep-rooted corruption, tribal culture, and devastation from war the past decades. In my view, the odds were clearly stacked against a COIN approach. Afghanistan had earned its repute as the "graveyard of empires" for a reason. The whole notion of us going in there to bolster the leadership, educate the bureaucracy, establish rule of law, modernize in terms of energy and infrastructure, and bring resources to the people—and that they therefore would side with us and the government and give up the insurgency—seeme'd somewhat naïve. It turned out to be very difficult.

In an irregular warfare campaign, the enemy forces blend in with friendly and neutral forces; there are no fronts. They also lack high-technology weaponry. In an IW environment, the traditionally recognized ability of airpower to strike at the adversary's "strategic center of gravity" will likely have little relevance due to the decentralized and diffuse nature of the enemy. The amorphous mass of ideological movements opposing Western influence and values generally lacks a defined command structure that airpower can attack with predictable effects. Still, airpower holds a number of asymmetric trump cards—capabilities the enemy can neither meet with parity nor counter in kind. For instance, the ability to conduct precision strikes across the globe can play an important role in COIN operations. Numerous other advantages—including information and cyber operations; intelligence, surveillance, and reconnaissance; and global mobility—have already proven just as important. These capabilities provide our fighting forces with highly asymmetric advantages in the IW environment, but in my view, we too often forgot these advantages. Many of the named ground operations in Afghanistan resembled the conventional approach to warfare. We were trying to put the square conventional-warfare peg into the round irregular-warfare hole. To an extent, they functioned more as morale-building for friendly forces. It was like being forced to take a kind of "operational middle ground" between conventional war and irregular warfare because we did not have the manpower or doctrines to do proper counterinsurgency. If you really believe in how to defeat an insurgency, it is about living among and controlling the population and having the citizens gradually come over to your side because they believe the government is a better option. Instead, many of the large operations would be of short duration, forces moving into an area or village to clear it of insurgents and then returning to their fortified forward operating bases. The insurgents who often fled before the force reached the village would come back, penalize those who cooperated with us, and continue controlling the village.

In fairness, there were some operations that I consider well targeted, but to me, the more effective approaches were often the day-to-day grinding of the opponent—especially from the SOF component. They were critical in identifying specific networks that needed to be taken down, killing the leadership, disabling those who were handling the money and the weapons which enabled the insurgency, and, most importantly, gleaning intelligence that would lead to future effective operations. Airpower, both conventional and special operations–specific, played key roles in the effectiveness of the counterterrorism mission.

While there surely are asymmetrical advantages that airpower brings to the fight, there are also clear limitations. When we have good intelligence, airpower can achieve astonishing results. When such intelligence is hard to come by, as often is the case in COIN operations, those limitations become more evident. We got a lot of questions from people in the headquarters about the use of airpower: "Why do we not seal off the border with airpower, why do we not protect the infrastructure with airpower, be more offensive, and don't just support the Army." Most of the people with these "great" ideas were not very familiar with Afghanistan and Iraq. An example: the borders of both countries were (and remain) relatively porous. Some people entered through the legal checkpoints; many did not. But for generations, people had been crossing back and forth across these borders with their livestock and goods for trade. Some were smugglers, some were members of borderless tribes, and in more recent times others were jihadists spoiling for a fight against the "infidels." But it is very difficult to evaluate which is which from the air. Airpower brings incredible capabilities, but it has its limitations. Airpower tends to be most effective when coupled with precise intelligence. While some intelligence can be gathered from air and space (including electronic intelligence, surveillance, and overhead imagery), sometimes operatives on the ground provide the best intelligence, particularly in IW. Airpower is clearly less effective in an insurgency, where it is difficult to tell who is on what side. Still, to counter these bands of insurgents in Iraq and Afghanistan with more of our own forces on the ground, more trucks, more artillery, and so forth did not seem to play to our strong suit, given that our main asymmetric advantage was what airpower brought to the fight.

Air-Land Integration

During the initial phases of operations in both Iraq and Afghanistan, the air component commander was the "supported commander" for various missions, all successfully accomplished. Both conflicts evolved into land-centric operations. In retrospect, I believe air-land integration achieved only a portion of its full potential; this needs to be addressed more rigorously in training, planning, and education in the future. Typically, the ground forces moved their headquarters to Iraq or Afghanistan with what was largely a ground-force staff. Those responsible for current and/or future operations would be Army dominated, as were most key positions in the headquarters. There were a limited number of Airmen there, but they tended to staff positions of limited influence. This normally led to operational plans that followed a pattern of planning the ground scheme of maneuver and then determining if air support might be helpful. Operation Anaconda in 2002 was perhaps the most infamous example of this in Afghanistan, to the point that *Anaconda* became a verb roughly translated as "to be blindsided." We pressed our air component coordination element (ACCE) directors and air liaison officers to proactively insert themselves into the operational planning processes at their headquarters.

Some of this friction is related to the land force emphasis on "decentralized command/decentralized execution," which enables task force or ground commanders to plan and execute operations within their AOR. Airmen subscribe to the concept of "centralized command/decentralized execution," which enables more effective use of finite airpower resources. Thus, planners in air headquarters tended to have limited influence on decentralized planning at lower-level Army headquarters. We would have liked to be more involved in planning, tasking, and execution at a much earlier stage of the operations. Occasionally we discovered ground commanders with limited understanding of the strengths and weaknesses of airpower who did not facilitate a process that included airpower as part of the plan. Adaptions and flexibility from both land and air forces were needed to succeed in IW.

There were some air-land integration success stories. One involved development and employment of the remotely operated video enhanced receiver (ROVER). If lasing a target from an RPA made close air support easier, the invention of ROVER was yet another significant leap forward. ROVER enabled a JTAC to communicate through a targeting pod, or other means, directly with the aircraft performing close air support and see exactly what the pilot in the cockpit saw. Communicating with each other while looking at the same imagery represented a quantum leap in the effectiveness of the air-ground team. Targeting pod–equipped aircraft provided nontraditional ISR (NTISR) of infrastructure and monitored ground operations, with real-time visual information exchanged between the pilots and ground controllers.

As previously mentioned, this level of integration between air and ground units requires a significant investment in personnel, training, and equipment. The United States learned the hard way that shortcuts in this investment increase the risk of collateral damage and fratricide. At the direction of the commander of CENTCOM and the CFACC, tests of air-ground integration were conducted in fall and winter of 2005–06 at each provincial reconstruction team to build confidence that air support would be available and effective should the PRT come under heavy attack. The NATO countries were required to certify their JTACs per STANAG 3797,[3] but there was understandable concern that training, communications, or language limitations would hinder the already challenging business of employing ordnance in close proximity to friendly forces.

The Iraq-Afghanistan Relationship

When analyzing the use of airpower in Afghanistan from a US perspective, it is impossible not to view Afghanistan in relation to Iraq. First, both theaters were in the area of responsibility of CENTCOM, which meant the resources of CENTCOM and CENTAF

(CENTCOM Air Forces) were applied to joint force requirements across the AOR, including both Iraq and Afghanistan. That meant that operations and priorities in one area often impacted another. For years, the main focus was Iraq in almost all aspects. Iraq was where we were taking casualties on a daily basis and where a substantial amount of US treasure was directed. The war in Iraq was under the continuous scrutiny of worldwide media, and it was where we struggled the most militarily. It was the main focus of US foreign policy for years and a place where the United States struggled to uphold its international prestige as the sole remaining superpower. Afghanistan had few of these characteristics, and resources were apportioned accordingly.

In the summer of 2001, the US-built CAOC facility was completed at Prince Sultan Air Base (PSAB) in Saudi Arabia. Joint Task Force Southwest Asia (JTF-SWA) moved its CAOC from Riyadh to PSAB shortly before 9/11; thus the new CAOC immediately got its baptism of fire as it controlled the air war in Afghanistan in the fall of 2001. So, even though we were still executing the decade-long Southern Watch in Iraq, the weight of effort was now on Afghanistan.

Then the planning for Operation Iraqi Freedom began, and it is no secret that *that* took on a quite separate urgency. Planning and providing adequate forces for the likely campaign in Iraq now became center stage. One concern was the relationship with the Saudis. From a long-term standpoint, with us fighting a war in Afghanistan and Iraq, the Saudis might impact our operational flexibility. The key reason the Saudis let us occupy the command and control facility at PSAB was the enforcement of the Iraqi no-fly zone. There was always some concern related to executing operations in other theaters of war from the CAOC inside Saudi territory. Depending on where we wanted to operate, they might decide to put some restrictions on us. So we started to look at our base at Al Udeid in Qatar. The Qatari government wanted to form an agreement with its Western allies because they had some security concerns of their own in the region. It is my impression that they made some strategic calculations and thought that if they had the US military in their country, that would have to be part of any potential adversary's calculus. The USAF built a new CAOC at Al Udeid to conduct air operations in Afghanistan, while the Saudi-based CAOC focused on Operation Iraqi Freedom.

When the initial phase of OIF ended in May 2003, it became pretty clear that Iraqi military forces were no longer an imminent threat to

Saudi Arabia. As noted, our relationship with the royal family as the keeper of the two mosques and the cradle of the Islamic faith had always entailed a certain "cost-benefit" calculation to both the Saudis and to us. The royal family knew they opened themselves to criticism by forces within their own country asking why "infidels" were allowed to operate from Saudi soil—particularly when attacking other Islamic countries. We were basically told that this would be a good time to disassemble the CAOC at Prince Sultan Air Base and move the command and control of coalition air operations elsewhere. This facility, which had only been in operation since 2001 and cost about $50 million, was dismantled in short order in May of 2003. The command and control of theater airpower for CENTCOM moved to Qatar. Al Udeid became a theater hub, with both a CAOC and a large number of air assets stationed there.

The CAOC, while USAF-built and led, was truly a combined headquarters at the operational level of war. Officers from other US services and other coalition nations held key leadership, staff, and liaison positions. Flag officers from the UK and Australia held positions as CAOC directors overseeing the five divisions: strategy, plans, operations, air mobility, and ISR. The CAOC included representation from all of the OIF and OEF coalition countries, including France, Singapore, Japan, Qatar, and others.

This USAF-led, multinationally staffed CAOC planned, tasked, executed, and assessed air operations in support of both OIF and OEF. As the insurgency gained strength in Iraq, the situation gradually deteriorated despite the efforts of the OIF coalition. In balancing the effort between OIF and OEF, the preponderance of effort was on OIF because the number of friendly force casualties was staggering, the infrastructure attacks were soaring, and the Iraqi military was not progressing satisfactorily to become self-sufficient.

Keep in mind the CAOC, in supporting the commander of CENTAF, had responsibilities that stretched across all 27 countries within the CENTCOM AOR—support for JTF–Horn of Africa, engagement activities and exercises across the region, missile defense responsibilities, airspace control responsibilities, and so forth. So to parse the effort into "Iraq versus Afghanistan" does not do justice to the intricacies and magnitude of the requirements. With the nature of airpower less subject to artificial or geographic boundaries, many of the mobility, ISR, and some kinetic assets could swing from one operation to the other based on joint force requirements.

The OEF-ISAF Relationship

Prior to and including my tenure as deputy CFACC for OIF and OEF airpower, the US-led coalition and ISAF coexisted peacefully, with ISAF operating in Kabul and in the relatively quiet northern Afghanistan region. ISAF, under NATO leadership, expanded its area of responsibility in stages. In May 2006, Stage 2 added Regional Command West to ISAF's jurisdiction and doubled its responsibilities. Stage 3—expansion into the volatile RC South, including the Taliban homeland of Kandahar—was under way in the summer of 2006 as I departed the scene, with Stage 4, assuming responsibility for stability operations across the entire country, targeted for October 2006 completion.

Seen from an overall big-picture perspective, the increased involvement of NATO and ISAF in Afghanistan was fundamentally a good thing. It was important for several reasons, not least the fact that they put an international face on a conflict which otherwise could be characterized as "the United States going it alone" once again. Some noted facetiously that NATO could assist the United States in terms of strategy, referring to the US "OODA loop" as "observe, overreact, destroy, apologize." Then again, others have found somewhat illustrative definitions for the acronym *NATO*, but I choose to leave that for another occasion.

At the same time it is no secret that in terms of airpower, ISAF's contributions paled in comparison to the combat power being exercised by the OIF/OEF coalition. As a general rule, ISAF crews and aircraft performed well, but those assets were very limited in quantity, amounting to perhaps a half dozen or so sorties each day. In many ways the ISAF contribution was as much political as it was military. ISAF also was limited in its ability to provide infrastructure and command and control of its airpower assets, relying heavily on the OEF coalition capabilities. This would prove to cause some friction, since there was a certain discrepancy between the political will to provide assets and infrastructure in theater and the ambition for NATO and ISAF to maneuver for leadership roles in the command and control of air assets in Afghanistan.

The OEF coalition was engaged on a daily basis against al-Qaeda leadership through offensive targeted operations. These operations were performed mainly with special operations forces, coalition airpower, or a combination of the two. This was a role that NATO and

ISAF had not signed up to do. Thus we ended up with two separate but intertwined operations in Afghanistan—ISAF's stability operations and the US-led Operation Enduring Freedom, including its counterterrorism objectives.

This, in turn, invoked some of the more problematic issues of alliance warfare that we remembered all too well from our past experiences in the Balkans—most notably in the 1999 Kosovo campaign, with nations putting national restrictions ("caveats") on the use of their force contributions. Alliance and coalition warfare has always been a challenge in this regard, but the construct of ISAF as a more defensive "security assistance force" versus OEF as a targeted and offensive air operation more susceptible to collateral damage made this even more politically sensitive. Some nations had to distinguish between these two operations for political reasons and had caveats and national rules of engagement that precluded participation in the latter. But for the OEF coalition, the very reason for being in theater was to root out those al-Qaeda groups that posed a direct threat to Western interests. It would remain a challenge to unite the two operations into one cohesive campaign. The situation led to nations imposing various caveats and limitations on use of their forces—some could only support their own troops, some had their own ROE on collateral damage approval, and so forth. We had to design specific matrices describing what each nation's forces could do and what they could not do—which proved to be a real challenge for those fighting the war on a daily basis.

There was some tension marking the relationship between the United States and ISAF regarding the preference of the NATO leadership to gain—in NATO terms—"operational command (OPCOM)" of national air assets, including air-to-air refueling (AAR); intelligence, surveillance, reconnaissance; unmanned aerial vehicles (UAV); fighters and bombers; and combat search and rescue (CSAR). OPCOM authority would, in their view, enable ISAF to plan and execute operations in a flexible manner to achieve their objectives in Afghanistan. Needless to say, there was great reluctance to accommodate this within the US chain of command for a number of reasons. The OIF/OEF coalition needed flexibility to achieve its objectives, including destruction of the al-Qaeda leadership, offensive operations, operations close to the Pakistan border, and a number of other sensitive operations in which the ISAF nations had not agreed to participate. We did not want to end up in a situation where we had an urgent need to respond to a surfacing high-value target and find that we had to "borrow" our assets from ISAF to conduct the mission. There was also a concern that putting US assets under NATO control would deter other NATO nations from filling the Combined Joint Statement of Requirements (CJSOR)—the list of requirements that NATO military commanders argued were necessary to achieve their objectives. NATO had no mechanism to force its member nations to provide assets and resources in relative proportion to their overall wealth or their stake in the outcome. Thus the CJSOR for NATO operations routinely came up short. ISAF leaders lamented the shortfall in assets—having only a half dozen or so fighters and little in the way of key assets such as ISR, aerial refueling, or CSAR. For example, only 1.5 of the 6 required intratheater airlift assets were pledged for the transition to Stage 2, and routinely the assets provided were encumbered by national caveats. When ISAF was to assume control of the southern and eastern provinces of Afghanistan by summer 2006, its leaders approached the OEF coalition with a list of shortfalls it needed to adequately fulfill the mission.

On the other hand, the OIF/OEF airpower coalition was robustly equipped for its mission. On a daily basis the CAOC oversaw roughly 300 coalition sorties. Within limitations of speed and range, the airpower was apportioned between OIF and OEF (to include JTF–Horn of Africa) based on CENTCOM priorities. About half of the sorties each day were airlift missions (C-130 and C-17), carrying an average of 2,600 passengers and 600 tons of cargo from one location to another. Typically 20–25 percent of that effort supported OEF. Two or three dozen more missions moved distinguished visitors, R&R Soldiers, and detainees. Thirty aerial refueling missions offloaded 2.1 million pounds of fuel to upwards of 175 receivers, with about 20–25 percent of those supporting OEF. Airdrop missions supported OEF almost exclusively; up to 15 missions per week conducted precision airdrop of supplies to forward-deployed forces in Afghanistan.

The apportionment of CFACC-controlled ISR between the three primary customers (Multinational Force Iraq, the Combined Joint Task Force in Afghanistan, and the Combined Joint Task Force–Horn of Africa) was very closely managed by CENTCOM. A weekly Joint Collections Management Board (co-chaired by the CENTCOM J2 and J3) gathered ISR requirements and made decisions regarding weights of effort. Various low-density, high-demand assets (U-2, RC-135, Nimrod, P-3, and Predator combat air patrols) were apportioned among the joint force commanders for the following week. In terms of pure assets, on a day-to-day basis the numbers were roughly 75 percent supporting Iraq versus 25 percent in Afghanistan, although weights of effort shifted based on operations and threats.

The requirements-driven apportionment for other mission types was similar. Typically 75–80 kinetic-capable (fighter or bomber) missions were flown each day, most of them extended with aerial refueling, with about 25 percent flown in OEF. Each air tasking order (ATO) period averaged 20 EW missions and 20 ISR missions; roughly one-third of those missions supported OEF. On any given day the coalition forces responded to 20–40 troop-in-contact events, in which fighters or bombers were dispatched from their NTISR locations to establish contact with a JTAC associated with the unit in contact with enemy forces. The goal was to have airpower on station within 10 minutes of the call for help in Iraq; in Afghanistan, given the distances, communications challenges, and lack of infrastructure, that goal was 20 minutes. These urgent calls for airpower were routine events—during the period that I was deputy CFACC, coalition forces conducted some 2,000 shows of force and dropped 1,100 precision weapons in support of joint forces on the ground. This required a significant investment not just in airpower technology, but also in personnel trained and equipped to perform the incredibly complex business of integrating airpower into the ground scheme of maneuver. Although OIF may have received the preponderance of air effort, the amount apportioned to OEF was considerable in absolute terms, enabling the ground forces in Afghanistan to extend influence well beyond their organic capabilities. Airpower provided the "high ground" for our forces engaged in stability operations.

Since the CFACC was designated the airspace control authority for Iraq and Afghanistan, the CAOC managed the airspace over both countries, integrating combat operations with commercial operations and commercial overflights. This involved a 24-hours-a-day complex and dynamic blending of battle management and air traffic control functions. My point is that the CFACC was charged with significant air component responsibilities across the theater. Our preference would have been to integrate the ISAF assets and requirements into the theater operations conducted by the CAOC. For a variety of political reasons, ISAF was reluctant to turn over management of its air operations to the CAOC.

Still, the US-led OIF/OEF coalition was committed to its support of ISAF, and in that sense we never viewed ISAF as lacking access to air-to-ground assets when required. This goes to the heart of the discussion. From an air perspective, we were working to achieve *unified command, distributed control,* and *decentralized execution* as the fundamental principles for the execution of air operations. We would have preferred to have one large airpower pool, overseen from one facility, under an air component commander responsive to a joint force commander, as recommended by joint and NATO doctrine.

One very important factor shaping our discussions on command relationships was a sense that the NATO and ISAF facilities were not up to the task of conducting robust airpower C2, to include planning, tasking, executing, and assessing airpower for the Afghan theater. When I visited the NATO tactical air operations center (TAOC) in Kabul on several occasions, I was generally impressed with the personnel, yet underwhelmed by the facility's capabilities. It had a small staff and some ability to communicate with aircraft but lacked the ability to develop strategy, provide a master attack plan, perform the ATO production and dissemination, and so on. It did not have an adequate combat operations center with a capability of real-time monitoring and directing aircraft, orchestrating the ISR platforms, generating intelligence and requirements—the whole package of modern air operations. I stress, this is not an indictment of the NATO personnel; just as when I served in 1999 in the Vicenza CAOC supporting the CFACC (Lt Gen Mike Short), some of my very best planners were from NATO nations. But NATO had simply not made the investment in deployable C2 capability. As noted, over the years the United States had made this incredible investment in C2 capability in theater, and for those who had the chance to see the facility in Kabul in comparison to what had been constructed for the CAOC at Al Udeid, the difference was stark.

The role of the TAOC post–Stage 4 was a source of continual discussion. NATO efforts to obtain blanket approval for its personnel to gain access to the Al Udeid CAOC did not gain traction with the host-nation government, which insisted on bilateral agreements with each country. An alternative suggestion was to move the TAOC to Bagram Airfield in Afghanistan and consolidate with the coalition C2 facilities there, but the NATO leadership was resistant, opting to preserve the ISAF C2 node at Kabul to oversee ISAF-dedicated missions.

One aggravating factor was that Afghanistan, as a country, posed extremely difficult challenges to conducting effective command and control. In Iraq we had near-instant ability to see and communicate with aircraft throughout the country. Afghanistan was a different story, given its lack of communications infrastructure and the incredibly rugged terrain. This was not for lack of trying—ground radio relay stations were built, FACE (fighter aircraft communications enhancement) radio relay pods were carried by A-10 aircraft, JSTARS (joint surveillance target attack radar system) and AWACS aircraft were occasionally pressed into service to perform this function, but we never achieved the robustness of communications connectivity that we enjoyed across most of Iraq. If there ever were a country in need of air and space capabilities to overcome the cards that nature dealt it, it is Afghanistan. Still, the ability to command and control forces in Afghanistan from the CAOC at Al Udeid was significantly more advanced than what NATO had established in Kabul. Contrasting that, the OIF/OEF coalition had the equipment, experience, and knowledge already available. We were in theater with intelligence and space assets no one else could match.

Finally, there was a distinct difference between ISAF and CENTCOM during this period in supporting the civilian authorities in Afghanistan. ISAF, at the time, had a relatively narrow view of the mission, while the CENTCOM CFACC was charged with air operations across the theater and across the spectrum from humanitarian operations to combat missions. This is one reason for the reluctance to divert OEF air assets and C2 capabilities to ISAF, lest it limit the much needed flexibility to perform this broad range of missions. A few examples:

- During my tenure, we placed a priority on building host-nation aviation capabilities, both the nascent air force and the air traffic control capabilities. The USAF took a lead role in planning the transition from combat airspace management to enabling civil aircraft to access the airspace. In mid July 2005, I participated in a ceremony marking the opening of the US-funded Kabul Air Control Center, from which combat and civil operations were to be coordinated. Opening the airspace above FL 360 (36,000 feet) to civil overflights shortened air routes for commercial carriers and provided a revenue stream to the Afghan government estimated at some $60 million a year. Our State Department and Federal Aviation Administration worked to send Afghan citizens to English language and air traffic control training (with limited success, unfortunately). It would have been good to have more ISAF/NATO participation in this effort, but it was expensive, and there did not seem to be an appetite on the part of ISAF/NATO leadership to add this boulder to their knapsack.

- In both OIF and OEF, for various reasons, we were figuratively well behind the power curve with respect to redevelopment of the Iraqi and Afghan air forces. We recognized that part of the coalition's exit strategy in both countries relied on the ability of the host nation to take over the functions that were being performed by coalition forces, such as air defense, air transport, search and rescue, reconnaissance, and direct support of ground forces. This proved a particular challenge in Afghanistan due to geography, lack of resources and infrastructure, low literacy rates, and other factors. Vetting potential service members—who might eventually control aircraft equipped with weapons—was particularly challenging in Afghanistan: during 2011 and 2012, we began to see a disturbing rise in "green-on-blue" attacks, which speaks fundamentally to the vetting challenge.

- On 8 October 2005, a 7.6-magnitude earthquake struck northern Pakistan. Pakistani national relief capabilities were quickly overwhelmed: the quake left an estimated 75,000 people killed and hundreds of thousands homeless as winter approached. International relief agencies responded, but the call quickly went out to coalition military forces to help. Much of the airpower effort was managed from the CAOC while still overseeing combat operations in Iraq and Afghanistan. Air Mobility Command sent a contingency response group to the Chaklala airfield (now PAF Base Nur Khan) in Pakistan, augmented with theater personnel including medical personnel, rescue forces, airfield cargo handling specialists, and air traffic control experts to support the joint task force established under then-RADM Mike LeFever. The US-led operation delivered more than 5,500 short tons of relief supplies and deployed two field hospitals that were manned with US Army and Marine personnel. They helped bring order from chaos, facilitating the transfer of humanitarian supplies onto helicopters (including

Pakistani and US Army/Marine) and trucks for distribution to the affected region. I believe we built considerable good will through this effort to ease the immense suffering of the affected Pakistanis.

It is important to appreciate the scope of the effort overseen from the CAOC and, hence, the reluctance to parcel out pieces of those capabilities to ISAF. We genuinely felt ISAF represented a step forward in many ways. We saw the political benefits of coalition warfare and welcomed more increased diversity of assets provided, but some infighting ensued when the draft plans from NATO appeared to put non-US officers in key positions to get more control over how airpower was used. This was resisted by the OIF/OEF coalition leadership.

In addition to requiring a cadre of trained personnel to maintain, operate, and protect the airfields, the cost of running the Kandahar airfield was about $250 million a year for construction, infrastructure, maintenance, food, fuel, and other expenses. Sticker shock set in and discouraged countries who had initially expressed willingness to take lead roles. US taxpayers had funded very expensive runway and ramp projects (among many other construction projects at Kandahar and Bagram), while many NATO countries were quite content to show up with a handful of airplanes and personnel, occupy dorms and ramps, and consume the food and fuel provided. In August 2005 one major NATO nation withdrew its TACAN navigational aid from the Kabul airfield—a relatively miniscule expense compared to the cost of running an entire airfield—leading to a request to the United States to backfill this capability (even though we were already operating both Bagram and Kandahar). Individual NATO nations showed very little appetite for doing the economic heavy lifting necessary to maintain the infrastructure and logistics in these remote locations. NATO leadership eventually designated Kandahar as an aerial port of debarkation (APOD) in 2005 to make it eligible for NATO organizational funding, and the United States was asked to maintain lead nation status at the airfield for at least another 12 months while NATO attempted to source personnel and equipment to assume responsibility.

As ISAF expanded operations, command relations for airpower and SOF in Afghanistan proved to both be knotty problems. The doctrinal principle of unified command argued for a single CFACC for CENTCOM and ISAF operations, overseeing all air operations and able to apply airpower's flexible capabilities against the highest priority requirements. This would logically have placed the CENTCOM CFACC as the DCOM (deputy commander)–Air. However, NATO's leadership was resistant to placing a US three-star in the ISAF command chain.

The NATO staff pushed for a DCOM-Air to issue direction and guidance for ISAF air operations. My personal recommendation was that the CAOC be responsible for orchestration of air operations, and give the ISAF DCOM-Air the responsibilities of base operating support infrastructure and senior airfield authority at airfields with significant ISAF presence, such as Kandahar and Kabul. This did not sit well with those in the NATO chain, and various proposals and counterproposals were bounced back and forth between CENTCOM and NATO headquarters. In late October 2005, Lt Gen Buck Buchanan met personally with his German air force counterpart at the CAOC to try to resolve the differences. The end result was a compromise of sorts—in May 2006, the DCFACC position was to be designated as a NATO billet, working *with* (or *for*, depending on whom you asked) the ISAF DCOM-Air. Liaison elements led by general officers would be dispatched to each other's headquarters (a NATO air coordination element to the CAOC and a CFACC air component coordination element to Kabul) to facilitate the exchange of information. They agreed that the ISAF DCOM-Air would serve in the capacity of "senior air advisor" to COMISAF, but "not as a CFACC."

At a CENTCOM conference in January 2006, terms like *Hand-CON* or *WarCON*, instead of *OPCON* or *TACON*, were used to describe the proposed command relationships, acknowledging that well-intentioned people in both organizations would have to make a less-than-ideal, convoluted command-relations spaghetti diagram workable. This nondoctrinal arrangement, with the deputy CFACC essentially working for two different bosses and supported by exchanged liaison elements, supporting related but distinct missions with liaison elements as intermediaries, would lead to rather predictable friction over the next couple of years.

Epilogue

The war in Iraq is instructional in understanding the war in Afghanistan in terms of political support, military apportionment, economy, technology, and focus. In this chapter, I attempted to put the ISAF mission in the context of the CFACC's theaterwide responsibilities. The transition to ISAF was an important step and one that was supported by the leadership of the OIF/OEF coalition. I also tried to show why allocating OIF/OEF forces to operate under NATO OPCOM in Afghanistan would have been suboptimal and could have hindered the OEF mission. As I departed the theater, ISAF was in the process of expanding its AOR to include much more volatile regions of Afghanistan. This would require a true joint force approach—a combined force prepared to conduct offensive and defensive operations on a regular short-notice basis. I left the theater confident that although the C2 arrangements were far from perfect, if ISAF ground forces needed airpower, it would be there. ISAF's ability to effectively employ that airpower, however, remained a question mark.

Notes

1. See Peter Baker and Elisabeth Bumiller, "Obama Considers Strategy Shift in Afghan War," *New York Times*, 22 September 2009, http://www.nytimes.com/2009/09/23/world/asia/23policy.html.

2. Bernard B. Fall, "The Theory and Practice of Insurgency and Counterinsurgency," *Naval War College Review*, Winter 1998, http://www.au.af.mil/au/awc/awcgate/navy/art5-w98.htm.

3. NATO Standardization Agreement (STANAG) 3797, *Minimum Qualifications for Forward Air Controllers & Laser Operators in Support of Forward Air Controllers*, 27 April 2009.

Part II

ISAF Assumes Responsibility
for Afghanistan

Chapter 3

Operation Medusa

Maj Gen Charles S. "Duff" Sullivan, Canadian Forces, Retired

*Co-President of the Combined Investigation Board
convened by Commander, US Air Forces Central
Command to investigate the A-10 friendly fire
incident during Operation Medusa
September–December 2006*

*NATO Air Component Commander to Afghanistan,
Deputy Chief Joint Operations
Director Air Component Element (ACE)
November 2008–November 2009*

Introduction

Operation Medusa was a major military offensive conducted by NATO's International Security Assistance Force along with the Afghan National Army 1–17 September 2006. Preparatory operations to shape the battlefield had been conducted for several weeks before. The region—the district of Panjwayi in Kandahar Province some 30 kilometers west-southwest of Kandahar City—had been a long-standing Taliban stronghold. The objective of the operation was to establish government control in the area. In military terms, ISAF intended to clear the enemy sanctuary by rooting out the insurgents and reinstate local, legitimate governance. ISAF forces designated to achieve this objective were mainly Canadian troops.

In early September 2006, the commander of US Air Forces Central Command (AFCENT), Lt Gen Gary North, ordered an investigation into a friendly fire incident that occurred during Operation Medusa, in which a US A-10 fighter-bomber aircraft inadvertently strafed a Canadian army battle position, killing one soldier and wounding 36 others. At the request of AFCENT, Canada agreed to support the Combined Investigation Board (CIB) and offered to deploy a brigadier general fighter pilot to serve alongside Brig Gen Stanley (Sid)

Clark, USAF, as co-president of the investigation. I received a phone call in the middle of the night from the Air Staff in Ottawa and by first light the next morning was making arrangements and packing my combat kit for an imminent departure for Afghanistan. The CIB was comprised of 15 members, support specialists, and observers. Within a few days of the friendly fire incident, the team was assembled at Bagram Air Base in northern Afghanistan ready to begin its investigative work.

The CIB focused its initial investigative efforts on the A-10 pilot and other members of the fighter squadron involved. At the end of the second week, the CIB deployed to Kandahar Airfield to interview members of Canada's 1 Royal Canadian Regiment (1RCR) battle group, most of whom were still on the frontlines of Operation Medusa where the incident had occurred. The CIB also interviewed key operations personnel who manned the battle group's fire support coordination centre (FSCC) and ISAF's theatre air control system (TACS).

During the interview process with soldiers and TACS personnel in Kandahar, we discovered there were significant, unexpected, systemic deficiencies within ISAF and the Canadian military with respect to air-land integration and the unsafe and ineffective application of air effects and enablers during combat operations. These unexpected findings resulted in the CIB devoting extra time to interviewing land-force personnel from the Canadian army and Regional Command South (RC-S).

Following a few more days back in Bagram, we spent the final 10 days of our in-theatre investigation at the CENTCOM CAOC in Al Udeid, Qatar, where the team had access to applicable operations files and intelligence information related to Operation Medusa and the friendly fire incident. ISAF's air planning and liaison staff permanently based at the CAOC also assisted in providing expert knowledge of ISAF's Deputy Commander–Air (DCOM-Air) organization, the relationship between ISAF and the US CFACC, and applicable operational activities across Afghanistan, including Operation Medusa. We conducted additional interviews via teleconference with several wounded soldiers who had been emergency-evacuated to Europe and North America immediately following the incident. Prior to leaving the theatre, the CIB had the opportunity to meet with senior members of NATO's investigation team,[1] which was commissioned to investigate the same friendly fire incident and ISAF's command

and control of joint operations. Canada and NATO had each commissioned their own independent investigations into the friendly fire event. The CIB pointed out to the NATO team several areas of interest and concern for further investigation that fell outside the CIB's mandate but were considered important to identifying and assessing factors that may have contributed to the incident from a higher headquarters and C2 perspective. The Canadian investigation team did not arrive until well after the CIB had completed its in-theatre work and had redeployed to North America to write its final report. Both the NATO and the Canadian investigation teams were disappointed the US military would not authorize release of all the information related to CIB findings, observations, and interviews.

The CIB redeployed to AFCENT headquarters at Shaw AFB in South Carolina in early October to brief Lieutenant General North on the findings and observations of the investigation and to write the final report. The board succeeded in completing its investigation and submitting its draft report to CENTCOM within 30 days of the friendly fire incident. In the months following, members of the CIB provided face-to-face briefings to the senior leadership of US Central Command, US Air Combatant Command, Canada's Chief of Defence staff and air force and army chiefs, the families and soldiers of Canada's 1RCR, and several special interest groups and military HQs.

Operation Medusa was considered an important event for NATO as it represented ISAF's first major attempt at joint operations since the expansion of its military authority beyond Kabul. ISAF assumed command of the southern region of Afghanistan on 31 July 2006, and Operation Medusa was its first significant encounter with the Taliban. Touted as the largest offensive operation in NATO history, Medusa was planned and executed by Regional Command South in August and September of 2006. Much has been said and written about the operation;[2] however, what really took place in the lead-up to the operation and on the Medusa battlefield itself remains shrouded in the bravado, hyperbole, and "communications campaign" championed by those who prefer to have the operation remembered as some kind of momentous tipping point in the battle against the Taliban in and around the city of Kandahar.

This chapter deals with the main points from Operation Medusa and supports the conclusion of how years of neglect and indifference toward air-land integration and the methods and practices of applying airpower in joint operations led to the defeat of the Canadian army during a major joint operation and the tragic and unnecessary casualties incurred by the 1RCR battle group in Panjwayi in August and September 2006.

Operation Medusa

As outlined in Regional Command South's operational plans, the purpose of Operation Medusa was to establish government control over an area of Kandahar Province in the vicinity of the town of Panjwayi 30 kilometers west of the city of Kandahar. The operation followed preparatory activities by units under the RC-S commander. Some of the most notable pre-Medusa operations were conducted by the Princess Patricia's Canadian Light Infantry (PPCLI) battle group. On 3 August 2006, they performed a most courageous effort that unfortunately resulted in several Canadians being killed and wounded on the battlefield. The PPCLI effort was meant to thwart insurgent plans to launch attacks on Afghanistan government locations in Kandahar City; however, the Taliban instead attacked the Panjwayi district centre on 19 August, Afghan "Independence Day," which threw the forces of RC-S into a desperate defensive battle that stunned unsuspecting coalition commanders.

Some of the fiercest fighting experienced by the military forces of RC-S in early August was recounted by the PPCLI commander, and a few handpicked members of his battle group at a strategic gathering of Canadian general officers in November 2006 in Gatineau, Quebec. Testimony of the heroic efforts of the soldiers of the PPCLI as they went head to head with Taliban fighters was truly awe-inspiring, with the most striking comments coming from the commander himself as he described the casualties his battle group suffered and how they battled enemy insurgents without the effects and enablers needed to underpin success.[3] The PPCLI's effort in the Panjwayi was to be their final major action in RC-S, as the 1RCR had already started arriving in theatre to relieve the battle-weary "Patricias." Under pressure to reverse the surging and ubiquitous Taliban in and around the approaches to Kandahar City, RC-S inched closer to Operation Medusa, which would see an increase in shaping actions in the latter half of the month in preparation for the "strike phase" that would be led by the Canadian 1RCR battle group during the first week of September.

In the days leading up to the much-anticipated strike phase of Operation Medusa, Charles Company of the Canadian 1RCR battle group deployed to its initial battle position south of the Arghandab River near Ma'sum Ghar in Panjwayi district and prepared to lead an assault against the burgeoning Taliban forces.[4] Their initial advance was planned to be a "feint" maneuver designed to draw out Taliban fighters and expose their positions. Once the disposition of enemy forces was identified, a two-to-three-day airstrike phase would follow, which would target all known and suspected Taliban locations. Following the airstrike phase, Charles Company would then advance to "clean up" any residual elements of a diminished Taliban force.

At least that was the tactical maneuver that the 1RCR battle group and its supporting elements had painstakingly set in place in the days and weeks leading up to the operation. However, on the afternoon of 2 September 2006, with only hours to go until the battle group was to initiate its feint maneuver, Charles Company was unexpectedly issued new orders by the Canadian Commander of RC-S. The general's new plan called for 1RCR to cross the Arghandab River and execute a direct assault on the Taliban force but without a feint maneuver and without the airstrike phase to target Taliban positions. As revealed in interviews with the CENTCOM investigation team, the senior platoon, company, and battle group commanders of 1RCR vehemently opposed and protested this change in plan; however, their objections had no effect on what was described as a troubling new approach coming from the commander of Regional Command South.

The extensive and detailed airstrike phase and the numerous air assets tasked to support the air effort had been "stood down" on orders from RC-S headquarters. The CENTCOM investigation team interviewed senior members of the battle group and RC-S staffs to learn more about the decision-making process that resulted in such a stunning change to the Medusa plan. However, no clear explanations were given, not even by the commander of RC-S himself to the co-presidents of the CIB. Some have speculated on the role of the legal advisor in influencing the commander's decision, others on pressure exerted by the ISAF deputy commander–Operations to "just get the job done," and still other observers on the lack of oversight of ISAF HQ. Some have even speculated that as tactically viable and sound as the original 1RCR plan was, the strategy of employing the land force as a supporting deception enabler to an offensive air operation as the "main event" did not resonate well with those in search of a land-force victory.

As ordered, 1RCR launched a direct assault on suspected Taliban positions at 0700 hours on 3 September 2006 but without the pre-planned feint maneuver to expose enemy positions and without the critical airstrike phase to target the Taliban force. As anticipated by the tactical commanders in the field that morning, the Charles Company advance did indeed expose the Taliban force; however, the advance was halted shortly after crossing the Arghandab River by overwhelming enemy fire, which quickly transitioned into a decisive defeat at the hands of the Taliban force, all within 20 minutes of the Canadians beginning their initial advance. With four Canadians killed in action, another six critically wounded, and three armored vehicles blazing on the battlefield, Charles Company found itself pinned down and taking devastating fire from well-placed and well-equipped Taliban fighters. As recounted during interviews by 1RCR soldiers, the unrelenting Taliban fire continued for two-and-a-half hours as they tried to withdraw to their initial battle position on Ma'sum Ghar. Interviews also provided several hours of testimony on the extraordinary acts of courage as Charles Company soldiers extracted their wounded comrades from the chaotic battlefield melee. Most troubling was the testimony revealing that members of Charles Company were completely unsuccessful in targeting any Taliban fighters on the battlefield that morning. Even when they were trying to provide covering fire to extract their dead and wounded, they recounted how they were shooting at shadows and puffs of smoke in a desperate attempt to pull back. Testimony on one attempt to provide emergency air support told of a 1,000 lb. high-explosive (HE) bomb that impacted the ground only a few hundred feet from the Canadian line and could have caused several friendly casualties. Fortunately, for some undetermined reason, the bomb did not detonate on impact. As noted by the CENTCOM investigation team, these frontline battlefield accounts were stunning admissions of a humiliating defeat and disappointing failure, all of which has since called into question the many official reports from RC-S, ISAF HQ, NATO, and scores of media headlines that trumpeted the tremendous success of Operation Medusa and the hundreds of Taliban fighters that were killed as a result of the Canadian-led operation.[5]

The investigation team learned from 1RCR soldiers and tactical ground commanders that following 1RCR's failed assault on 3 September, the plan for the very next day was to repeat the same maneuver and with the same tactical goals and objectives. Having observed Charles Company's first attempt from high atop a vertical feature just south of the Arghandab River near Ma'sum Ghar, a nearby special forces commander stepped forward to urge a different approach for the next day's attempt. However, Charles Company had their orders from their regional commander. Throughout the night of 3 September, the Canadian battle group maintained a steady barrage of fire, which included heavy artillery from a nearby forward operating base and close air support from US A-10 fighter jets on the previous day's suspected Taliban positions. Soldiers from the 1RCR recounted that even though there were no Taliban forces sighted, this long and steady overnight bombardment was conducted under the pretext of a troops in contact (TIC) declaration, which meant forces were authorized to return defensive fire in response to incoming enemy fire.

As dawn approached on day two, the soldiers of Charles Company were huddled around a large fire they had lit on their Ma'sum Ghar battle position to burn garbage and litter from their breakfast routine. Unfortunately, this predawn garbage fire was located only a short distance from the insurgent target area and was misidentified by one of the US A-10 pilots as the glowing remnants of a 500 lb. bomb dropped on a suspected Taliban position only 60 seconds earlier. The A-10 pilot, who had been targeting Taliban positions throughout the night under the tactical control of the Charles Company forward air controller (FAC), rolled in on what he thought was a recently bombed Taliban position.[6] The fighter pilot called "in hot" on his aircraft radio and received approval from the Canadian FAC on Ma'sum Ghar with Charles Company to release weapons on his intended target. As the pilot completed what he thought was a successful attack run, he heard the dreaded words "Abort! Abort! Abort! . . . friendly position!" He had just strafed Charles Company's battle position with his 30 mm cannon, killing one soldier and wounding 36 others, many critically. A second A-10 aircraft, which was only seconds away from strafing the exact same position, pulled away from the garbage fire that was still burning. During the hours that followed, air support and artillery fire were called in to provide cover for the massive casualty evacuation needed to transport the dozens of critically wounded soldiers to the Role 3 hospital at Kandahar Airfield. Sadly, less than 24 hours after being initiated, the strike phase of Operation Medusa was over with a total of five soldiers killed, almost 50 wounded, vehicles destroyed, and a clear tactical victory for the regional Taliban commander and insurgent forces.

Findings and Observations
from Operation Medusa

The causal finding of the friendly fire incident was established as "pilot error," since the pilot of the A-10 aircraft had misidentified a friendly position as his intended target. However, several additional contributing factors, findings, and observations emerged from the CENTCOM investigation and post-investigation consultation sessions with the Canadian air force, army, and expeditionary force headquarters which revealed disturbing deficiencies within Canada's military and within the ISAF coalition itself.[7] As mentioned above, a critical finding was the distracting presence of the predawn garbage fire lit by the battle group on their position. However, several other troubling circumstances added to the challenges that faced NATO aircrews that night, including the absence of "identification friend or foe" (IFF) measures to mark the position of the Canadian battle group to friendly fighter aircraft, the absence of proper communications and target-designation equipment to provide control and coordination to NATO air support aircraft, and the lack of training, qualifications, and accreditation for the Canadian FAC.

The CIB's investigative probe and follow-on consultative sessions also revealed a dearth of trained and qualified personnel in the Canadian army and air force capable of planning, coordinating, and executing air missions in support of land-force operations. They also revealed the Canadian army's decision not to deploy tactical air control parties (TACP) and joint terminal air controllers to support their combat units, as well as the absence of fully qualified JTACs and air-power and air-land integration experts in the tactical operations centre and fire support coordination centre of the Canadian battle group.[8] At higher levels of responsibility and authority, air personnel at ISAF and Canada's task force headquarters lacked the most basic knowledge of air support operations and air-land integration methodologies and practices, according to the CIB report. Perhaps most troubling of all was the overall lack of awareness within Canada's air force and expeditionary force headquarters in Canada and across ISAF's air team of the difficulties being experienced by Canada's army in employing even the most basic elements of air effects and enablers in RC-S.

In November 2006, CIB members were invited to Ottawa to brief Canada's Chief of Defence on the official findings and observations from their investigation. Part way through the briefing, they were asked by an incensed Chief of Defence a most obvious question: How is it possible for a modern Western military like Canada's army to experience such difficulty in conducting operations against the Taliban in Regional Command South? The explanation offered by the investigation team centered on the fact that the Canadian army had suspended brigade-level training in the early 1990s, which denied its junior ground commanders and land force units the opportunity to train with the effects and enablers normally deployed to support such large-scale land-force training events. As a result, the training of subsequent army ground commanders resulted in their "not knowing what they didn't know" when it came to the employment of critical effects and enablers in joint war-fighting scenarios. They thought that they were "full-up," "good-to-go," and doing a great job, which seemed to have been the shared sentiment at all levels of leadership and decision making in the Canadian army in 2006.

The Chief of Defence agreed with the team's explanation and turned to his senior army and air force generals, who were also assembled to receive the briefing that morning. He declared that what had just happened (Operation Medusa) was "professionally embarrassing and humiliating" and he wanted it fixed immediately. The senior general from Canada's army was quick to add his indignation regarding Canadian soldiers going into combat without proper training and equipment. Follow-on discussions I had with other senior Canadian military leaders revealed that the commanders and senior staff at Canada's Expeditionary Force Command in Ottawa and its operational air force headquarters in Winnipeg were completely unaware of the army's struggles with air support and air-land integration in Afghanistan and were also professionally lacking in their understanding of the critical role that air support should have been playing at that time in Kandahar Province. A senior Canadian two-star army general made some very disturbing comments in November 2006 when he declared that deploying TACPs, which would have included dedicated FACs and airpower planners to support Canada's ground troops in Afghanistan, was a "throwback to the Cold War."

A chance encounter in the fall of 2007 at a conference near Oxford, England, with the commander of ISAF during Operation Medusa, Gen Sir David Richards, offered me an unexpected opportunity to brief him on the findings and observations of the CENTCOM investigation and the overall outcome of the operation. We had a lengthy conversation, and although he remembered the friendly fire incident, he was totally unaware of any of the difficulties experienced by the Canadian battle group during the operation or any of the deficiencies and failures related to the employment of air effects and enablers or the absence of critical air personnel and equipment. It was also mentioned during our conversation that the general had been out of theatre for an extended period of time due to a serious illness, at which time his command responsibilities had been delegated to ISAF's Deputy Commander Air, a Canadian two-star general officer.

Post-Medusa concerns centered mainly on the crude and unsophisticated ground–force operations conducted in RC-S and the lack of expertise in airpower and air-land integration methods and practices. Comments from an interview with the CIB captured in the investigation report transcripts from the lessons learned team from Canada's Army Doctrine and Training Centre asserted that the Canadian battle group's understanding of air-land integration and their application of basic air support was "amateurish."[9] As anticipated by many concerned observers, the findings of the Operation Medusa investigation initiated a flurry of activity meant to ensure that such a tragic failure would not be repeated. Based on a recommendation made by the CIB co-presidents, CENTCOM's CFACC directed the immediate deployment of his airpower and air-land integration experts to the NATO HQ in Kabul, which was later established as a full US "air component coordination element." The purpose of the ACCE was to augment ISAF's air staff and provide the much-needed expertise and knowledge for planning, coordinating, and employing the full spectrum of US airpower capabilities in complex joint operations. As I observed firsthand, the poor relations that had emerged in the wake of Operation Medusa between ISAF's DCOM-Air in Kabul and CENTCOM's CFACC and CAOC staff in Qatar prevented the ACCE from playing any meaningful role in the months that followed.

Notwithstanding the fractious leadership relationship between the US CFACC and ISAF's DCOM-Air, CENTCOM's CFACC arranged to make critical equipment and training available to ISAF units and, where needed, to upgrade the ability of coalition units to employ air capabilities and champion air-land integration. In coordination with the CFACC, NATO directed and sponsored JTAC training, certification, and accreditation programmes to better prepare FACs for their tours of duty in Afghanistan. To address the dearth of knowledge and expertise at all levels of the ISAF military structure, member nations of the NATO coalition were urged to deploy air-land integration and airpower subject matter experts (SME) to operational staff positions and combat army units across ISAF's theatre of operation.

Perhaps the most troubling of post-Medusa concerns related to the several thousand Taliban fighters—estimated at the time between 3,000 and 5,000—that had rallied across the region to challenge the forces of RC-S in August and September of 2006. These insurgents dispersed and melted back into Kandahar City and the neighboring towns and villages but were now fully energized, empowered, and emboldened as a result of their stunning victory against the forces of Regional Command South. As predicted, those very same insurgents continued to challenge the RC-S forces in a very significant manner. Soon after Operation Medusa, they no longer chose to take a "conventional" stand as they had in the Panjwayi in September 2006. Although their numbers grew and their attacks escalated, they became a highly adaptive insurgent force, reshaping their tactics to more frequently include roadside bombs and improvised explosive devices synchronized with complex attacks from multiple firing positions—all of which exacted far more casualties, both military and civilian, than several Operation Medusas could have ever inflicted.

Relearning Old Lessons:
From Operation Anaconda to Operation Medusa

The failure of Operation Medusa and the significant number of casualties incurred could have been avoided by simply identifying and applying recent lessons learned from operations such as Anaconda in March 2002. Canadian official sources placed most of the blame at the feet of the US A-10 pilot and did not address the potentially more troubling systemic doctrine and training failures in the Canadian and US armies and the ISAF command structure.[10] Indeed, the investigation carried out by the CENTCOM investigation team also cited the leading causal factor as the A-10 pilot; however, just as important was the case for a systemic review of the lessons learned and a critique of the superficial way in which lessons learned were handled. A review was also needed of the failures at senior leadership and decision-making levels that have not been addressed in any significant manner to date.

In 2008, the new four-star commander of ISAF, Gen David McKiernan, envisioned a new strategic approach for counterinsurgency in Afghanistan. Operations staffs intent on getting things right became preoccupied with quickly understanding the lessons of previous operations, and the ISAF senior leadership team embarked on an effort to understand and apply the most-relevant best practices and lessons learned from past operations in the Afghanistan theatre. Indeed, previous military efforts yielded volumes of valuable lessons and preferred practices; however, few could compare to the seminal events of Operation Anaconda in 2002 and Operation Medusa in 2006.

Just as Operation Medusa was ISAF's first major battle in Afghanistan, Anaconda was the first major battle for US forces in Afghanistan in 2002.[11] It was conducted against al-Qaeda and some Taliban forces that were using the Shahikot Valley to assemble and regroup their forces. This relatively small valley is located in Afghanistan's Paktia Province on the Pakistani border some 80 miles southeast of Kabul. While planned as a three-day battle with regular army, special forces, and ANA units, the operation ended up lasting 16 days, 2–18 March 2002. US casualties totaled eight killed and more than 50 wounded, and the operation became a symbol of inadequate joint air-land integration planning and execution within the US military.

Operation Anaconda offered several valuable lessons regarding the application and integration of airpower in US land-centric joint operations, all of which should have transferred to the ISAF mission. Perhaps most striking of all Anaconda lessons was the realization that if a country as militarily capable, disciplined, and experienced as the United States could experience such difficulty in integrating even the most basic elements of air support into the planning, coordination, and execution of an operation like Anaconda, how could a coalition of less-capable militaries be expected to succeed in a theatre of operation as challenging as Afghanistan and against a foe as cunning as the Taliban? The response to this rhetorical question is Operation Medusa.

Some of the more notable findings regarding the application of airpower during Anaconda include

- the absence of the air component in the planning phase of the operation,

- failure to share ground-force goals and objectives with the air component commander and staff once the operation had commenced,

- the absence of air- and space-borne assets to support the intelligence, surveillance, and reconnaissance effort,

- the absence of suitable air-ground integration and communications capabilities for air support coordination,

- an overall lack of tactical coordination of air support during all phases of the operation,

- the lack of understanding of air support targeting capabilities and processes,

- the inadequacy of the air command and control structure and the theatre air control system, and

- the overall failure to include airpower and air-land integration experts in the joint planning and execution phases of the operation.[12]

Some have surmised that the overall absence of a credible air support contribution in a land-centric operation such as Anaconda was the result of the interservice tension that existed between the air component arm of US Central Command and the land-centric staff of the CENTCOM headquarters itself.[13] Those familiar with the lessons from Medusa might not find it surprising to learn that the operation was nicknamed "Cana-Conda" by members of the CENTCOM team sent to investigate the friendly fire incident that ultimately terminated the ill-fated operation. With respect to air-land integration and the application of air effects and enablers in support of a land-centric operation, Operation Medusa was, in many respects, a repeat of Operation Anaconda.

The 24-month period following Operation Medusa saw coalition member nations scramble to address the errors and deficiencies identified in the many retrospective analyses of NATO's largest offensive operation. Within ISAF, individual coalition partners reinvigorated their air-land integration training programmes and scrambled to identify the personnel and resources needed to acquire new equipment and rebuild atrophied capability. But what they soon realized in the months following Operation Medusa was that the consequences of years of neglect and indifference toward air-land integration and the application of airpower in combat theatres of operations could not be reversed in a matter of months or even years. The damage had been done and it was going to take a very long time to rebuild and reacquire lost capability.

Special Thanks

I would like to end my chapter by giving special thanks to Dr. Dag Henriksen of the Royal Norwegian Air Force Academy, Trondheim, Norway; Dr. Alan English of Queen's University, Kingston, Ontario; Dr. Randall Wakelam of the Royal Military College of Canada, Kingston, Ontario; and Dr. Daniel Mortensen of the United States Air Force Research Institute, Montgomery, Alabama.

Notes

1. NATO's Bi-strategic Analysis Lessons Learned (BALL) Team was formed around a core of allied command transformation, including Joint Analysis and Lessons Learned Centre (JALLC) personnel with augmentees from the Supreme Headquarters Allied Powers Europe (SHAPE), the Canadian Ministry of Defence, US Joint Forces Command (JFCOM), and Allied Joint Force Command (JFC) Brunssum. The team makeup provided a balance of army and air force SMEs—as well as a mix of NATO, US, and Canadian personnel—to ensure an unbiased focus which would represent the views not only of the air and land components, but also those of both nations and both NATO supreme commanders. The BALL draft report stated that its mission was to identify areas in alliance lessons, systems, and procedures where improvement can be made in fratricide prevention at the operational level by conducting an analysis of the 4 September 2006 incident and NATO's operational systems, training, and tactics, techniques, and procedures (TTP) for the coordination of joint air-ground combat operations and fratricide prevention.

2. Several books and articles have been written on Operation Medusa: Adam Day, "Operation Medusa: The Battle for Panjwai," *Legion Magazine*, 1 September 2007; Col Bernd Horn, *No Lack of Courage: Operation Medusa, Afghanistan* (Toronto: Dundurn Press, 2010), with a foreword by retired General R. J. Hillier; and Maj Rusty Bradley and Kevin Maurer, *Lions of Kandahar* (New York: Bantam Books, 2011), which subsequently sparked Mark Thompson's "Inside the Battle for Kandahar," *Time*, 8 July 2011.

3. Ian Hope, *Dancing with the Dushman* (Kingston: Canadian Defence Academy Press, 2008). Lt Col Ian Hope was the commanding officer of Task Force Orion in February–August 2006.

4. The title *Charles Company* is the traditional way the 1RCR refers to its C Company.

5. For instance, BBC News wrote that "Afghan and NATO forces say a two-week operation has driven Taliban militants out of a stronghold in the southern province of Panjwayi. The British commander of NATO troops in Afghanistan, Lt Gen David Richards, said Operation Medusa had been a 'significant success.'" "NATO Hails Afghan Mission Success," *BBC News*, 17 September 2006, http://news.bbc.co.uk/2/hi/europe/5354208.stm. The *Washington Post* wrote that "warplanes and artillery pounded Taliban fighters hiding in orchards Sunday during a NATO-Afghan offensive in southern Afghanistan that the alliance said killed more than 200 insurgents in its first two days." Noor Khan, "Scores of Taliban Fighters Killed in NATO Offensive," *Washington Post*, 4 September 2006, http://www.washingtonpost.com/wp-dyn/content/article/2006/09/03/AR2006090300203.html. See also Sharon Hobson, "The Information Gap: Why the Canadian Public Doesn't Know More about Its Military," prepared for the Canadian Defence & Foreign Affairs Institute, June 2007.

6. A forward air controller (FAC) is a "member of the tactical air control party who, from a forward ground or airborne position, controls aircraft in close air support of ground troops." Joint Publication (JP) 3-09.3, *Joint Tactics, Techniques, and Procedures for Close Air Support (CAS)*, 3 September 2003, GL-10, http://www.bits.de/NRANEU/others/jp-doctrine/jp3_09_3(03).pdf.

7. Post-investigation consultation sessions with the commanders and staffs of Canadian Expeditionary Forces Command (CEFCOM) headquarters in Ottawa, the Canadian Army Doctrine and Training Centre in Kingston, Ontario, and 1 Canadian Air Division Headquarters in Winnipeg, Manitoba.

8. A tactical air control party is a "subordinate operational component of a tactical air control system designed to provide air liaison to land forces and for the control of aircraft." JP 3-09.3, GL-14. A joint terminal attack controller (JTAC) is a "qualified (certified) Service member who, from a forward position, directs the action of combat aircraft engaged in close air support and other offensive operations. A qualified and current joint terminal attack controller will be recognized across the Department of Defense as capable and authorized to perform terminal attack control." Ibid., GL-12. A fire support coordination center is a "single location in which are centralized communications facilities and personnel incident to the coordination of all forms of fire support." Ibid., GL-9.

9. The Canadian army had deployed its "lessons learned team" from the Army Doctrine and Training Centre in Kingston to Kandahar during Operation Medusa. The team lead was interviewed by the CIB.

10. Board of Inquiry conducted by the Canadian Expeditionary Force Command into the friendly fire incident during Operation Medusa, Executive Summary, 2006.

11. Among other places described in Lester W. Grau and Dodge Billingsley's book *Operation Anaconda: America's First Major Battle in Afghanistan* (Lawrence: University Press of Kansas, 2011).

12. David E. Johnson, *Learning Large Lessons: The Evolving Roles of Ground Power and Air Power in the Post–Cold War Era* (Santa Monica, CA: RAND Corp.,

2007), 97–103; and David J. Lyle, "Operation Anaconda: Lessons Learned, or Lessons Observed?" (master's thesis, Fort Leavenworth, KS, 2009).

13. Ibid.

Chapter 4

The US-NATO Military Dichotomy

Maj Gen William L. Holland, USAF, Retired

*US Central Command Deputy Combined
Force Air Component Commander
August 2006–August 2007*

By fall 2006 and spring 2007, the use of airpower in Iraq was largely on cruise control. We had adequate capabilities embedded in theater, and the tactics and operations were largely developed. In terms of airpower, we did not have to put a lot of effort into changing much—the system was working. The opposite was the case in Afghanistan. After Operation Medusa, it was clear to everyone that no system was in place. So, while the overwhelming focus and priority of the United States was in Iraq, the priority of effort and time *for me* was Afghanistan.

Squeezed between a Rock and a Hard Place

At first glimpse, Operation Medusa appeared to share a lot of commonalities with Operation Anaconda in that the immediate problem lay in astonishingly poor joint situational awareness. But while there were tactical and operational failures that explain Operation Medusa, the deeper problem causing the context of this failure was the organizational structure—the system—that NATO had put in place.

To be honest, I did not envy those officers leading the air effort at ISAF headquarters. In my opinion they were "stuck between a rock and a hard place." They had been given significant responsibility but very little authority. My perception of the situation, and I talked to a large number of people about this, was that the air element of ISAF was struggling on several fronts. ISAF was a land-centric headquarters, so the air element had to battle the organizational structures within the HQ to exert influence. Furthermore, my understanding at the time, after numerous conversations with the commander of ISAF, Lt Gen Sir David Richards, was that he felt that his deputy commander for air (DCOM-Air) and the air coordination element comprised a *staff* function and not a *command* function. They were to organize and overlook airfield performance and development, work strategic issues related to airpower at ISAF HQ, and the like—but when it came to operational planning, tactical execution, and command and control, it was the CAOC Al Udeid who was leading the effort. This would generate friction for some time. I do not think the Canadian DCOM-Air at ISAF readily accepted that construct. And as I admitted to him, if I were in his position I am not sure I would readily have accepted it either. He wanted ISAF Air to have more influence on the planning and execution of air operations in ISAF's AOR. And while he wanted ISAF DCOM-Air to be the air commander of ISAF as the senior airman on the staff, he could never accept that at the time he was a staff officer and did not have the capability to command and control air operations in Afghanistan. This triggered an effort in NATO and ISAF to build these capabilities and to lay the foundation for more ISAF involvement and authority in the application of airpower.

ISAF Air was experiencing friction within the ISAF HQ in terms of air-land integration and in terms of General Richards' viewing his own air element as a staff rather than a command function. This subsequently caused friction in air coordination and tactical execution with the CAOC at Al Udeid. Then came Operation Medusa and the A-10 friendly fire incident. Since ISAF's DCOM-Air was Canadian *and* most of the casualties in the air-related blue-on-blue incident were Canadian soldiers, he must have had a tremendous amount of pressure laid on him—not only within the Canadian chain of command, but also within ISAF HQ and ISAF Air's relations with the CAOC. It must have been difficult.

So, from my perspective, the use of airpower—the system—was not functioning adequately in Afghanistan. The handling of Operation Medusa serves as an example. After talking to numerous people and reading various reports, my clear impression was that ISAF did not comprehend the full magnitude of what had happened. Within ISAF, I believe, the situational awareness of the planning and execution of that operation—as well as what needed to be addressed to identify and implement the lessons learned in that operation—was barely visible to a small number of people. I believe it was barely understood even within the Canadian chain of command. The reason for this lack of focus within ISAF was partly because the Canadians took most of the blame. Secondly, the fratricide incident took much of the focus off of the real failure of planning and execution at the tactical and regional level. Consequently, I never felt the ISAF staff grasped the full impact of Operation Medusa, and I am not sure they really did their own full investigation. If USCENTCOM and the CFACC had not gone in to conduct the investigation, I am not sure one would have been done.

To understand why this was handled as it was, one must understand that ISAF HQ was a strategic-level *function*. In my opinion, it did not yet see itself as an operational war-fighting *command*. During the summer of 2006, it had divided its effort into a pragmatic geographical division of the country, with the United States taking responsibility for the eastern provinces. In effect, it had relegated the war fighting to its regional commands. That had significant implications for how the war was run, which processes were considered important, and the lack of unity of effort or an overarching unified strategy.

Strategy

The issue of strategy became a complex and difficult aspect of the war in Afghanistan. As I am sure other contributors point out, the US strategy in Iraq and Afghanistan became twofold: one objective aiming to root out insurgents and terrorists in targeted counterterror operations was done largely by special forces and airpower, hence the rationale for Operation Enduring Freedom. The other arm of our strategy became counterinsurgency, which was a completely different approach. It demanded different qualities of our forces and the way they operated. While the former included very familiar elements that the organization was trained and equipped to do, the latter provided huge challenges to the way we normally operate. It took quite some time to understand that.

The ISAF approach was different. It is the nature of a "security assistance force" to be less offense postured and to focus more on the broader aspects of assisting Afghanistan. I had several one-on-one conversations with General Richards in fall 2006, and I was impressed by his ability to articulate his visions and his intent in these sessions. His political-military vision and strategy more resembled counterinsurgency and were certainly not as combat-oriented as the US-led Regional Command East (RC-E). Still, even though General Richards seemed to have a clear view of what needed to be done in Afghanistan, I do not think his counterinsurgency strategy was clearly understood by the wider ISAF staff or the commanders of his regional commands. It became more an overarching guidance and vision rather than a concrete strategy. The lack of a strong unified strategy left more of the development to the regional commands, which had a very separate take on this issue.

It is important for the reader to know that by fall 2006, Afghanistan was not one cohesive theater of operations. It was one theater of operations in the east, one theater of operations in the south, and one theater of operations for the rest of the country. In reality, there were only the two regional commands, in the south and in the east, that had significant operational challenges and were involved in the planning and execution of real war-fighting operations. Each of these two theaters was organized differently, with different focuses and priorities. In effect, I felt as if I were cooperating and working with two separate and distinct theaters of operations within Afghanistan. Since the strategy from ISAF HQ was loosely formulated and not followed by a vigorous effort to have everyone follow the same line of thought, the forging and cohesion of military strategy, operational planning, and tactical execution were relegated to the regions. What puzzled me was that this did not simply happen—it was devised this way by intent.

Regional Command East was basically a US endeavor. Here we had a fairly robust command and control structure in place because it was US-led and devised mostly in accordance with US doctrine. The main focus was combat and counterterrorism-related. There was less sense of prudence or overly focusing on counterinsurgency. A lot of our unilateral OEF-targeted air operations were conducted in this region. The US domination of RC-E became somewhat of a problem after ISAF formally assumed responsibility for the region, because it was an uphill struggle to change the perspectives and culture to recognize that US forces had to do things in accordance with NATO and ISAF HQ. We pushed really hard to the commander in RC-E at that time to make sure he understood this was no longer a US-only operation.

RC-S had a separate approach, more in line with General Richards. Its focus was more toward counterinsurgency and nation-building but still with heavy emphasis on combat operations as a necessity for security and to set the conditions for engaging the local population in the counterinsurgency effort.

It was obvious to me that there was a disconnect in the whole approach of defining a commonly agreed upon strategy that ensured a cohesive effort in theater. The US effort ended up being both counterterrorism and counterinsurgency. ISAF and General Richards had their own version of counterinsurgency, but it was largely disconnected from the regional commands. The regional commands had huge leverage in terms of planning and executing combat operations, and with little strategic guidance, they devised their own. I was focused on getting the regional commanders to help *me* understand what *their* strategy was, because I felt that, from a tactical standpoint, I was supporting their strategy much more so than the ISAF operational strategy. There were some attempts to rectify this and have the regions adopt General Richards' vision, but these attempts were rare and inadequate. This resulted in some operations having a counterinsurgency focus and some a counterterrorism focus, and sometimes operations flew in the face of each other.

In retrospect, looking at the longer line of strategic thinking in Afghanistan, I believe Gen Dan McNeill, USA, who succeeded General Richards as commander ISAF, had an understanding of what Richards had tried to do. I think he embraced that to a certain point but felt he had to push forth with an increased war-fighting focus because the situation in Afghanistan warranted that at the time. I believe General McNeill understood that the time had not yet come for a strong traditional engagement counterinsurgency approach, and that he needed to await that transition until more of the insurgents had been defeated and better security established. General McNeill brought that US war-fighting effort into ISAF, which was necessary at the time. When he ended his tour in summer 2008, Gen David McKiernan, USA, inherited a situation that gradually opened up to a counterinsurgency approach. McKiernan was able to articulate more clearly the type of strategy that I believe Richards was defining in his one-on-one discussions with me. But General Richards was ahead of his time, and he did not adequately address the need for a "preparation phase" for the counterinsurgency to succeed. He relegated that fighting to the regional commanders, but I do not think the security aspect in the regions was yet realized. Therefore the need for attention to the importance of the preparation phase before going directly into a counterinsurgency population engagement modus was disconnected. Obviously, Richards was very bright and intelligent; it is just my impression that he was ahead of his time and that ISAF was not prepared to execute his strategy. McKiernan then laid the foundation for the counterinsurgency strategy that we have seen the past years. When Gen Stanley McChrystal, USA, assumed office as commander ISAF in summer 2009, the media portrayed McKiernan as an "old school" general who did not understand counterinsurgency, leading to his being replaced by McChrystal. I believe that was fundamentally misguided. General McChrystal came in and reamplified the effort, but the foundation was already there when he assumed command. In my view, there has been too little recognition of McKiernan's work in establishing a counterinsurgency approach in Afghanistan. But back in fall 2006, ISAF was not prepared or equipped to conduct an adequate counterinsurgency campaign, and the strategy was by no means rooted in the various regions which, on a daily basis, were fighting a war and interacting with the Afghan population based largely on their own strategic understanding.

Regional Command South

Having the US-led RC-E work more in line with the ISAF approach to Afghanistan was a challenge, but daily operations created little friction on the part of the air community. Regional Command South was a different story.

One of the first issues I noticed was that RC-S tried to distance itself from us and Operation Enduring Freedom (OEF). I could understand that from a political standpoint, but from an operational military standpoint, it made no sense. They tried to solve their air challenges by limiting themselves to ISAF air assets. We had to pull really hard to get General Richards to stop that, because if they insisted on using only the embedded and very limited ISAF air assets, they would shoot themselves in the foot. We had a lot more assets theaterwide and a lot of capabilities they simply did not have in their inventory. Such a stovepipe approach would greatly reduce the efficiency of their operations. It became an uphill climb to establish a sound working relationship because they often did not include us in their planning, and changing that mentality took a lot of effort. The CAOC was seen as a US function that primarily was focused on Iraq—which, in many ways, it was—but it was still doing a lot to support the Afghanistan theater. Prior to fall 2006, it had primarily supported what would become RC-E because the operational tempo required that and only

US assets could engage in counterterrorism. But ISAF's expansion into RC-S and RC-E—and particularly the seminal event of Operation Medusa—changed all that.

I personally went to RC-S after Operation Medusa to talk to the commander, his staff, and the personnel at the regional air operations center (RAOC). After studying both US and NATO doctrine, the whole construct of a RAOC was incomprehensible to me. What was its purpose? What was its task? Which authority and what capability did it have? So I went to talk to them and see how they were running their business. It turned out that the majority of the manning of that RAOC, which I believe was only 4–6 people, was not even what we would have had as a US division-level air support operations center (ASOC). It was undermanned, it did not have good direction and guidance on what it should be doing, and it had poor command and control and communications capabilities at the time. It was not integrated in a lot of the planning in RC-S because the planning in most cases was being done by ground forces out in the field. The regional command would come up with a broad overarching plan and push that guidance down to the task forces and tactical-level units for more detailed planning.

From the air perspective, there certainly was not much joint planning at the regional level. In a conversation with the RC-S commander in his office in spring 2007, he argued there was no need to include air in their planning—he simply expected air to be available when the operation commenced. There was absolutely no understanding of the benefits of having experienced airmen involved in planning who could advise in terms of capabilities, effects, and tactics that would enhance the operation. I told him that this was contrary to the lessons of history as well as every doctrine I had ever read. I tried to explain that he needed to include the air planners in the operational planning—if not to enhance the effectiveness of the operation, at least to enable air to provide a more robust rescue if his forces ran into problems. He did not seem to understand either *why* or *how* to do that.

It became obvious that the RAOC construct and air side of RC-S was not very effective. They might be very efficient but not very effective. I discussed my findings with the RC-S commander and tried to make sure that the RAOC knew what kind of assets it needed. We had a good capability in RC-E, and I knew I could take elements from that capability to strengthen RC-S. But no one ever told us they needed more assets until after Operation Medusa. Operation Medusa became the seminal event that made people understand the system was broken. We needed to reorganize the planning and strengthen the ability to monitor and control air operations. I suggested moving the ASOC from RC-E to ISAF HQ in Kabul and started the process of getting approval from the US chain of command to do so. ISAF was standing up a big combined joint operations center (CJOC) to do more centralized planning and operational oversight, and an ASOC would be a tremendous asset in this regard. It would potentially make it easier for ISAF Air and the CAOC to cooperate and communicate with each other. Gradually the challenges of RC-S improved. It was a process that took some time and was not without friction.

Air Challenges in Afghanistan

The area of air-land integration and the inadequate joint perspective of our collective effort was an obvious shortfall of the entire operation. The sad fact is that the terms *airpower* and *jointness* were an afterthought on behalf of the regional commanders at the time. In my opinion this was a general trend, although US ground commanders tended to be more aware of the utility of airpower than their non-US NATO counterparts. There seemed to be a culture within the ground forces that they owned the planning process in the AOR they were handed, and they appeared to view airpower through very narrow kinetic lenses that reduced it to a constant that simply was expected to be there once the troops established contact with the enemy. It is difficult to understand how this persisted despite the recent lessons of Anaconda and Medusa—not to mention our lessons from World War II, Korea, and Vietnam. Part of this is individual personalities. Some have a more joint focus than others, naturally, but I do think there is an educational disconnect here. For colonels or one- or two-star generals, the knowledge of airpower and the emphasis of a joint approach should be an integral part of their understanding of war. It was not. RC-S HQ was not a joint headquarters during my tenure as deputy CFACC. There were hardly any influential senior airmen on that staff, and more often than not, the planning was performed on a lower level where no airmen were involved. So there is an educational aspect, a cultural aspect, and an organizational aspect which converge into a dysfunctional structure that inadequately releases the potential of the resources available. There were several operations that were highly successful because of sound air-land integration in planning, but they were few and far between. When we integrated air planners into upcoming division-level operations, they often proved to be successful. We discussed the operational use of airpower with the ground forces, and together we developed the "air presence" construct, which meant that close air support–capable aircraft were overhead and visible when our ground forces were advancing. It led to ground forces actually putting in requests for air cover and not just requesting kinetic fire once they got into trouble.

Some have argued that airpower was somewhat reduced to a "911 call" for the ground forces. I guess that is right, and to a certain extent it was the nature of the beast. Afghanistan was engaged in a civil war with an elusive protracted enemy that provided few opportunities for strategic attacks. It was an army-dominated operation with no cohesive strategy or clear sense of what airpower could bring—as well as one gradually leaning toward a counterinsurgency that emphasized the Afghan population as the center of gravity. Thus, the war in Afghanistan was not a classic air campaign. The very nature of this war did not provide opportunities for huge strategic attack or interdiction campaigns. To be honest, we did not have the capability to find, fix, and attack that many targets. It was almost to the point where we had to commence an operation to find, fix, and attack targets, so by nature it turned into a close air support (CAS) environment. The United States had organized, trained, and equipped its air forces to handle such scenarios. Supporting the ground force was a necessary and important role in the overall effort. Still, I would argue that we continuously challenged ourselves to figure out better ways to include air. We looked at developing operational capabilities and ways to help prepare the battlespace using ISR, transport, humanitarian relief, counter-IED, and so forth. But until someone suggests something that we should have done and we did not do, I believe we did a fairly good job.

Perhaps contrary to popular belief, I never felt a shortage of assets in Afghanistan. Surely the apportionment was heavily in favor of Iraq, but a large portion of the forces that were not bedded down in Iraq were in support of Afghanistan. The infrastructure in Afghanistan was still under construction, but it was being built up rapidly. We were constantly looking at what more we could put closer to the war in Afghanistan, but I never felt that Afghanistan lacked significant resources from an air support standpoint other than maybe some ISR assets. ISR collection capabilities, processing, and dissemination requirements for Afghanistan were not nearly as sophisticated and developed as we wanted them to be. Even if we could have put more assets there, I am not sure their products could be maximized. All things considered, the availability of assets was not a significant limitation on our theaterwide effort. Our key challenges lay significantly more in our structural, organizational, cultural, and conceptual approach to this war.

One of the issues we struggled with, which became very apparent after Operation Medusa, was the inadequate training, equipment, organization and competence of many joint terminal attack controllers in theater. This was particularly true of non-US nations sending JTACs to Afghanistan and was an important problem addressed by the incoming ISAF DCOM-Air. He recognized that despite the "standardized agreements" (STANAG) for NATO's JTAC training, equipment, language skills, and level of proficiency, there were still huge problems related to bringing all JTACs up to an adequate level. The first thing we did to assist this effort was to identify a US expert—a colonel—and attach him to ISAF's DCOM-Air to do an inventory and assist in getting an overview of the situation—to analyze the in-theater JTACs' training status, their operational background, their communications capabilities, and so forth. It became a combined effort of both ISAF HQ and the CAOC to identify the shortfalls and rebuild the JTAC structures to provide safe and timely coordination of ordnance dropped in theater.

Another issue brought to our attention by ISAF's DCOM-Air in fall 2007 was the perception that certain US platforms were using unwarranted heavy-handed force in theater—that certain US bomber squadrons were dropping a significantly higher amount of ordnance on targets than other allies or even other US platforms operating in similar situations. This indicated a certain culture or philosophy that was contrary to our ambition of a proportionate and discriminate use of force. The ISAF DCOM-Air and his staff were right, and we immediately addressed that issue. I think one explanation of the problem was related to competence. If you have a significant CAS capability and are trained to do it but you are not a full-time dedicated CAS expert, you tend to rely more on those individuals you believe are the experts. In this case it was easy to rely on the JTAC, who coordinated on behalf of the ground commander with full situational awareness. If the bomber crew heard, "I want a string of six on this compound," they did not question that. Contrast this to an A-10 pilot or somebody who does close air support for a living, who might respond differently and point out, "Listen, I think two bombs on that compound is sufficient, and I would rather save the other four in case another incident occurs." It probably was a combination of factors like training, culture, the "heat of the moment," and so forth. Once we became aware of this issue, we implemented better procedures among the aircrews, JTACs, and ground commanders to avoid this unnecessary use of force. As far as I know, we succeeded in rooting out this problem by the end of the year.

Epilogue

The United States often has a different approach to military operations than NATO. NATO is as much a political organization as it is a military organization. In broad terms, the United States still appears to fall back to the Powell Doctrine, preferring to go in with overwhelming force and thereby hopefully set itself up for rapid success. NATO, on the other hand, often comes in with minimal force and builds the structures needed for success. If that does not work, it gradually and collectively tries to provide more forces. So the philosophies are inherently opposite, and it is quite hard for either side to comprehend the other's approach. The NATO nations often seem to think that the United States too often is coming in with a big footprint and taking over the entire operation. The US perspective is often that NATO provides inadequate resources to win the wars quickly. There seems to be a certain dichotomy there, and this time it influenced the war in Afghanistan in general and the ISAF Air–CAOC relationship in particular.

If there is anything I would like to change looking back at my tenure as deputy CFACC, it would be the perception of many that the CAOC in Al Udeid was a unilateral US CAOC. It was not. Surely it was a US "backboned" CAOC, but a number of nations—perhaps most notably the UK, Australia, and New Zealand—provided officers who filled key positions. Still, that did not seem to convince a lot of actors in the Afghan theater that this was not entirely a US-only endeavor. I worked hard to change that perception but realize I did not succeed as much as I would have liked.

This in turn had ramifications for the working relationship between ISAF Air and the CAOC. We understood that NATO had its own chain of command, but also that the United States was providing the overwhelming majority of air assets. That was the direct reason for—during Lt Gen Allen Peck's tenure—providing a NATO hat to the US DCFACC. It meant that the DCFACC formally was the air component coordinator for ISAF. In effect, that made the DCFACC the senior operational air commander for ISAF. We brought the Canadian DCOM-Air, as well as his Dutch successor, to the CAOC to discuss that in fall 2006. From my perspective this organization secured "unity of command" on the air side, and it enabled a degree of "centralized control, decentralized execution" that we believed was the right way forward. NATO and ISAF, on the other hand, wanted to control the assets in Afghanistan and provide unity of command within ISAF through changing the command and control relationship. The challenge, of course, was that NATO did not want to provide resources to achieve that, and so we were asked to let our assets be controlled by ISAF. It did not adequately address our need to think in much broader terms, having another war to fight in Iraq as well as other operations within CENTCOM's AOR. This remained a source of friction for years.

Chapter 5

From Saint-Mihiel (1918) to Afghanistan

Lt Gen Frederik H. Meulman, RNLAF, Retired

*ISAF Deputy Commander Air and Director
Air Coordination Element (ACE)
January 2007–February 2008*

Sometime in May 2006, the commander of the Royal Netherlands Air Force (RNLAF) told me that the Netherlands had to fill the position of ISAF deputy commander–Air (DCOM-Air) in Kabul in early 2007. He wanted me to take the job. After a few years of relative calm in Afghanistan, the Taliban and other antigovernment forces were continuously challenging the authority of the central government in Kabul and creating an increasingly volatile environment, so the offer to serve as ISAF's air commander represented a challenge. I had spent the better part of my career studying and lecturing on strategy, strategy development, and the planning, tasking, and execution of airpower.[1] Combined with my tactical and operational experiences,[2] this made me feel I was ready to assume this responsibility, so I decided to take the job. On a cold morning in early January 2007, I was on my way to Afghanistan. It would prove to be one of the most rewarding experiences of my life.

I have spent quite a lot of time thinking about what to include in this chapter. My period in Afghanistan included a broad spectrum of personal and professional experiences, mostly fulfilling and exceptionally positive, but also experiences marked by friction and less admirable features. I have decided to be open, direct, and candid in my approach. The intent of this book is to provide lessons and understanding of the application of airpower for a wider audience and the upcoming generation of officers. To gain insight into the internal dynamics in ISAF headquarters and the deliberations, friction, and dialogues with other institutions and partners shaping our effort will hopefully highlight some key lessons we need to address in future operations.

There are, of course, dilemmas involved in such an approach. While my time at ISAF was very positive and rewarding, I risk focusing on lessons of a less positive nature that might give the chapter a certain "negative" outlook. I refer to processes and individuals who might have a different perspective on the same issue and have no opportunity to include their alternative sentiments in this book. In criticizing some US policy and decisions, I risk that this may overshadow my deep respect for the US military's general professionalism and overwhelming effort and sacrifices in Afghanistan.

It is important to understand that it is *my story* and *my perception* of events. I am aware that much more can be said about the planning, tasking, and execution of air operations. One must realize that this is just a short synopsis, a narrative that captures the main aspects as I see them.

Discussing airpower as a unilateral military tool gives little meaning. It is paramount that the use of airpower—like every military tool—be viewed in relation to all other means of power to employ it in a manner that will bring us closer to achieving the overall ambition of our involvement in Afghanistan. Thus the overarching strategy and a number of other factors must be included to evaluate *why* airpower was used the way it was in Afghanistan in 2007 and to what extent there was cohesion between strategy, operational planning, and the tactical execution of air missions. This has guided my approach to this chapter.

The Troubled Relationship

In November 2006, while still holding a national position in the Netherlands, I visited the US CENTCOM combined joint force air component commander (CJFACC) for a courtesy visit at the US CAOC in Qatar. Knowing there had been some friction between the US chain of command and ISAF, I wanted to get off to a good start with my US counterpart. He was very friendly and cordially welcomed me as the upcoming ISAF DCOM-Air. Then he started a monologue, lasting some 45 minutes, in which he told me in the most transparent way how he felt about the different roles between ISAF and the US air organization, the role of the US CENTCOM air forces (CENTAF), and the planning, tasking, and execution of airpower over Afghanistan. The United States provided 85 percent of the air assets and 98 percent of the ISR assets in Afghanistan, and for this reason it was for him—and him alone—to act as the CJFACC. ISAF's

DCOM-Air in Kabul, he told me, was relegated to the position of commander, air force forces (COMAFFOR), a position unknown to those not familiar with the US air organization.[3] From that visit, it instantly became clear how the United States—and in particular the CENTAF commander—viewed the role and command relationship between CENTAF and ISAF. Needless to say, the view appeared somewhat different from NATO's JFC Brunssum perspective, which was the formal chain of command through which I reported. The coming months would show the friction and inefficiency of this approach and the need to sort out these complicated overlapping command relationships.

The day after I arrived in Kabul, I met my Canadian predecessor as DCOM-Air. He did not refer to *any* lesson from Operation Medusa; the operation was not part of the in-brief. In retrospect, that was a mistake. NATO's and ISAF's lessons from that operation would have been hugely beneficial to me as the incoming DCOM-Air—it should have been self-evident to include these lessons. If not self-evident to the outgoing DCOM-Air, it should have been part of an institutionalized process within ISAF as an organization determined to learn from its experiences. It was not, and my staff and I had to relearn *in theater* many of these lessons ourselves during 2007—lessons that we otherwise could have received upfront.

My predecessor was quite outspoken on other issues and immediately identified what he perceived as my main challenge: "Your biggest problem will be the US CAOC in Qatar," he told me. He referred to the ongoing discussions involving the air command and control structure, a relationship the CENTCOM CJFACC had explained to me in no uncertain terms when we met in November 2006. Furthermore, my predecessor confided in terms of allied priority and information-sharing in theater, "first and foremost this revolves around the US. Then there is nothing. Then it is the UK. Then nothing for a while and somewhere down the road the other Anglo-Saxon countries (including Australia and New Zealand). After that maybe Germany, the Netherlands, France, etc." His assessment implied that information-sharing was dependent on where you fit in the intelligence-sharing mechanism—that is, if you were included in the "two-eyes," "four-eyes," or other intelligence-sharing arrangements. It also implied that as a member of the command group, you had only partial information and were not fully involved in every discussion. In other words, it was not your position that determined the level of information you received but your nationality—a situation that was highly undesirable to properly conduct the job.

In retrospect, his assessment proved to be exactly right. Let me give a few examples to illustrate this point. ISAF DCOM-Air was not involved in the ISR planning, tasking, and execution process. This was dealt with through the intelligence community, located in a classified area in the HQ to which I did not have access. The targeting process involved a similar situation. Although the standard operating procedure (SOP) proclaimed that ISAF DCOM-Air had a backup/supporting role in the targeting process, it was only in the first half of 2007 that I became involved in the process. This was only because DCOM-Security, who had the lead responsibility in the targeting planning process, became so overtasked (especially during night-time) that he asked for my support. After the new DCOM-Security was appointed in May 2007, DCOM-Air was once again no longer involved in the process; it stayed almost completely within the US planning/targeting realm.

I mention these issues because I believe it is important to understand the relationship between ISAF and the US chain of command upon my arrival. The US CENTAF had dominated the Afghan theater for a long time. After ISAF assumed responsibility for the entire country, Operation Medusa had presented a number of shortcomings at ISAF's tactical and operational level that produced increased strain on an already "troubled" relationship. For some officers serving in ISAF in fall 2006, Operation Medusa and other factors had become so mired in friction that it influenced their personal relationships within the chain of command, not least, my predecessor as DCOM-Air. While it is certainly true that CENTAF dominated in air resources, it was equally clear that NATO had assumed responsibility for ISAF operations in Afghanistan. That meant political-military guidance and direction were provided by NATO headquarters in Brussels, with the North Atlantic Council and the Military Committee as the main players. The formal chain of command thus ran through the JFC Brunssum and SHAPE. There was no appetite to take orders unilaterally from USCENTCOM through its CAOC in Qatar, even though CENTAF provided the bulk of air resources. In simple terms, at the time of my arrival the command relationship was troubled.

Strategy

The fundamental problem for ISAF in early 2007 was the lack of an overarching political-military strategic plan for Afghanistan from which operational-tactical campaign plans could be derived. Although the in-theater operational-strategic headquarters in Afghanistan, we simply had no long-term vision or focus. Operations were concluded without proper analyses of effects and/or how to build on the operational gains for more long-term stability. The operational tactical scope for ISAF HQ was only a couple of weeks instead of months or years.

In 2006, NATO adopted its so-called effects-based approach to operations (EBAO) and comprehensive approach concepts,[4] with the latter focusing on coordinating all instruments of power and not just the more narrow use of military force. It immediately became clear to us that such an approach was necessary. Still, this concept remained in its infancy throughout 2007. First of all there was no fully coordinated, let alone integrated, approach among the key players—ISAF, the United Nations Assistance Mission in Afghanistan (UNAMA), and the government of Afghanistan (GIRoA)—in the realms of the three defined "lines of operation," (1) security operations, (2) reconstruction and development, and (3) governance. Second, there was the enduring tension between ISAF and OEF. The former focused on supporting the government of Afghanistan in establishing a safe and secure environment and creating the conditions for reconstruction and development. The latter focused primarily on countering terrorism and preventing Afghanistan from again becoming a safe haven for terrorists. This lack of unity of command and effort had to be remedied, which among other things caused significant challenges in terms of coordinating and unifying our strategic communication. Third, as noted, the politico-strategic guidance was lacking in 2007. This meant that the planning, tasking, and execution of ISAF's mission at the military-strategic and operational-strategic level were predominantly left to the military. This should be viewed in the context that, upon our arrival in Afghanistan in late January 2007, it became clear to us in ISAF's command group that ISAF was not yet fully ready to cope with the developing security environment, reconstruction and development, and/or governance support. There was hardly any experience dealing with the whole spectrum of issues influencing stability in Afghanistan. Thus, in early 2007 there was little cohesion between politico-military guidance, strategic thinking, operational planning, and tactical execution of military operations.

It is important to distinguish and nuance the level of guidance, strategy, and campaign plans in Afghanistan. When criticizing the levels of cohesion and clear guidance, I do not mean to say there were none. ISAF's overall mission was to assist the GIRoA in establishing and maintaining a safe and secure environment, with full engagement of the Afghan National Security Force (ANSF), to extend its authority and influence, thereby facilitating Afghanistan's reconstruction and contributing to regional stability. From a political-military strategic point of view, this may have seemed a sufficiently clear intent. It was not. And for those of us who tried to make operational plans from this political "guidance," there was little concrete in terms of what to achieve.

Still, to achieve this general guidance, ISAF's campaign design consisted of the aforementioned lines of operation: security, reconstruction and development, and governance. Security was ISAF's primary responsibility in terms of supporting the GIRoA, whereas the other lines of operation were more focused on creating the conditions for success. In reality, the focus was on security and the use of military force. Reconstruction and development and governance development were not really part of the deliberations, and only a few times throughout 2007 did ISAF HQ address these issues in some detail.

ISAF's mission planning was conducted formally at three different levels. First, at the SHAPE level, the Supreme Allied Commander Europe (SACEUR) was responsible for planning the military-strategic operations plan 10302. Next, at the level of JFC Brunssum, operation plan 10302 was translated into operation plan 30302 with its broad operational-strategic "vision of resolution" and related lines of operation. Finally, ISAF's operation plan 38302 translated the higher-level guidance into campaign plans. The intent was to demonstrate NATO's commitment to the security (and creating the conditions for success in terms of reconstruction and development and governance) of Afghanistan and thereby demonstrate the requisite respect for the Afghan people and their culture to ensure their support of ISAF's endeavor. The methods ISAF used were threefold: first, securing freedom of action; second, aiding in the development of Afghan national and regional capacities; and third, striving to fully integrate forces, methods, and resources in theater.

For the duration of 2007, however, it was clear that, although there were military-strategic and operational-strategic plans, one thing was missing in this chain, and that was a comprehensive politico-strategic plan for Afghanistan with a clear description of the desired strategic outcomes—what we were to achieve or an end state—an "exit-strategy." The political-strategic guidance from HQ NATO in Brussels did not provide that.

Here lies perhaps one of the main failings of NATO and ISAF in Afghanistan. There have always been more-or-less-loosely articulated ambitions for Afghanistan. It is easy to state that one wants security, stability, development, and good governance, but that is not a strategy. The problem during my tenure was that the main part—clear political-strategic guidance, a strategy—had not been articulated and laid down as the centerpiece of the operation. What did it mean to "assist the Government of Afghanistan in the establishment and maintenance of a safe and secure environment"? Should it be counterterrorism or counterinsurgency? Both? Something else? What body or organization should ensure the "comprehensive approach" and how to balance these efforts with the GIRoA? There was little political consensus on these issues, and we operated accordingly. In practical terms, it meant that without clear political-strategic guidance or an articulated strategy, all the subordinate plans would also lack precision. So we realized there was no clear campaign plan, no clear "vision of resolution," no clearly established "air estimate," no clear joint air operations plan, and no clear idea in terms of how to support the joint force commander.

Adding to this was the realization that the United States was somewhat pushing us into the counterinsurgency domain. It became obvious that the link between COMISAF and USCENTCOM was very strong and directly influenced the planning and execution of ISAF operations. Subsequently, COMISAF issued his "Commander's Intent" on 1 March 2007. As far as I could determine, it was written in isolation by the commander himself. There was no communication at all in advance, and any idea of a combined/joint approach was lacking. He simply did not involve the full ISAF command group. This process resulted in a lot of comments and complaints within ISAF HQ—including on both the US and UK sides. The main reason for his decision was apparently that he was not happy with the concept of "Afghan development zones," a concept inherited from the previous ISAF mission that geographically defined areas in which to focus development spending and security efforts. He had the opinion that the concept was flawed and the Afghans themselves did not properly understand the concept. Contributing to this, the security situation was rapidly deteriorating in early 2007, further supporting the rationale for a change of direction. Suddenly, ISAF was going to conduct an all-out COIN strategy to defeat the insurgency. What did that mean? There was no discussion or elaboration on the content. The process made it clear that COMISAF was not a strong communicator and that he did not emphasize a "combined" effort by including his international players within his HQ. It was not clear to me—and presumably neither to the others in the command group—*if* and *how* the "Commander's Intent" was discussed with higher headquarters and whether it was in line with the overarching operation plans. The only reference made was to FM 3-24, a US field manual on counterinsurgency that had its origins in the US military experiences in Iraq.[5] Although this field manual has received a lot of attention since, hardly anyone in ISAF HQ, perhaps with the exception of many in the US contingent, was familiar with it. Furthermore, it was a US field manual which did not reflect a combined-joint NATO doctrine on COIN.

COMISAF wanted to defeat the insurgency through a consolidated tactical campaign on the ground. In my view, that strategy resembled the failed approach to the Vietnam War. To me such an approach seemed too rigid and too limited and would not lead to a successful outcome of our endeavor. Afghanistan *was* and *is* related to a comprehensive approach that includes issues like security, reconstruction and development, governance, corruption, and so forth. Thus, in the executive meeting of 5 March 2007, I raised this very issue and explained that the process and content of the "Commanders Intent" were not fully transparent, adequate, and sufficiently clear. I received no reaction whatsoever.

So the overarching strategic and operational "architecture" was not in place, and the cohesion of our effort was hurting. The command relationships were unclear, and since there was no commonly agreed strategy on Afghanistan, ISAF's military-strategic mission was predominantly left for the military to devise without proper guidance. At the time, ISAF HQ did not have the experience or competence to devise a coherent and encompassing strategy or fully implement the three main lines of operation. We had a lot of work in front of us.

The Dynamics of ISAF HQ

Besides the limited overarching structures guiding the use of airpower, the dynamics of ISAF HQ were important factors influencing our ability to utilize airpower in a manner that would increase the overall input to our collective effort in Afghanistan.

With the exception of COMISAF and DCOM-Security, ISAF's leadership met for the first time in late September/early October 2006 for leadership and predeployment training. The initial gathering at JFC Brunssum in the Netherlands proved to be a good beginning. All were eager to get to know each other and start working together. Still, two and a half days in Brunssum was not long enough to get acquainted and make a team out of them. Also, the weeks in Stavanger, Norway, for predeployment training did not meet all our requirements, perhaps particularly because, from my point of view, the training lacked any focus on airpower. Except for a minor portion in the targeting process, the exercise play simply did not include the air portion of the campaign. At that time, it was already apparent that ISAF HQ's focus was and would be land-centric.

My first encounter with the upcoming COMISAF was during our predeployment training. He was a typical US infantry officer who had dealt with operations more or less continuously since Vietnam—a very experienced warrior *pur sang*, including a lot of operational experience in Afghanistan, but he appeared to have less experience at the political-military strategic level. The general had meetings with everybody in the ISAF command group. In my case he was more interested in my vision of Afghanistan, not so much the role of airpower. He made clear that he favored an air coordination element (ACE), an organizational model that fit US doctrine and probably his own experiences. Our conversation and the subsequent initial period in ISAF HQ showed some of the shortcomings of COMISAF and our headquarters: (1) airpower was hardly an issue at HQ Kabul; (2) the HQ and COMISAF were very land-centric; and (3) COMISAF's focus was predominantly on the US information lines and special operations in particular. It was too much US and US doctrine oriented, and if you were not trained in the United States, it was not easy to properly understand the specific lines of reasoning. And the US staff rarely asked themselves if the others were on board or not. They picked and chose their people and manned specific groups of particular importance. COMISAF would often make up his mind with a few US insiders and execute the tasks at hand. This would be the default approach in ISAF HQ throughout 2007.

Let me give one example: In the first weeks after our arrival in theater, COMISAF had very little interaction with the rest of the command group. In our scheduled plans meeting on 1 March 2007, we discussed the intelligence we were fed and what it meant. The command group showed no agreement on the intelligence picture. Without further deliberation or agreement, COMISAF suddenly ordered the execution of Operation Baaz Achilles. This came as a surprise to all of us. We later learned that he had met with a small group of US insiders the night before and made his decisions on the operation. When I noted that the role of airpower in this operation was unclear and that it would be helpful if I as DCOM-Air had been invited to the meeting the night before, the chief of staff looked at me and answered, "We thought that you were not here." It illustrates the atmosphere at the time, and it proves that I had to fight my way in and become involved in the planning discussions in COMISAF's office from the beginning. In this particular case, air was not sufficiently involved in the planning for Operation Baaz Achilles. What was clear, however, was that the strategic focus, campaign plan, and long-term vision for this operation were largely nonexistent. Furthermore, the process preceding this operation proved that we had to fight for airpower involvement in strategic-operational and tactical planning across the theater from the outset. This situation improved over time, but airpower was still viewed as a distant element of the campaign, an auxiliary force, and not an integrated part of the fight. Changes of existing orders to subordinate and supporting commanders—so-called fragmentation orders (FRAGO)—were being developed within the headquarters in which airpower was not necessarily an integral part of the document; it often simply did not have an air portion. One day I was utterly fed up and refused to sign off on the document before the air portion was included. It was unprofessional not to incorporate airpower as an integral part of all planning, but it was not easy to bring that sentiment across in early 2007.

The headquarters had more structural issues. ISAF HQ in Kabul was the first composite ISAF headquarters, consisting of some 2,000 representatives from more than 40 countries, mainly military personnel with a wide variety of backgrounds and experiences. While this had some fundamentally positive political effects for NATO/ISAF, it also meant the HQ had to overcome the problem of differing

experience, various levels of training, and the inevitable friction related to language skills and social/cultural backgrounds of its personnel. With representatives from more than 40 countries, we had to
cope with differing national interests. One might, perhaps, assume
that an endeavor like Afghanistan would create a situation where nations would be willing to set aside national interests, but nothing
could have been further from the truth. It was a challenge to act in
accordance with the collective will of the various nations and to pull
in the same direction to achieve agreed objectives in a synchronized
and coordinated manner. Interests often diverged, and national interests often defined the role and ambition of each individual in planning, tasking, and execution of ISAF missions. Some nations' interests were limited to just being in theater to show their political
support. Some adopted more responsible attitudes and positions but
still did not come close to what was actually asked of them. And some
extended or even overextended their contributions in terms of what
could realistically be expected from that particular nation. Almost
every country had "caveats" which limited the operational effectiveness of ISAF. Adding to this, the headquarters was quite a bureaucratic place in early 2007.

During my predecessor's tenure, there was a tight schedule of
meetings to cope with the combined joint effects task order (CJETO)
process, a model that was very process-driven and not predominantly
focused on the security requirements of that time. In my view, the
CJETO process was actually focusing too much on joint effects without setting the proper conditions to achieve them. The CJETO "business model" became a force in itself, but the conditions in Afghanistan
and our level of comprehensive approach were not mature enough to
run the CJETO paradigm effectively. The lack of experience, limited
language skills, national caveats, and over-reliance on the CJETO process implied, in my opinion, that the level of effectiveness of ISAF HQ
did not exceed 30–40 percent. Over time, the situation would improve, but it would not exceed the 60-percent mark. Finally, the
methodology in ISAF HQ, and especially in the command group, did
not involve very intense dialogue. There were few real overarching
discussions on strategy, and the way ahead was mainly determined
through the US chain of command. The real influential nations besides the United States were the UK and, to a lesser extent, the other
Anglo-Saxon countries, and then the rest. In my view at the time,

ISAF HQ did not represent a real joint-combined approach in its effort to handle the complexities of Afghanistan.

Airpower in a Land-Centric ISAF Headquarters

The use of airpower in Afghanistan was not a traditional air campaign as we had all learned it at various academies and staff colleges. This time, of course, there was no need to establish air superiority. And the conditions were not inviting the often doctrinaire solution of—once air superiority has been established—how to proceed to conduct an offensive air interdiction and/or strategic air campaign to defeat the enemy. In reality, ISAF's air campaign was much more fragmented, consisting essentially of four parts: (1) an *air-to-ground/close-air-support campaign* in support of the forces on the ground, including time-sensitive targeting/dynamic targeting; (2) an *air transport campaign* conducted in theater through the intratheater airlift system (ITAS) and other nationally provided capabilities; (3) an *ISR campaign*; and (4) a *space campaign*.

The *ISR* and *space* campaigns were predominantly planned and executed with US assets and through US command and control. The *close air support* and *air transport* campaigns were based on ISAF inputs but were planned by the CAOC and executed with a variety of national assets. Apart from ISAF "dedicated" resources, the Americans (and to a lesser extent the British) unilaterally had considerable numbers of available aircraft stationed in the Middle East and/or in theater—including B-1B bombers, tanker aircraft, and the complete range of ISR capabilities. Also, US aircraft carriers with F-18 Hornets and A-6 Prowlers, among other assets, were available on a regular basis. These resources were planned, tasked, and executed by the US CAOC in Qatar on a day-to-day basis to support ISAF or US-led coalition operations, depending on the situation. Space resources were also made available to ISAF to enable communication, weather analysis, navigation, and targeting support.

The main airports used by ISAF were Kabul International Airport, Kandahar in the south, Herat in the west, Mazar-e Sharif in the north, and Bagram and Jalalabad in the east. There were also Termez (Uzbekistan) and Dushanbe (Tajikistan), as well as important US bases like Al Udeid Air Base (Qatar) and Al Dhafra Air Base in the United Arab Emirates.

As ISAF's DCOM-Air/director ACE, I had four main tasks: (1) be COMISAF's substitute in his absence; (2) advise COMISAF regarding air operations; (3) be responsible for monitoring ISAF air operations, which was done in close cooperation and coordination with the US CAOC in Qatar; and (4) serve as the official representative at ISAF headquarters responsible for the reconstruction and development of Afghan civilian aviation.

The rapidly deteriorating security situation in Afghanistan in 2007 meant that air-land integration and the establishment of more robust and focused air command and control arrangements would become my priority. Air-land integration proved to be the most neglected area of operations. One sunny morning in spring 2007, the Regional Command South commander entered my office and started discussing the availability of airpower. The operational tempo had gone up drastically the past few months, and security of our forces was always the number one priority. The RC-S commander made clear that as far as he was concerned, there was no need to plan for the use of airpower. His adage was, "we don't plan on the use of airpower, because if we need it, we expect it to be there." What he presumably perceived was that airpower would be available in sufficient quantity to provide support *when* and *where* he as a commander needed it. Also implicit was the conventional view that airpower somehow equaled close air support that needed less preplanning and coordination. I explained the reality of the situation and warned him of this approach. Taking into account the deteriorating security situation, high operational tempo, and available air assets, there would be a fair chance that one day we had to say, "No, unfortunately, there are not a sufficient number of aircraft available to meet your needs." This story illustrates the attitude of some ground commanders and their lack of understanding of how the planning and use of airpower actually should work.

I was astonished to realize that a modern fighting force like NATO/ISAF could operate so unsophisticatedly. After yet another fight to bring across the importance of airpower and the need to implement it in our planning efforts, I proclaimed in the headquarters that "we still haven't learned the lessons of Saint-Mihiel, 1918," referring to the operation during World War I in which airpower was applied for the first time in a large joint-combined operation and with overwhelming success.[6] It appeared as if the most basic lessons from history had eluded us in terms of air-land integration.

Clearly, there was a need for better prioritizing and allocation of available air assets in theater. From a strategic perspective, air-land synchronization became the key challenge. Air-land synchronization implied that air and land planners first of all had to know and understand each other. Second, it was essential that those doing the planning at the different levels have a clear understanding of what was being planned at the strategic, operational, and tactical levels and vice versa. Understanding each other's intentions, requirements, and capabilities and capitalizing on each other's strengths was of the utmost importance. Only by knowing what the respective levels wanted to achieve and sharing those thoughts was it possible to provide the right air support at the right time with the right means. Ground commanders needed to stop requesting specific platforms for support and instead tell us the *effect* they wanted to achieve. Instead of asking for a B-1B, for example, they could ask for CAS, in which case we could allocate an F-16 to do that job while finding a more suitable mission for the B-1B. Once the desired effect was clear, the CAOC in Qatar or the ASOC in Kabul could easily task the right asset to do the job in direct cooperation and coordination with the JTAC. The CAOC and ASOC level had the competence, oversight, and experience to determine which asset should be allocated to which situation.

In reality, many of these problems arose from the different doctrinal or philosophical approaches to planning and execution. The adage for land planners was "decentralized planning and decentralized execution." This implied that the ground commander at the tactical level planned and executed the operation. For instance, Task Force Helmand would plan and execute operations within its area of responsibility. This was contrary to air planners' doctrinal philosophy which was fostered on "centralized planning and decentralized execution." As has often been the case, airpower in Afghanistan had a relatively small number of expensive, technologically advanced platforms available. It would be a huge mistake to divert those assets to individual ground commanders. Limited assets with the ability to reach any point in Afghanistan, literally within minutes, meant that centralized planning had to be the guiding principle for airpower employment to provide the flexibility of prioritizing which operation/situation needed the resources the most.

This worked both ways: the airpower community needed to understand the needs of the ground commanders and the modalities of their planning process to properly support them. Conversely, the ground planners needed to understand the challenges of planning and executing airpower and the variety of effects modern airpower could provide. It was time to move away from the unsophisticated demand of just wanting a B-1B bomber overhead when moving into side valley X in operation Y and, rather, create planning structures before each operation involving both land and air planners to discuss which effects were needed where and at which time. Based on the collective competence and in-depth knowledge of various air- and land-based systems, we could not only significantly increase the effectiveness of the operation at hand, but often limit and specify resources to avoid duplication and unnecessary use of air platforms that could otherwise be put to better use elsewhere. These two planning paradigms were at odds in early 2007, presenting a situation that had to be solved.

On the air side, this meant we had to focus initiatives to cope with the more complex environment and the increasing number of "troops in contact." ISAF was moving into the new HQ in Kabul, which provided multiple challenges. ISAF HQ established the combined joint operations center, which brought ground and air officers into the same room for current operations. For the air component, this entailed a considerable increase in materiel, competence, and personnel capacities. At the same time, the United States made a national air operations control center (AOCC) available that acted as an air support operations center, which became an integral part of the CJOC structure. This was moved to ISAF HQ from the US in-theater hub, Baghram Airfield, and represented a formidable increase in ISAF HQ's ability to direct air operations. In effect, the ASOC (code-named Trinity) was instrumental—through coordination with the CAOC in Qatar—in allocating air resources and running the day-to-day air war in theater.

Another big issue I had to deal with was the FACs/JTACs.[7] The "blue on blue" incident involving the Canadians during Operation Medusa raised many issues regarding JTACs and their concept of operations. In early February 2007, I was briefed on the action plan that NATO's Air Component Command (ACC) Ramstein developed to handle this problem. At the same time NATO's Allied Command Transformation formed a group that investigated the situation and reported on its findings and recommendations—the Bi-Strategic Analysis Lessons Learned, or BALL report. The ISAF HQ air organization embraced the findings of both the ACC Ramstein plan of action and the BALL report.

It became clear that the situation with the FAC/JTAC teams was far from adequate. ISAF HQ in Kabul had basically no idea who was a FAC/JTAC in theater at the time, no standardization, no idea of their level of equipment, training, language skills, or whatever. The report led to a number of improvements. These include

- creating dedicated crisis establishment (CE) positions at ISAF headquarters to deal with JTAC issues;

- standardizing documents to improve the training, equipping, and reporting procedures of JTACs;

- creating a consolidated JTAC webpage to provide continued direction and guidance, create the conditions for theater qualifications, provide introduction briefings, and establish a JTAC action tracker list;

- producing an ISAF JTAC handbook to provide current doctrine;

- collecting and disseminating mission reports and establishing a dedicated link with all the regional commands through the regional air operations control centers (RAOCC);

- ensuring that JTACs were properly briefed and assessed when entering the operational theater before starting their challenging work out in the field; and

- requiring the US commander at ACC Ramstein to make a substantial number of ROVER systems available to NATO,[8] thereby providing the FACs/JTACs the capability to directly and digitally communicate with the pilot and significantly improve the quality of so-called talk-ons to the target.

The improvements in FAC/JTAC education, training, and in-theater reception and deployment kept us busy throughout 2007. Still, I have to admit that we had not solved all the issues by the beginning of 2008.

Another issue was the heavy-handed *kinetic* application of airpower. The use of airpower, especially in the kinetic domain, increased substantially in the early months of 2007. ISAF alone dropped almost 3,000,000 lbs. in 2007. This figure does not include OEF bombs. What was remarkable was the high payload dropped per mission/sortie, even if the number of so-called desired mean points of impact (DMPI) was very few;[9] 20,000–25,000 lbs. per mission was quite common. The question was "why?"

Per international law, *proportionality* became a key factor throughout the planning, tasking, and execution process. The United States worked from the premise that once the target was designated as legitimate, the bombs dropped would be governed less by proportionality and efficiency than by effectiveness. So, even if the target could be neutralized using a 500 lb. bomb, the use of more 1,000 or 2,000 lb. bombs was just a matter of ensuring that it was properly destroyed. For instance, we observed that a B-1 selected a particular geographical area and simply dropped enough bombs to neutralize the entire area, thereby ensuring that the three or four insurgents somewhere in that area would be killed. There was a certain culture for this approach. It was not uncommon to hear a JTAC request another bomb on target "just to make sure." To a certain extent you can understand the tactical logic, but it is ethically and politically questionable at the same time. If there is no substantiated need to drop a bomb, we should refrain from doing it.

We informed the US CAOC about our concerns and emphasized that proportionality was the driving criteria in our planning and execution of air operations. We argued that we should lower the current level of kinetics and noted that our effectiveness in theater would not be reduced if we adhered more to the principle of proportionality. Finally, this heavy-handed approach might draw attention contrary to our collective ambition in Afghanistan. All units should adhere to the agreed rules as much as possible to prevent unnecessary use of force, thereby reducing the potential for civilian casualties. From the second quarter of 2007, the situation improved, and the high-payload missions decreased substantially. I must emphasize that this only refers to the extended use of force on legitimate and authorized targets. Whenever airpower was planned, the targets underwent a very strict collateral damage assessment process to ensure they were legitimate military targets that could be attacked in accordance with international law.

Battle damage assessment (BDA) was yet another concern. It was not easy to get first- and second-phase BDA results after we struck a target, which made it hard to assess the effectiveness of each mission/sortie. This was especially a problem in the first few months of 2007 when the expended ordnance exceeded all previous levels by substantial margins. Even detailed and informative "mission reports" were hard to get in this period, making it difficult to determine the outcome of an attack. The CAOC did not want to provide the mission reports to ISAF DCOM-Air, informally labeling them "none of his business," even when dedicated NATO/ISAF assets were involved. The CAOC finally concurred after many discussions and numerous elaborations on the necessity of having this information at the head-quarters in Kabul. Later that year, it provided all information required in a direct and timely manner. The situation improved substantially after the incorporation of the ASOC in ISAF HQ, largely due to the active role of the ASOC/CJOC in executing the daily ATO and dynamic targeting (DT) situations.[10]

ISAF Air Command and Control in a US-Dominated Environment

One of the most complex aspects of my work as DCOM-Air was the command and control structure. To understand the complexity of the situation, one must understand that the US view of C2 arrangements in Afghanistan diverged from the NATO perception of air C2 in theater.

As noted, the CFACC within CENTCOM was responsible for planning, tasking, and execution of all US air operations in Afghanistan, Iraq, and the Horn of Africa. The United States provided the bulk of air assets and almost all the strategic enablers to execute air operations over Afghanistan. Furthermore, the principle governing US doctrinal thinking was unity of command, which made the CFACC responsible for all applications of airpower in theater. The United States wanted its CFACC to have unity of command for all of Afghanistan—including ISAF.

Within NATO, however, the ISAF DCOM-Air was assigned to act as the "CFACC" of ISAF's air forces. NATO, too, wanted unity of command. CENTCOM is not in the NATO chain of command, and particularly since we wanted to distinguish between ISAF and OEF, the command relationship became an issue. DCOM-Air was responsible for drafting the air estimate (i.e., what was needed to successfully carry out the assigned tasks) and for ISAF's part of the joint air operations plan as well as, on behalf of COMISAF, the direction of air operations. The two perspectives on air command and control in Afghanistan did not coincide and were a daily source of friction.

The relationship between ISAF-Air and the CAOC reached its bottom in late spring 2007. A particular issue kept me busy as DCOM-Air in the first half of 2007—the role and position of director of the air coordination element. The ACE was formally an integral part of ISAF, but it became clear that the one-star general assigned as director ACE in early 2007 was of the opinion that he represented the CAOC in Qatar and was therefore not meant to be linked to NATO/ISAF's DCOM-Air organization. Taking into account the very fragile and sensitive relationship between Kabul's DCOM-Air and CAOC Qatar at the time, his attitude did not ease the tension. In fact, it sparked many discussions and friction, since from an ISAF perspective he was part of the DCOM-Air organization. His lack of respect for the role and position of DCOM-Air and ISAF's chief of staff only added to the tension, which peaked when an e-mail from the director ACE was "intercepted." It was written so as to bypass ISAF's leadership—in particular, the chief of staff. His attitude toward superior officers in the ISAF chain of command in general, and the content of this e-mail in particular, led to a decision to relieve him from his position. COMISAF had already agreed before the director ACE's national government sent a request to find a solution to "save face." A number of meetings were held between a representative from this nation, ISAF's chief of staff, the DCFACC/CAOC, and myself. Finally, we agreed on a way forward which clarified the role and position of director ACE, and the interrelationship strengthened. The one-star general was reprimanded for not being straightforward and fully reliable and for insubordination. He sent formal apologies to the Air Staff organization in HQ Kabul explaining what had happened and why. As DCOM-Air, I had a long talk with him to explain the whole situation. It was a difficult discussion but ended with the proper understanding. The one-star general understood quite well the "yellow card" that had been handed out and that a second issue would definitely relieve him from this position. After this incident there were no further negative interferences, and the one-star general worked in a very cooperative mode. When he left the theater in fall 2007, I was absolutely pleased with this general officer, who had learned some hard lessons but turned himself into a team player and a dedicated and focused professional. He was—and still is—a very knowledgeable airman, and he became a huge asset to us in the end.

I mention this story because it signified both the lowest level of relations with the CAOC, but also one of the key factors that spurred a process leading to improvement. Finally, we sat down with the CAOC staff and discussed the issues and our working relationship thoroughly. Combined with the increased tempo in air operations in summer 2007, this led to a new air C2 structure clearly depicting the different roles, tasks, and responsibilities between NATO/ISAF and the dual-hatted US authorities in the air C2 chain. Partly out of necessity, it paved the way for better cooperation and dialogue. In my view, the main reason for this friction was that the US CFACC found it hard to conform to the tasks, responsibilities, and authorities of ISAF's DCOM-Air. As a result, the CFACC initially made hardly any use of the direction and guidance from ISAF HQ. He demanded overall authority to issue the joint air operations plan and felt that he was the sole CJFACC responsible for air operations in the Afghan AOR. After the incident with the one-star general and the increased tempo of air operations in Afghanistan, the process moved forward. The US DCFACC in Qatar, by his personal character and commitment to finding solutions, managed to define and agree on solutions and working relationships between our two air organizations. A key factor was the creation of a dual-hatted command relationship for the DCFACC. The CFACC, who was also commander of Ninth Air Force, was normally based at Shaw AFB in the United States. The DCFACC was present on a daily basis in Qatar as the "forward-deployed CFACC." By making the US DCFACC fully responsible for ISAF's air operations and the official who considered all requests for deployment of air forces, it was possible to develop an optimal apportionment. Frequently, nationally retained US resources were assigned to ISAF for certain tasks (e.g., fighters, tankers, and ISR). Only in this manner did it become possible to support all requests with the right overarching perspective and subsequent priorities. We also developed the Qatar-based ISAF Detachment CAOC Central (IDCC), a body of 14 people manning positions throughout the CAOC structure in direct cooperation with ISAF headquarters staff. The CAOC staff and the IDCC team displayed great mutual respect, which clearly strengthened the operational output of the CAOC.

The personal aspect is worth emphasizing. While the DCFACC in spring 2007 was prone to flexibility and compromise, resulting in significant progress, the subsequent DCFACC was more in line with the US CJFACC's approach. Thus, the process did not further improve in the fall of 2007. I must admit that I, too, was a part of this process and must shoulder some responsibility for a working relationship that was marked by friction, particularly during the first six months of my tenure. In a formal sense this was based on instructions from the highest level in JFC Brunssum. A key problem was that we rarely met in person to discuss issues we needed to solve. Another was the non-availability of classified means in HQ ISAF in Kabul to communicate with the leadership in Qatar. For this reason, situations too often arose without us communicating adequately to prevent misunderstandings. For example, one day in late spring 2007, a US colonel entered my office with a letter stating that the United States would shortly send a US Air Force two-star general (ACCE) to HQ ISAF. There was no mention of the why, when, and what it would mean for the working relationship in HQ ISAF. I sent a short memo to COMISAF asking for further clarification. I wondered why this two-star general was needed, especially since we had finally adapted and focused the air C2 structure between HQ ISAF and the CAOC. I received no reaction. So, in the summer of 2007, a US major general suddenly showed up in the early morning commanders' update and assessment briefing. The US Air Force ACCE came without any introduction or explanation. This created a lot of questions and even irritation within ISAF HQ. What was his role? Who was he representing? What were his tasks, roles, and authorities? Other than COMISAF himself, the attitude of the staff became one of complete neglect. To be honest, it was quite embarrassing. Even during morning commanders' briefings, the major general was not offered a chair and therefore had to remain standing while others were seated. NATO's approach was that the US ACCE was not needed and was a duplication of the position of DCOM-Air. Since his assignment had not been discussed in advance, it was somewhat confusing. It led to irritation even at the level of commander, JFC Brunssum.

The approach of COMISAF was completely different. Even while the US ACCE was standing during the morning briefing, COMISAF approached him as a trusted agent, asking him questions during the briefing, and giving him particular taskings. In my view, the absence of any information or clarification of the role, tasks, and authority of the US ACCE created a situation that was highly undesirable. He proved to be a very positive, forward-leaning general officer, who many times offered his support as a "two-star action officer." We got along fine, but the process proved to once again lack the most basic information and dialogue. The deputy commander of Ramstein tried to explore and explain why this officer was sent to ISAF HQ, and it appeared that the chief of staff of the US Air Force himself asked for a two-star ACCE presence in theater as his direct representative. The reason was never fully disclosed; the US loop was closed, and personal interrelationships were strained yet again for reasons that could have been easily addressed, communicated, and resolved.

A few words are in order on how we were actually organized to plan, task, and execute air operations. Each ISAF regional command had its own regional air operations control center, or RAOCC: Mazar-e Sharif in the north, Herat in the west, Kandahar in the south, and Bagram in the east. The fundamental role of the RAOCCs was to tailor the airpower needs of each regional command and to translate requests for aircraft into airpower effects. The RAOCC construct ensured the bottom-up integration of airpower with land operations and set real-time regional requirements. In cooperation with ISAF HQ's ASOC, they took care of the daily input for the ATO to the US CAOC. The RAOCCs were responsible for monitoring and, if necessary, adjusting the daily ATO. The latter was done by so-called dynamic retasking. During execution of air operations, the ISAF HQ ASOC was in constant contact with the RAOCCs, air liaison officers (ALO), and JTACs. Moreover, there was constant coordination with the CAOC in Qatar. Manned with exceptionally well-skilled and dedicated personnel, the US CAOC was instrumental in planning and executing the air war and bore the actual responsibility for execution of the air operations in Afghanistan.

To make sure that the required airpower was available, two air request procedures were established: the *deliberate* and the *dynamic* planning and tasking processes.

In the *deliberate* planning process, air requests originated from the ground task force, who considered its need for airpower in upcoming operations. It forwarded requests to the RAOCC/ALO, which formalized them in the format of a joint tactical air request (JTAR) to HQ ISAF's ASOC. The ASOC would gather all JTARs, prioritize them, and forward them to the CAOC Qatar to be put on the ATO. Thus, ground commanders could read which resources were allocated to support them in the ATO.

Of course, the enemy has its own will, and not everything can be planned in an ATO. *Dynamic* tasking implied that airpower would be used in support of emerging situations that demanded immediate and direct action. Situations such as troops in contact or specific targeting opportunities (dynamic targeting) called for more flexible solutions. Aircraft were tasked for ground or airborne alert and could be made available in situations of this nature. These requests often came from ground forces through the FACs/JTACs via their respective RAOCC to HQ ISAF's ASOC who, in cooperation with the CAOC Qatar, decided which resources to allocate where. Normally, we would have enough airpower available to handle all upcoming situations. The statistics of 2007 showed that the direct support for ground forces was provided in almost 100 percent of requested situations, with a reaction time of 15–18 minutes—quite a credible and trustworthy support for the men and women of ISAF and its coalition partners in often critical situations. I must note that at certain times, ISAF was only capable of providing the much-needed air support through US unilateral support from its aircraft carriers and nationally retained theater capabilities. The overwhelming US resources were often a tremendous and lifesaving asset.

In late 2007, we changed the internal organization of ISAF-Air. DCOM-Air actually became the new director of the air coordination element (director ACE). The formalization of the new ISAF structure, whereby it changed from three DCOMs to one, occurred in November 2007. In the new structure, director ACE provided COMISAF's "air direction and guidance" to the DCFACC in Qatar. The direction and guidance consisted of ISAF's input into the joint air operations plan, COMISAF's monthly guidance in the form of the actual air operations directive, and a weekly air prioritization matrix that was used for daily prioritized input from HQ ISAF in the ATO. This matrix prioritized the allocation of airpower according to importance of planned land operations. Director ACE also monitored the execution of ISAF's air mission on behalf of COMISAF. Deputy director ACE for plans and projects, commander Kandahar Airfield, and commander Kabul International Airfield were under direct command of and reported directly to director ACE. Their responsibilities involved complex issues such as the takeover by NATO of the US-led Kandahar Airfield, NATO's infrastructural rehabilitation of Kabul International Airport, and also matters such as air basing, airspace management, and flight safety.

The regular C2 structure implied that ISAF HQ communicated through JFC Brunssum in an "L-construct" toward Component Command Air (CC Air) Ramstein. In practice, however, there was a direct "functional link" between CC Air Ramstein and the air organization at ISAF HQ. Although CC Air Ramstein did not have a formal C2 relationship, it acted as the supporting air command to HQ ISAF. Ramstein provided reach-back support by manning critical slots in ISAF's air organization. For example, the chief air liaison element plans and the chief and deputy chief RAOCC South and East were provided by CC Air Ramstein. Ramstein also provided expert consultation in the development of the air estimate and JAOP formulation and expertise in the realm of air campaign planning. Finally, Ramstein provided reach-back support for several reviews (e.g., the ITAS and JTAC survey, the airspace review, and the formulation of the minimum military requirements for the establishment of a recognized air picture and a common operational picture). The relationship with Ramstein matured further throughout 2007 to the extent that its support was indispensable for adequate execution of ISAF's air mission in Afghanistan.

All in all, this was not a doctrinal and straightforward setup. It did not completely solve the issues of a US versus a NATO chain of command, but it was the best that could be achieved at the time. The agreements led to an effective organization of the planning, tasking, execution, and monitoring processes for air forces in Afghanistan. It ensured an adequate procedure for the necessary air support, and in the end that was what we needed.

The Use of Airpower—Some Observations

The most significant overall conclusion for the application of airpower is that it played a very important role in Afghanistan; without airpower, ISAF's operation would have been doomed to failure. Our most basic challenge was to have everyone in theater understand the role and flexibility of airpower, to integrate its use in planning, and to create the understanding that airpower includes capabilities that go far beyond "flying artillery" or an "auxiliary force" for tactical-focused ground commanders. For me it was a surprise that ISAF had not come farther in its joint thinking on this issue and that air-land integration had not come farther since the battle at Saint-Mihiel during World War I.

Another observation is that the team that took over ISAF HQ in January 2007 was not fully ready to conduct the full spectrum of operations and a synchronized air campaign throughout the Afghan AOR, for reasons that I have already mentioned. It took the organization the better part of 2007 until a much better synchronized air-land integration and optimization of the planning and execution of airpower became the standard. Actually, 2007 was a year of organizing and creating the conditions for success in the years to come. It was only after the development of a clear vision of resolution that the interdependencies between the different lines of operations became clearer and more synchronized. It was also the year in which it became clear that it would be a long-haul operation in Afghanistan. In particular, that was related to the return of the insurgents in 2007, who made it clear they were completely back in theater after a number of years "licking their wounds" in Pakistan. It was this deteriorating security situation in different parts of Afghanistan, especially in the south and east, that ISAF had to cope with first to create the conditions for a parallel process of reconstruction and development and governance-building.

I believe that the use of airpower, unfortunately, was most effective at the tactical level. From a strategic perspective, however, the security situation and the number of incidents actually increased during 2007. At the end of the year, it was hard to say whether ISAF, from a strategic point of view, had created the required conditions for tipping the balance in favor of the Afghan government. There was this discrepancy throughout the year: when airpower was applied at the tactical level, it was effective. Some 14,000 CAS sorties in support of troops in contact were flown, and almost 2,500 requests for TIC air support were made, most of which were granted, with a reaction time that was acceptable for those who asked for the direct support. Still, the overall situation looked bleak. In retrospect, I must admit that most of the time the application of airpower to provide support to the ground forces was not effects-based. The fact that the majority of sorties flown were in support of troops in contact implies that air support was mainly requested to solve an immediate problem. Especially for preplanned operations, it became more and more important to define in advance the effect that airpower had to achieve. Air-land integration progressed throughout 2007. The insufficient knowledge base across theater was improving, and planning commenced well in advance. CAOC and air planners were detached to assist with the planning and better integration of air assets; CAS was better apportioned across the theater. And lastly, mutual trust and understanding were also enhanced, but overall there was still room for further improvement.

Air-ground support did not include weapons on every occasion. The range of deployment options also included the so-called show of presence, show of force, strafing of ground targets, and psychological operations (e.g., dropping leaflets). Medical evacuation with helicopters and fixed-wing aircraft also proved to be of great value. Almost 900 medical evacuation missions were flown in combat support mode, and not just to give succor to ISAF troops. The Afghan National Security Forces and the civilian population also benefited from the help, and the "golden hour" principle—the guarantee that a casualty would be picked up within the hour and taken to a Role 2 or 3 hospital—was truly practiced.

Command and control and flight safety were challenging issues in Afghanistan. Most of the airspace was uncontrolled because there was insufficient real-time radar and radio coverage. Only around Kabul, Kandahar, and Camp Bastion in Helmand Province was positive control of air operations the standard. Due to these airspace management limitations, "see and avoid" became the default procedure while executing a mission. It was clear, however, that this hampered the safe and secure execution of air operations. For example, during Operation Chakush in RC-S, it took the air organization a couple of days to create safe and secure deconfliction of the very congested airspace where slow and fast moving jets, RPAs, artillery, and mortars all used the same airspace at the same time. The situation became even more complicated because the JTACs' span of control was too broad, so they lost situational awareness and were further challenged by CAS aircraft not properly following standard communication procedures. Airspace deconfliction became even more complicated when special forces planned and executed their high-density airspace control zone (HIDACZ) without coordinating with the CAOC that had also planned a HIDACZ for its own set of operations. This all meant that there was a clear need for coordination and adherence to procedural separation and optimization of the radar and radio coverage over Afghanistan.

Adding to this was the persistent challenge of coordinating ISAF, OEF, and ANSF activity. In the absence of unity of command, unity of effort had to be ensured. The challenge was to ensure a timely and proper consultation and coordination process and the establishment of adequate structural arrangements to facilitate this process. A complicating factor was the absence of a unified C2 system and the complexities of interoperability linked to the wide array of systems. Not only was disclosure a limiting factor while working different systems and sharing information, but a real-time unified C2 was not possible because many nations used their unique national assets and systems—systems like ISAF Secret, NATO Secret, secure internet protocol router (SIPR), CENTCOM regional intelligence exchange system (CENTRIX), theater battle management core system (TBMCS), interim CAOC capability (ICC), German air force command and control information system (GAFCCIS), and others. It was hard to assess the impact of this complicated C2 architecture on the planning and execution of operations, but it must have complicated and delayed effective execution of command and control in theater.

The ISAF intratheater airlift system transported freight and personnel on a large scale, involving thousands of flying hours and more than 80,000 persons/troops and tons of freight. Many missions were flown for logistic support besides ITAS. In particular, the many platoon bases, company outposts, and forward operating bases in Afghanistan received logistic support from the air. What was remarkable was the increase in 2007 of the use of containerized delivery systems—pallets with logistic supplies, sometimes satellite-guided, which were air-dropped very accurately. In an environment with such a difficult landscape and infrastructure as Afghanistan, the deployment of air forces was indispensable. Throughout Afghanistan there was a need for airlift capabilities with "defensive aid suites," because the number of small arms fires increased throughout 2007. That meant that the air threat level in Afghanistan called for capabilities like missile approach warning systems, radar warning receivers, flares, and distinctive procedures for landings and takeoffs. Without these defensive aid suites and procedures, aircraft were limited to certain areas and airfields, which would significantly reduce the campaign's effectiveness. Finally, I mention a factor that hugely influenced our transport campaign but is rarely highlighted: VIPs were always welcome, but they travelled extensively, consuming almost 25 percent of the scarce transport assets. The fact that VIP flights consumed such a great amount of the available hours led to the need for a proper procedure and prioritization. Overall, ITAS VIP transport was highly effective, but its efficiency could have been better.

"Strategic communication" was a huge issue. ISAF did all it could to prevent collateral damage through precise rules of engagement, a stringent collateral damage estimate (CDE) process, the requirement of positive identification and correct information on the local population's ways of life (pattern of life), and the right choice of weapons. Regrettably, in spite of all the precautions, it was not possible to fully avoid civilians being killed. What must be noted here is that in some cases the opposition deliberately positioned civilians in dangerous situations to discredit the foreign troops in Afghanistan so as to conduct strategic information campaigns. This in turn challenged us in terms of handling information. In more than one instance, an incident would happen in which opposing military forces claimed large numbers of civilian casualties. Afghan and international media immediately reported these claims. The process of establishing all the facts is, of course, largely more cumbersome. It takes time to carefully scrutinize cockpit videotapes, interview involved personnel, and assemble all the pieces to provide adequate information in extremely serious circumstances. The often incorrect information coming from the opponent, who, for instance, did not discriminate between a deployment of ISAF resources and one of the coalition/Operation Enduring Freedom, was impossible to counter adequately. By the time the "truth" was out in terms of civilian casualties, the damage had been done. An accurate presentation of the facts by ISAF in retrospect did not compensate for the negative media. We were losing ground in the information domain.

The critical importance of sufficient basing capabilities should be mentioned. The year 2007 showed a continuous increase in air assets in theater. The beddown options were limited because of limited ramp space, reception criteria that prevented effective beddown, and insufficient subsistence facilities. For this reason, ISAF and the coalition developed plans to increase the beddown, reception, and support capabilities at Kandahar Airfield, Kabul International Airport, Herat, Mazar-e Sharif, Bagram, and Jalalabad.

We saw a massive increase in ISR missions throughout 2007, and with that, the use of RPAs. The ISR requests ran through the intelligence organization of the headquarters in Kabul to the CAOC in Qatar, where they were planned for execution in a dedicated "ISR air task order." The year 2007 also saw an enormous increase in the use of medium-altitude long-endurance RPAs like the Predator (MQ-1) and Reaper (MQ-9), which could be used for information-gathering and/or direct attack.

Rebuilding Afghanistan's Civil Aviation Sector

In retrospect, the perspective and mind-set in ISAF HQ in 2007 was predominantly military and operational. Reconstruction and development and governance development were not really part of the deliberations, and only for a few times throughout 2007 did ISAF HQ address these issues in any detail. This focus was understandable, but the approach should have been comprehensive from the very beginning.

One of the important projects we were able to assist GIRoA with in 2007, and which really deserves to be emphasized, was the reconstruction and development of Afghanistan's civil aviation sector. Civil aviation is of utmost importance for Afghanistan because it is a landlocked country and its road infrastructure is very limited in capacity. Thus, airfields in Afghanistan are the gateways to the world but also for regional outreach of government officials to different provinces and districts. Developing Afghanistan's airfields meant large distances could be covered in a relatively short period of time and peripheral areas could be made accessible.

The aims for the civil aviation sector had been laid down clearly in the Afghan National Development Strategy (ANDS) and the Afghanistan Compact of 2006. The air transport goals and timeline (outlook till the end of 2010) were as follows: (1) Kabul International Airport and Herat were to achieve full International Civil Aviation Organization (ICAO) compliance; (2) Mazar-e Sharif, Jalalabad, and Kandahar were to be upgraded with runway repairs, air navigation, fire and rescue, and communications equipment; (3) seven other domestic airports, including Bamyan and Tarin Kowt, were to be upgraded to facilitate domestic air transportation; and (4) air transport services and costs were to be increasingly competitive with international markets and rates. Apart from the 14 airfields included in the Afghanistan Compact, Afghanistan had some 40 locations that could qualify more or less as airfields and also required further development.

One of the subsectors of the ANDS was the Regional Airports Task Force, which focused on the rehabilitation and developments of the airfields in Afghanistan. The task force was cochaired by the deputy minister of transport and civil aviation (MoTCA) and ISAF's DCOM-Air. They made great progress, not only with respect to infrastructure, but also airport functions such as training of specialists (meteorology, firefighting, air traffic control, etc.). They also invested much time in improving management and control at the ministerial and airport levels. This enabled the Afghans to better define, initiate, and realize their own needs. It must be noted that the leadership at the MoTCA was a real issue. There was hardly any institutional, managerial, or focused expertise. Planning, programming, and budgeting were underdeveloped. Personal connections more than expertise influenced assignment of functions. One task we attempted to execute in 2007 was to provide an overall picture of requirements and projects for the civil aviation development and reconstruction in Afghanistan and link available money to these requirements and projects. This proved to be a very hard nut to crack. Still, by the end of 2007, the three large airfields (Kabul, Kandahar, and Herat) were better equipped than ever before. This was a positive situation for 2008, indeed, but we knew that it was necessary to keep moving ahead with unrestrained energy and dedication to succeed.

The Status of the Comprehensive Approach in Afghanistan

Even though this book and this chapter focus on airpower, the broader perspective must be included to understand the potential utility of this tool. At the end of 2007, a couple of months before the end of my tenure as ISAFs air commander, I drafted a paper called "Stovepipes and Caveats: The Need for a Comprehensive Approach and Strategy in Afghanistan." It was an assessment of the status of the comprehensive approach as I saw it. The paper had COMISAF's approval and was written in cooperation with the senior civil representative of NATO in Afghanistan, Amb. Daan Everts. I was supposed to speak at a conference in the Netherlands based on the paper but was ultimately asked not to participate. The main reason was that the content might have sparked a debate not supportive to the discussion at that time about extension of the Netherlands mission in Uruzgan Province.

It was clear that by the end of 2007, Afghanistan was at a crossroads. Either it would develop into a relatively stable and secure country with sufficient prospects for political, socioeconomic, and cultural-religious development, or it would fall back into a pre-2001 situation with all the accompanying ramifications. By the end of 2007, it was by no means clear which way this would go. Although an incredible amount of work had been done by a myriad of players, and billions of dollars and euros had been spent, the future was unclear. The question was whether reconstruction and development were perceived as moving fast enough and with sufficient credibility that the people of Afghanistan would not be disconnected from their government, and thereby from the international community and ISAF. If they became disconnected, it implied that other forces would start to dominate the political and socioeconomic landscape and prevent the establishment of a country where people could live in a safe, secure, and prosperous environment.

The difficulties and complexity of Afghanistan were reflected in the interplay of a weak government disconnected from the traditional and predominant tribal-oriented provinces and districts; fragile institutions; narcotics; a high level of crime; an insurgency, especially in the south and east; a very high percentage of illiterate people; poor infrastructure; ethnicity and language issues; a challenging geopolitical situation; and uncertain developments of government and parliament. Governance was still immature, especially at the provincial and district level. Narcotics and corruption were strangling the country, and the people's perception of security had deteriorated. It was clear that the insurgency in Afghanistan could not be won militarily. The geopolitical situation, especially the situation in Pakistan, was not promising for the future and would allow insurgents safe havens in the border areas between Afghanistan and Pakistan for the foreseeable future.

The much-needed interplay between the government of Afghanistan, the international community, and ISAF was not optimal. It lacked a sense of urgency, will, and proactiveness. It was not based on a common politico-military strategic approach that could guide the way to further successful development. It was the lack of a comprehensive approach that was of great concern. The "Report of the NATO Parliamentary Assembly" provided some honest assessments, and as NATO's senior civil representative, Amb. Daan Everts, pointed out in the report,

> Afghans must step up their ownership of the reconstruction effort. Within the ISAF mandate of security, governance and reconstruction, it was governance that was the weakest leg of the chair. Other international organizations had not demonstrated effectiveness in the Afghan context. The UN was not stepping up to its role as overall coordinator of reconstruction efforts, and officials away from the capital suggested that the UN lacked significant presence, especially in provinces like Helmand and Kandahar, where UNAMA has declined to

establish field offices until security is improved. NATO had offered, without success, to provide security to potential UN offices in order to encourage further UN involvement. Non Governmental Organizations, for their part, were often reluctant to work with NATO or other international military forces, for fear of losing the distinction between military and civilian efforts and potentially becoming considered as combatants. . . . [There is] a lack of consensus among national views on the role of the military in operations such as Afghanistan, and on how to deal with warlords, as well as on counter narcotics efforts. . . . [There is no consensus on] how to find the proper balance between military and political efforts in the counter-insurgency. These fundamental political differences made it extremely difficult to reach a consensus view on an overall strategy for NATO in Afghanistan.[11]

I must note that it was not just the NATO parliamentary assembly that was critical in terms of a certain lack of comprehensive approach in Afghanistan. There was a general feeling that a comprehensive approach was missing, especially at the grand-strategic level—the intertheater perspective—in Brussels (EU), New York (UN), and various capitals. The same feeling was shared at the politico-military strategic level within NATO's command structure and intratheater headquarters in Afghanistan. The feeling existed, but to a lesser extent, at the operational and tactical execution level.

The overriding question was first and foremost, What do NATO, the international community, and the government of Afghanistan want? That was not clear by late 2007. In my view, a comprehensive approach should focus on getting the key players around the table, getting all relevant players involved in achieving mutually agreed objectives, coordinating and integrating activities, and communicating accordingly. To move in one direction required a comprehensive concept based on an agreed analysis of the situation, a politico-military strategy accepted by the key players, and a coherent approach guided by an integrally focused organization. Thus far, in theater, it was ISAF that had taken the initial steps in addressing these issues. ISAF had little real success by the end of 2007.

So why did the comprehensive approach not work in Afghanistan? In my view, this had to do with the difference between theory and practice. The comprehensive approach was still predominantly an intellectual undertaking. The practical realities were insufficiently understood and acknowledged. It was almost Clausewitzian by nature. A comprehensive approach can perhaps only be successful in an ideal, abstract world, without any limitations. Just as war is never an isolated act, the same holds true for a comprehensive approach. The results will therefore always be suboptimal due to political factors, socioeconomic factors, and local/provincial powerbrokers—and the lack of money, competence, and capacity to provide adequate reconstruction support. Thus far the overall conclusion was that there was no coherent unified direction and guidance from ISAF HQ or the regional commands. In the absence of unified guidance and direction, national influence prevailed.

ISAF's primary focus was the "security line of operation." If ISAF was the proponent for security until the Afghan National Security Forces developed, matured, and could take over the job, the conditions must be put in place to create this stable and secure environment. By late 2007, this had not been achieved. The reasons were twofold. First, NATO's force structure in Afghanistan was insufficient to carry out its mission successfully—that is, with long-term effects. With its 2007 force structure, ISAF was only capable of gaining ground but not of holding it; once NATO left the area, it was just a matter of time until the insurgents reinfiltrated. Second, the buildup of the ANSF was too slow, especially the Afghan National Police, who in the end must be the guardians of the rule of law.

Without adequate security, sustainable reconstruction and development are not possible. Without reconstruction and development to create much-needed long-term solutions, it will not be possible to gain the trust and support of the people of Afghanistan. And that is what it is all about. If the people cannot see a structural advantage of our presence in terms of stability, security, reconstruction, and development, they will decide in favor of the insurgents and distance themselves from the government as well as ISAF and the international community. This is the link between all our "modern concepts" like the comprehensive approach, counterinsurgency, effects-based approach to operations, and winning hearts and minds.

While the military unfortunately lacked unity of command, the international community lacked unity of effort—the most basic comprehensiveness. Hundreds of international and nongovernmental organizations, governmental organizations, donor agencies, and so forth each had their own different interests characterized by a stovepipe approach and numerous caveats.

The question is how we can improve the comprehensive approach in Afghanistan. In my view, there are a number of preconditions to success. The key is to adopt an approach that takes into account the ever-existing difference between theory and practice, which governs a more realistic level of ambition and aspirations. Furthermore, there is a need for stronger commitment by the involved parties, which means they have to really buy in to the strategy. They must understand that there is no such thing as a free ride. What is really needed for nations to commit is a strategy—the "what to achieve" part of our collective effort. This has to be in place. The comprehensive approach would then be the "how to do it" or methodology of the effort. This should include the pragmatic realization that a comprehensive approach by itself does not guarantee success or the achievement of the desired end state in Afghanistan.

The best single strategy for success by late 2007 was the Afghanistan Compact,[12] established at the London Conference in 2006. This document identifies three focus areas for campaign progress: (1) governance, rule of law, and human rights; (2) security; and (3) economic and social development. The Afghanistan Compact further describes progress along these lines in terms taken from the interim ANDS. Each sector is described as a sequence of benchmarks and milestones spanning a five-year period ending in 2011. These are the international community's collective conceptual views of an acceptable strategic end state. Although there is no real prioritization and no real link among the respective pillars of the ANDS, it and the Afghanistan Compact are vital documents and central to any sensible strategy for Afghanistan. They are the key documents and basis for ISAF's approach in this country.

To further improve and develop the comprehensive approach in Afghanistan, a common sense of *urgency* needs to be established. A new international conference—like the Bonn Conference in 2001—should be held to address the objective assessment of the current situation. The aim would be to structurally reengage those in charge and agree on a way forward. Once the stakeholders have agreed to a common strategy and plan, the coordination mechanism must be established to monitor and, if necessary, navigate the comprehensive plan forward. There are a number of ways to do this, but what is really needed is a credible, forward-leaning, and empowered group of principals or a powerful individual—a "super-coordinator" for Afghanistan. Still, it must be kept in mind that Afghanistan is not the Balkans, and where the high commissioner in the Balkans had full powers, this will not be the case in Afghanistan. This can only be done through coordination and cooperation with the government of Afghanistan. For example, ISAF and the GIRoA would be responsible for security.

The GIRoA and UNAMA would be responsible for reconstruction and development, as well as for governance. A Group of Principals—possibly under the chairmanship of the super-coordinator and consisting of, for instance, the GIRoA, UN, EU, NATO, USA, and UK—would gather on a weekly basis and monitor, assess, and discuss issues from a comprehensive perspective. The advantage is that consistent direction, guidance, and signals could be given. This Group of Principals could be backed up by a monthly meeting of political directors from the various capitals. At subordinate levels, a principals approach could be established as well, for instance, in the respective regions.

As noted in the beginning, by late 2007 Afghanistan was at a crossroads. The most fundamental precondition for success was the establishment of an agreed comprehensive approach, based on a common strategy that includes the Afghanistan Compact, a COIN strategy, and a government-building approach. Through my own experiences as ISAF air commander, I have seen the results of taking a comprehensive approach within my own microcosm of Afghanistan's civil aviation sector. Without this approach, a realistic and effective rehabilitation and development program for the Afghan civil aviation sector cannot succeed. It is partly this experience that convinces me that a similar approach at the macro level can succeed.

Epilogue

This short narrative of my experiences as DCOM–Air/director ACE between January 2007 and February 2008 ends here. I would like to end this chapter on a more personal note. First and foremost, I would like to express my gratitude and appreciation to the experienced, dedicated, and focused airmen and women who worked relentlessly throughout the air organization in Afghanistan and in the US CAOC in Qatar. If for whatever reason the crisis management could not be handled or tasks could not be supported from within the theater of operations, CC Air Ramstein provided the needed support. The personnel at JFC Brunssum and at SHAPE also stood ready to provide timely and professional support. It was a great pleasure to be surrounded by such a wonderful group of people. A special word of thanks goes to the largest member of the alliance, the United States of America, which provided key resources and key enablers while supporting operations when needed. The professionalism of these highly trained and proficient airmen serves as an example to us all. Having participated in their professional military education system improved my understanding of their national and combined way of thinking with regard to airpower. The dedication of the men and women of ISAF was astonishing. Inevitably in the circumstances we operated in, personnel died while serving in ISAF and paid the "last full measure of devotion." I pay tribute to all these men and women who paid so dearly and to their families who still suffer. It was an honor to serve in Afghanistan with ISAF X. The question that often comes to mind after my tenure is, Was it worth it? For me, the answer is a resounding "yes." ISAF X was a mission worth serving. Afghanistan was a place worth serving. I sincerely hope that our children and grandchildren, who will be better positioned to evaluate the long-term effect of our endeavor there, will support my feeling that it really was worth it.

Notes

1. I studied at the College of Aerospace Doctrine, Research, and Education (CADRE) at Air University, Maxwell AFB, AL; graduated from the US Combined Joint Force Air Component Commanders course; and lectured for a few years on the broad aspects of airpower at the Advanced Staff College in the Netherlands.

2. Among a number of positions, I served as a base commander and as deputy commander, combined air operations center (CAOC) 2 at Kalkar, Germany.

3. Apparently, COMAFFOR is the senior air force officer over those air forces assigned or attached to a joint force commander at the unified combatant command, subunified combatant command, or joint task force level.

4. "NATO Riga Summit Declaration," press release 150, 29 November 2006, http://www.nato.int/docu/pr/2006/p06-150e.htm.

5. The US Army and the US Marine Corps Counterinsurgency Field Manual (2006) has received quite a lot of attention. The field manual was produced under the oversight of Gen David H. Petraeus and has since been considered an important publication in terms of influencing the US Army and US Marine Corps thinking and execution of counterinsurgency operations.

6. The battle for Saint-Mihiel (France) on the western front during World War I raged from 12 to 16 September 1918. Led by Gen John Pershing, it would be the first significant battle for the American Expeditionary Force (AEF) in World War I. Facing heavy entrenched German opposition, the operation proved to be very successful and is remembered as particularly innovative and well performed in terms of its joint and combined approach to operations. With the air portion often referred to as the "brainchild" of Gen William "Billy" Mitchell, the use of airpower in this joint combined environment displayed the largest assembly of aviation assets in the world up to that point, including some 1,476 allied airplanes. James H. Hallas, *Squandered Victory: The American First Army at St. Mihiel* (Westport, CT: Praeger, 1995); David Bonk, *St Mihiel 1918: The American Expeditionary Forces' Trial by Fire* (Oxford, UK:

Osprey Publishing, 2011); Walter J. Boyne, "The St. Mihiel Salient," *Air Force Magazine*, February 2000; George M. Lauderbaugh, "The Air Battle of St. Mihiel," air campaign planning process background paper, Airpower Research Institute, Maxwell AFB, AL; Michael J. Tashner, "Examples of Airmindedness from America's First Operational Air Campaign: The St. Mihiel Offensive, 1918," Air Command and Staff College, Maxwell AFB, AL, March 1997.

7. A *forward air controller* (FAC) is a "member of the tactical air control party who, from a forward ground or airborne position, controls aircraft in close air support of ground troops." A *joint terminal attack controller* (JTAC) is a "qualified (certified) Service member who, from a forward position, directs the action of combat aircraft engaged in close air support and other offensive operations. A qualified and current joint terminal attack controller will be recognized across the Department of Defense as capable and authorized to perform terminal attack control." Joint Publication 3-09.3, *Joint Tactics, Techniques, and Procedures for Close Air Support (CAS)*, 3 September 2007, GL-10, GL-12, http://www.bits.de/NRANEU/others/jp-doctrine/jp3_09_3(03).pdf.

8. *ROVER* stands for "remotely operated video enhanced receiver." The system "allows forward ground controllers to see what the aircraft is seeing in real time. The usage of ROVER greatly improves a forward air controller's reconnaissance and target identification. . . . Before ROVER capability, ground controllers had to rely on visual talk-on to hunt for IEDs, track insurgents or follow suspicious vehicles. The ground controller would have a map to guide the pilots where they needed to go. The ROVER gives the FACs more confidence when making decisions such as dropping bombs, because they have the same real-time bird's eye view as (the pilots)." US Army Combined Arms Center, "Remotely Operated Video Enhanced Receiver," 2008, http://usacac.army.mil/cac2/call/thesaurus/toc.asp?id=35613.

9. Simplified, DMPIs are "recommended aim points (otherwise known as desired mean points of impact [DMPI]" for bombs; i.e., the point on target in which we want the bomb to hit." Air Force Doctrine Document (AFDD) 3-1, *Air Warfare*, 22 January 2000, 53. The US *Dictionary of Military and Associated Terms* defines *DMPI* as "a precise point, associated with a target, and assigned as the center for impact of multiple weapons or area munitions to create a desired effect. May be defined descriptively, by grid reference, or by geolocation. Also called DMPI." JP 1-02, *Department of Defense Dictionary of Military and Associated Terms*, 12 April 2000 (as amended through April 2010), 137.

10. The *air tasking order* is a large document that lists air sorties for a fixed period of time, with individual call signs, aircraft types, and mission types. The ATO for Afghanistan was organized and produced at the US CAOC in Qatar. It is officially "a method used to task and disseminate to components, subordinate units, and command and control agencies projected sorties, capabilities and/or forces to targets and specific missions. Normally provides specific instructions to include call signs, targets, controlling agencies, etc., as well as general instructions. Also called ATO." Targets handled within the concept of *dynamic targeting* are previously unanticipated, unplanned, or newly detected targets that are generally of such importance to higher authority that they warrant rapid/immediate action (prosecution within the current execution period). DT is defined as, "Targeting that prosecutes targets identified too

late, or not selected for action in time to be included in deliberate targeting." JP 3-30, *Command and Control for Joint Air Operations*, 12 January 2010, GL-7, GL-9.

11. Lt Gen "Freek" Meulman, RNLAF, "Stovepipes and Caveats: The Need for a Comprehensive Approach and Strategy in Afghanistan," NATO draft assessment paper, October 2007.

12. The Afghanistan Compact was produced during the London Conference on Afghanistan held 31 January–1 February 2006. It can be downloaded from http://www.nato.int/isaf/docu/epub/pdf/afghanistan_ compact.pdf.

Chapter 6

Airpower as a Second Thought

Maj Gen Maurice H. Forsyth, USAF, Retired

*US Central Command Deputy Combined
Force Air Component Commander
June 2007–June 2008*

When the United States sent forces into Afghanistan on 7 October 2001, we did so almost exclusively alone. In the ensuing weeks, we largely defeated the Taliban and pushed them out of Afghanistan. Al-Qaeda was obviously still a viable foe, but we believed that targeted operations over time would shrink its leadership and operatives further. Our strategy was never entirely clear on whether we were pursuing a counterterrorism or a counterinsurgency operation. We ended up doing both. The political and military costs of a unilateral operation in Afghanistan pursuing the counterinsurgency dimension were such that our senior leadership wanted to bring an international force into the country and try to build the security in Afghanistan from within. In cooperation with Afghan authorities, the UN, and our allies, ISAF was introduced to provide security and start building up the Afghan National Security Forces.

This enabled the United States to limit its military commitment and redirect attention to other parts of the CENTCOM area of responsibility. While I believe this was the right thing to do, two factors would significantly impact this approach: First, ISAF was founded on a mandate to provide security and train Afghan security forces—not to fight a prolonged counterinsurgency operation. But as things progressed, the mission obviously changed. Second, our focus shifted. As the war unfolded in Iraq, it became obvious that our resources had to be focused there. Our priority was—without question—Iraq first and then Afghanistan.

I remember a conversation I had with COMISAF in spring 2007. By then we were working hard to increase the ramp space at the Kandahar and Bagram airfields to allow more planes to operate inside Afghanistan and make the airpower contribution even more robust. He told me that not only was he asking for more air support, he needed more ground forces as well. He told me he had asked Secretary of Defense Robert Gates for more troops every time he came by, and Gates had told him to "keep asking, but you are not getting anything, because we need to win the war in Europe before we go to the Pacific"—an obvious analogy to World War II, when General McArthur and Admiral Nimitz had to tread water in the Pacific until victory was secured in Europe. So he knew that the war in Afghanistan had to largely be put on hold until Iraq was handled. *He* knew that, *I* knew that, *all Americans* knew that, politically, we had to win in Iraq because of the way we went into that war. This, of course, influenced the strategy in Afghanistan.

Strategy

In my view, there simply was no coordinated strategy between NATO, ISAF, and CENTCOM by spring 2007. Many nations did not want to sign up for the counterterrorism operations of OEF, which was a priority for the United States. One way ISAF tried to fix this, from my perspective, was by dividing the country into regional commands. I can understand this from a political perspective, but in terms of military operations and a cohesive effort utilizing our collective resources, it generated all sorts of problems. Every week we had a meeting with COMISAF, and each regional command reported on its limited sector. You certainly got the feeling that their outlook rarely was on the overarching success of this war, but rather very much focused on their own limited AOR. What happened in other sectors appeared to be of less concern. The Americans operated in the east, and the British and Canadians operated in the south, while the other regions were relatively calm at the time. Each region appeared to have its own strategic outlook, way of doing business, and approach to Afghanistan. As alluded to earlier, it was not a cohesive effort.

I would describe the strategy in Afghanistan from 2002 onward, in effect, as one of "holding." By late 2002, we knew Iraq was to be the US priority, and the NATO/ISAF nations had limited interest in the Afghan war. It became clear that troop contributions would be limited for years—too limited to change the long-term dynamics in Afghanistan. So the strategy—or rather, the emphasis—was to build up the NATO PRTs and forward operating bases (FOB) in Afghanistan, keep the Taliban on the ropes, try to build a security force, and just hold until more resources could enter the theater.

Although I did not perceive ISAF to have a clear, cohesive strategy that was adhered to by all regional commands, I believe COMISAF felt he had to handle several strategies in a practical manner. It was clear that the United States had a counterterrorism strategy in the east that he certainly was involved in, but one to which many nations were unwilling to contribute. He also had the mandate which dictated that the main purpose of ISAF was to train the ANSF and assist the GIRoA in rebuilding key government institutions. Finally, he knew that he had too few forces to achieve this and thus adopted a variation of the holding strategy, requiring a pragmatic approach of balancing these sometimes competing strategic outlooks.

Air Strategy and the Ownership Debate

This holding strategy had ramifications for the use of airpower. In a sense, we seemed to believe we could divide Afghanistan into regions that hardly coordinated their efforts with each other and had divergent business models for approaching this conflict and then just put a layer of airpower on top of it all—that airpower was an instrument not needing broader cohesion among strategy, operational planning, and tactical execution, but rather one that should meet the tactical demands of each task force on a short-term notice. This notion ended up shaping the use of airpower. While I was DCFACC, the air strategy was relegated to a reactive response to troops in contact, or TICs. In terms of kinetics, that was almost all we did—respond to TICs.

The COMISAF in 2007, Gen Dan McNeill, was well aware of this. His two metrics were (1) how long would it take for air to respond to a TIC? and (2) how often in that response did we have to go kinetic? His desire was to decrease the *kinetic* approach and increase a posture of *show of force*. This was a logical approach, of course, when trying to gain the trust of the population of Afghanistan in a counterinsurgency effort.

Obtaining a clear strategy was not easy, and crystallizing overarching military thinking on how to utilize airpower—air strategy, if you will—was very difficult for a number of reasons. I have already touched upon the broader issues shaping this effort. As noted, many NATO/ISAF nations were fighting among themselves as to whether or not to contribute to the counterterrorism mission of OEF. Under the original mandate, ISAF was, by its very nature, limited mainly to "security" and "assistance." Subsequently, it was less prone to do hard, prolonged fighting. The participating nations had different takes on this. Just their diverse ROEs for ISAF were difficult to handle and convert into an effective fighting force. The volume summarizing the restrictions and ROEs imposed by the various ISAF countries was two inches thick. That alone is an indication of some dysfunctional structures that needed to be mitigated.

Perhaps the most disappointing feature I experienced during my tenure as DCFACC was the pettiness of a continuous, prolonged, and unproductive debate on air ownership. A British general officer speaking on his experiences in Afghanistan noted that "children debate ownership," indicating his take on the command-and-control debates in theater. In my view, that was actually a somewhat fair description of what was going on in Afghanistan. I had to use significant resources to handle what for many actors in theater was the overriding question with regard to airpower: Who was going to own what? If I were to break down most of the C2 debates in both Afghanistan and Iraq from an air perspective, they generally boiled down to the fact that everybody wanted to own the air assets themselves. COMISAF wanted the air assets, ISAF staff and their DCOM-Air wanted the air assets, CENTCOM wanted to control the air assets, the ground force commanders wanted to have their own air assets, SOF wanted their own air assets, and so it went. It was like a surreal revisit to debates a century ago. Everyone looked at their own limited AOR and had little or no appreciation for the consequences of carving up the scarce air resources and dividing the pieces to accommodate the tactical needs in compartmented geographical and operational AORs. The argument of "unity of command" to establish a system that would allocate limited resources throughout the theater of operations to best serve the overall effort and those most in need seemed to be lost in short-sighted and narrow-minded perspectives on airpower. It seemed like a century of hard-earned lessons and military history had been lost.

The entire time I was there, only one service allocated all of its assets to the combatant commander—the US Air Force. Everybody else kept assets for themselves. They called them "organic assets." Of all the airplanes operating in Iraq and Afghanistan—U-2s, Predators, C-130s, tankers, whatever—the air component only had operational control over 55 percent of them. Many called upon the CFACC to receive more air resources that it simply did not control. Many organizations had their own. They never gave them up; they did their own thing with them and rarely coordinated their effort with other agencies. The Marines are a good example. Once they took over in western Iraq (Al Anbar), they wanted everyone else out. I was discussing control of the airspace in a theater like Iraq and Afghanistan with a good friend and Marine officer with whom I had attended the Naval War College. At some point in that discussion, my friend simply stated, "I will own the airspace over my Marines!" That is the way the Marines approach war and their role in it.

But in fact, the sentiments of my friend were very similar to those of NATO/ISAF during my tenure. They wanted to do it on their own. Once they had their piece of ground in Afghanistan, they wanted to have their air assets and their command and control to do it themselves. It was certainly not a joint approach, nor was it just a non-US problem. The compartmented approach in RC-S was equally matched by the unilateral approach of the United States in RC-E.

It is important to note that every person I ever met in theater, no matter from what country or what organization, wanted to do the right thing. I do not know of a single incident in which an individual maliciously withheld forces or did something because of malicious intent—that was never the case. But the discussions with ISAF's DCOM-Air in fall 2007 illustrate the ongoing ownership debate. I have great respect for the ISAF DCOM-Air at the time. (The title was changed to "Director Air Coordination Element" in fall 2007.) We got along. We had our disagreements, but we could agree to disagree, and in that I found, quite frankly, a familiarity that was much appreciated. One factor in our discussions was that his professional background was as an air defender—the senior airman on the ISAF staff never flew an airplane. In my view, that was sometimes reflected in a position where he would argue for defensive and reactive solutions rather than exploiting the offensive potential of airpower. One of our main problems in Afghanistan was the reactive nature of our effort, and the ISAF DCOM-Air never pushed for proactive air solutions. In this regard, we appeared to be opposites in our philosophical approaches to this war.

Our most profound disagreements were related to command and control of air assets in Afghanistan. In my view, ISAF Air wanted to use US air assets but did not want to recognize the US CFACC, Lt

Gen Gary North, as the air component commander. When we were briefed on the air organization at ISAF HQ, their diagrams showed the CFACC far up in the right corner as an adviser to COMISAF. And while I, as DCFACC, was subordinate to the CFACC, in my NATO hat I was supposed to get my direction and guidance from the director ACE (formerly, DCOM-Air). It was just amazing from my perspective that anyone would think this kind of command and control relationship was functional.

Among other things, this structure was rooted in the fact that General North was a three-star who outranked everyone at ISAF except General McNeill. He required a NATO "flag-to-post" agreement not to be outranked in the decision-making process. To me, this was not a C2 relationship built for success. It was often built on the peculiarities of individual nations rather than sound logical thinking and military experience. Too many times I was approached by individuals who informed me on behalf of their country of behind-the-scenes political play that needed to be debunked. For example, one nation was maneuvering for a particular general officer position, which triggered anxiety from another nation which was lobbying for a different solution. It felt absurd at times. You sometimes felt like sitting everyone down and saying, "Listen, how about we just calm down, build the command and control structure needed to succeed, and then find out who will fill the positions, rather than the other way around."

In short, ISAF Air had very limited air resources and wanted the United States to release its air assets so they could be controlled and apportioned by ISAF. To underscore my point: in July 2007, the United States was providing 83 percent of all the close air support in Afghanistan—and ISAF's DCOM-Air wanted US air assets to work for him. I do understand that he was the DCOM-Air for ISAF and that ISAF was responsible for the whole of Afghanistan, but ISAF did not have adequate assets. I believe there were 6–8 non-US fighter aircraft allocated to ISAF in 2007, and their C2 capability was very limited and hardly comparable to US resources in theater. It was a difficult discussion, and we had to agree that we disagreed in the end.

In many respects the US approach was not much better. SHAPE's Operations Plan 10302 was signed in April 2006, which allowed the United States to support ISAF with airpower. But it was limited to what would be called "collective self-defense." In practical terms, this meant that if ISAF had a TIC, CENTCOM air assets could respond and assist. On the other hand, if COMISAF called the CAOC and had a target he wanted to hit and it was not an imminent threat to anybody, we had to call CENTCOM for approval. The fact that COMISAF deemed it necessary was evidently not enough. So in each case, we needed to call the chief of operations (J3) in CENTCOM back in the United States, and this officer would decide whether our CENTCOM air assets could strike targets designated by COMISAF—a very cumbersome and dysfunctional process that illustrates the inefficient need for ownership and control that should have been delegated and adjusted to fit the needs in theater. In the end we managed to change this particular example, and CENTCOM finally gave COMISAF what it called "target of execution authority." But for a whole year, if he had a target ISAF wanted to hit with US assets, we had to ask CENTCOM to be able to use them, because they were not there for ISAF; they were there for OEF missions.

Just to make it more discombobulated in terms of the leverage to develop any air strategy, the number one US priority was to support the special operations forces. So whenever Gen Stanley McChrystal, the Joint Special Operations Command commander, needed SOF support, he would get it. To his defense, he did not play that card very often. When we got a call from him requesting air support, he really needed it. But it illustrates a wider challenge and the matter of priorities for the air component of CENTCOM: first it was supporting SOF forces, then those assets identified in the ATO, and then ISAF.

In regard to the possibility of overarching thinking and developing any form of air strategy, it all morphed into a battle rhythm in a manner and scope over which the air component had limited influence. Routines were so ingrained in theater with respect to supporting TICs, how ISR was requested, and how one got other airpower capabilities or other air support missions, that one could not break the rhythm. It went on autopilot. Neither the Army/Marine doctrine publication FM 3-24 (2006) nor the US Air Force's subsequent doctrine on irregular warfare (2007) had any influence in theater. This was to a very small degree driven by air force demands and to a much larger degree driven by the ground-centric advocates in theater. Their competence, knowledge, and vision regarding the full potential of airpower were, to put it mildly, not always all that impressive. My initial observations upon arrival in theater were that the way this was set up was very much dysfunctional.

Air-Land Integration

One of the most troubling features of this war from my perspective—both in Afghanistan and Iraq—was that the air component had to continuously fight for a place at the table when operations were being planned. Airpower was a second thought. Ground commanders planned operations within their limited AORs and somehow expected air to be there if they needed help. It was not a joint effort to exploit the full potential of air and land power combined. I believe this was predominantly due to a ground-centric leadership at both ISAF and CENTCOM. Almost all the key leaders in joint positions were Army generals. The only senior officer from the Air Force was the CFACC, Lt Gen Gary North. And since he was dual-hatted as commander of Ninth Air Force at Shaw AFB, he had to stay in the United States most of the time. In effect, this reduced the influence of the airpower community.

To answer why, in the twenty-first century, the United States and NATO—the most formidable fighting forces in the world—proved so inadequate in terms of air-land integration is difficult. I believe one explanation has its roots in the 1991 war in Iraq. Airpower was so publicly displayed, influential, and decisive that it significantly hurt relations with the Army. For years you would not hear any senior Army or Marine leaders talk about the air portion of Desert Storm. It would be the "100-hour war," emphasizing only the ground portion of the effort. Subsequently, there was the war in Bosnia and the air operations (Operation Deliberate Force) in late August–early September 1995 that contributed significantly in paving the way for the Dayton Accords. A few years later (1999), the war against Serbia (Operation Allied Force) ended with the Air Force as the dominating service. I hesitate to use the word *service*, as I prefer a joint perspective, but in this case it was the air force—the airpower community of the United States and NATO—which for political reasons was the instrument of choice. Thus, the decade was very much influenced by airpower, and this did not play well with the ground-centric leadership.

That is not to say that ground forces were irrelevant in any way, but merely to say that the wars of the 1990s, the first decade after the Cold War, were predominantly of a political and military nature that made airpower a flexible choice that politicians appeared to prefer. And airpower did a fairly adequate job once employed. At the time—somewhat unreasonably, I might add—some people started questioning the need for the Army. It appeared the Army had a minor identity crisis—something the incoming secretary of defense, Donald H. Rumsfeld, seized upon, calling for a "leaner and meaner" ground force. To some extent, I believe the Army thought it was going to be subsumed, much like in the 1950s and early 1960s when significant portions of its budgets went to nuclear weapons and the US Air Force's Strategic Air Command (SAC). Army leaders feared they somehow would exert less influence on the American people and in the halls of Congress in terms of receiving adequate resources. So when the opportunity arose with the ground wars in Iraq and Afghanistan, they took full advantage to exert influence on budgets, on leadership, and in the public domain. While the 1990s may have been the decade of airpower, the first decade of this century would be that of ground forces and counterinsurgency. The US Army completely transformed itself with the budgets of these wars. Its leadership exerted great influence and dominated the public domain for years; thus the names of generals like McChrystal, Mattis, and Petraeus have become familiar throughout the world.

Besides the fact that the wars of Iraq and Afghanistan have not been particularly successful, the unfortunate result has been an over-reliance on ground power. While the wars in Bosnia and Kosovo precluded an Army presence for political reasons, such was not the case with regard to airpower in Iraq and Afghanistan. This had the full potential for a joint effort, as our military forces are intended to operate. But while great generals like Petraeus and Mattis have been heralded as substantial military thinkers, I believe history will prove them less champions of a joint military effort—so much so, that the original doctrine on counterinsurgency (FM 3-24) did not contain a single chapter on airpower. When this was noted, the document was amended to add airpower as an appendix at the end. In fact, to my knowledge, no senior airman was invited to contribute to the process of developing that doctrine. Excluding airpower from a counterinsurgency doctrine—even excluding the participation of senior airmen in the process—is quite remarkable and an indication of the low level of air-land integration and cooperation I unfortunately saw every day in the Iraq and Afghan theaters of war. It was an indication of the kind of leadership that persisted throughout my tenure. These individuals were great people and officers, and each tried to do the right thing. But by reducing airpower to an afterthought, largely institutionalized by their own doctrine, they missed an opportunity to exploit the full joint potential of our military force. We need to address that in the future. The issue concerns leadership and a sense of narrow-minded protection of one's own limited turf that is counterproductive to our collective effort.

The flip side of this coin is that we—the US Air Force and the wider airpower community—have allowed this to happen. Airmen tend to be more focused on flying and their careers within the Air Force. Educating and establishing senior air officers in joint positions have not been priorities. Gradually, air influence was lost in the joint community. Furthermore, those Air Force officers in key operational assignments in Iraq and Afghanistan were not promoted commensurate with Army officers in similar assignments. The Army has been much better structured for this. They have to a much larger degree focused on their leadership, given promotions for operational experience, and positioned their senior officers in key leadership positions to exert influence. Finally, for years our CFACC was located stateside, thus lacking the full influence of the only Air Force three-star in theater.

It will be interesting to see how the level of jointness develops in the years to come. The Libya operation has not been particularly emphasized in the United States. I do not think it is coincidental that a war fought predominantly by airpower has not received much attention among our military leadership. Many point out that the US public is weary of wars overseas. They point to air and naval power, and SOF, as the military forces of choice and say that we should let allies fight their own battles without a large US/allied ground force presence as in Iraq and Afghanistan. Whether or not the political needle again points toward any selected military services in the future is hard to predict. It depends on context, politics, and the uniqueness of each conflict. But facing rising challenges with the lack of jointness that has marked the wars in Iraq and Afghanistan is hardly the best solution.

Air Objectives, Focus, and Resources

In terms of OEF-ISAF air operations, the CFACC's objective as depicted on briefing slides at the time was "To support ISAF and neutralize and engage the insurgents, conduct Combined Joint operations and enable, establish and maintain a legitimate and credible government of GIRoA [*sic*]." Our air operations, also from the briefing slides, included

- close precision strikes,
- TIC response,
- named operations,
- nonkinetic air support,
- target presence show of force,
- electronic warfare,
- ISR,
- civil-military operations,
- humanitarian assistance, and
- air mobility.

Looking back, it is interesting that *civil-military operations, humanitarian assistance*, and *air mobility* were at the bottom of our priorities, given that this was largely a counterinsurgency operation seeking to gain the trust of the Afghan people. It is also interesting to see how *named operations* were a priority. I think the reason for this was Operations Anaconda and Medusa. Many of the mistakes in Operation Medusa in 2006 could have been identified by studying Operation Anaconda in 2002. Gen T. Michael Moseley, who was the CFACC (2001–03) during Operation Anaconda, ended up having extremely limited time to prepare the battlefield for that operation, and what little time he got was largely because an Air Force major forced himself into the Army planning conference and said, "You need air." It was an extremely poorly coordinated operation, a classic example of misjudgment of the capabilities of airpower, and a sad testimony to the frequent lack of jointness observed in theater.

It is my strong conviction that the reason the Afghan insurgents—the militias, the Taliban, and al-Qaeda—so publicly emphasized civilian casualties, presumably the result of air, was because they knew that the single foe they were unable to influence directly was airpower. This was our most influential asymmetric advantage, and they needed to reduce its influence as much as possible. They knew that if they could eliminate airpower altogether, they would win. In retrospect, I would say they did a good job curbing it. Surely, we need to stay within the boundary of international law, guard distinction, and ensure proportionality, but the inflated claims of civilian casualties represent a strategic communications contest we largely lost. The insurgents made it a strategy to blame airpower for incidents where airpower was not even involved, and since the gathering of facts is by nature cumbersome, our reports of innocence were often too late. Unfortunately, this relegated use of airpower to a last resort instead of a more proactive posture that would have enabled it to be more effective and save US/allied lives. Regrettable.

The use of ISR was steadily increasing during my tenure, leading to a continuous fight over who would receive it. Again, the C2 relationship was interesting. When the air component put up a new orbit or a combat air patrol (CAP) in theater, we had to meet with CENTCOM in the United States regarding who would get it. In other words, this was not only a question of *apportionment*; they reserved the right to *allocate* those resources as well. This was contrary to our doctrinal understanding, which says a service allocates resources to a combatant commander, who then apportions those assets through the components to support the objectives of the supported commander—in this case the land component commander. This was not the case during my time, as CENTCOM chose to retain the authority to allocate resources—yet another issue that deviated from doctrine, reduced flexibility, and put increased strain on a dysfunctional C2 construct.

During my tenure, we had A-10s and F-15Es in Afghanistan. All F-16s were operating over Iraq, and the B-1s supported both operations. I would estimate that the USAF had about 25–30 percent of its kinetic-capable airplanes in Afghanistan and 70–75 percent in Iraq. Of course, at the time, there was not nearly as much fighting in Afghanistan as in Iraq. Still, as I carefully noted in my briefings, tail numbers are not indicative of capability. What is important is the ability to create effects. In retrospect, I believe the effects that the air component was able to achieve in Iraq were significantly higher than in Afghanistan. That was not entirely due to the larger number of aircraft, but also to the nature of that conflict, the C2 infrastructure (which was much more difficult in mountainous Afghanistan), the way these resources were used, and the level of fighting. In Iraq, we regularly had JSTARS in theater, which was rarely the case in Afghanistan. We basically had a lot more capability and assets in Iraq than in Afghanistan. The level of fighting and incidents involving airpower in Iraq was roughly compatible with the 25–30 percent versus 70–75 percent apportionment. Iraq was still our main focus.

Epilogue

The first time I met with General McNeill, COMISAF, was in April 2007. He sat down with me and said, "I need some more help over here." I looked in his eyes and could see how frustrated he was that he did not get the level of resources he asked for and needed for Afghanistan. On the other hand, anyone who asked for anything in Iraq would have it shortly thereafter. I ended up having the utmost respect for General McNeill. I liked him as a commander and as a person. He was a very straight shooter. As I understand, he was about to retire when he was asked to become the supreme commander in Afghanistan. He accepted that challenge instead of retirement because he thought it was an important thing to do. I think he realized early on—perhaps he was even told before he took over—that he had to ensure that Afghanistan did not blow into something big, and that he knew he would not get the assets he needed until Iraq was neutralized. He knew that he was not going to be the priority. He could still ask, but he just would not get anything, at least from the United States. Additionally, NATO was very reluctant to send forces. Defense Secretary Gates had gone to the North Atlantic Council and said, "Look, we need your help here. We are engaged in Iraq; we need some more forces in Afghanistan." He did that over and over again, resulting in a lot of frustration. So I got the impression that General McNeill—at least back in April 2007—came to the conclusion that he would take anything and everything that was offered to him. He would do the best he could with it, but he knew that the best he could do with such scarce resources was to tread water until success in Iraq would free up more forces. He tried to work the NATO nations, tried to get more assets, tried to build more infrastructure, and tried to piece together a coherent strategy. But Afghanistan had been divided into regions, and it was difficult to break down some of the barriers that were built up between the various regional commands.

It is notable that when you used to hear about fighting in Afghanistan, you more often than not would hear about fighting in Regional Command-East, South, or North—you did not hear about the fighting in *Afghanistan* the way you heard about the fighting in Iraq. There was a certain geographical cohesion to a larger extent in Iraq than in Afghanistan. On the news, you could often hear the phrase, "There was fighting in Iraq today," and you had to listen to find out where.

News about Afghanistan, on the other hand, tended to be geographically specified by regions.

My impression was that General McNeill was tired when he left Afghanistan. Tired from his efforts of bringing together a coalition that had different ROEs, different caveats, and different political desires on how to achieve the outcome of this war. Tired of what I would call a certain pettiness in terms of who should get what, compartmented thinking, and a tendency by many nations to view Afghanistan through their national soda straw, focusing on their limited piece—often a PRT or an FOB. Tired of nations that regularly neglected the broader picture and what could actually be achieved if we devised a clearer strategy and used our forces in a more cohesive manner. I commend him for his efforts. I think that if he were to write a chapter on his experiences, he would say that he was not necessarily successful if the measure was to develop a broad comprehensive strategy and enable vast changes to Afghanistan. His job, with the limited resources and cohesion available at the time, was rather to "hold," create a foundation for progress, and ensure that the situation did not spiral downward until the international community decided to give more priority to this war. That is probably his biggest achievement and legacy.

Looking back on the war in Afghanistan, I feel strongly that someone should compare the use of airpower in Vietnam to the use of airpower in Afghanistan. I believe there are some important parallels and lessons waiting to be unveiled from such a study. In my view, the single most important issue stemming from the Vietnam War regarding the use of military force was that command and control was—to put it bluntly—a mess. Correspondingly, much of what will come out of the Afghanistan War with regard to the use of military force is that command and control was a mess as well. In Vietnam we won hundreds if not thousands of small limited battles with the help of airpower and ground power combined, only to give up our gains immediately thereafter, leading to us having to fight for those same gains again and again. The same thing was happening in Afghanistan. Sadly, I am not sure we learned a lot.

What I do know is that our ability to influence the battlefield from the air has exponentially increased in the past decades. Early in my career in the US Air Force, my colleagues at the squadron and I would go out in the F-4 and practice dropping bombs. We would practice and practice until we hit the target. Today, with the advent of modern technology, it is a given that you are going to hit the target—now you go out and practice not to miss. I believe the airman's perspective and the advantages that airpower brings to the fight today, as in Afghanistan, have the potential for providing different and vastly improved effects on the battlefield. This brings great improvements but also features we should think through more thoroughly. We have made great improvements in terms of how to use JTACs to affect the battlefield with air for a ground commander. We have learned that the Army and Marines can extend themselves further than they normally could because they can almost always depend on having air on hand to provide timely precision logistics and engagements when they need it. The importance and perception of airpower have reached a level in which it makes big news if air does not show up when troops are engaged with an enemy or a mistake leads to civilian casualties. The expectations of airpower have in many ways become ingrained as something one simply expects to be there in large quantities to assist troops in need and with a zero margin for error—a margin of error no other service operates with, much less is held accountable for by the public. Somewhat reluctantly, I have to say that in a counterinsurgency fight such as Afghanistan, I believe we have tweaked the system on the margins in terms of accuracy and our ability to use technology for command and control to get coordinates, positions, and the timely information needed to conduct real-time precision engagements. But in terms of affecting the battlespace and the larger objectives of these wars, from an airman's perspective, I believe we have a way to go. We need to improve on the overall cohesion between political goals, military strategy, operational joint planning, and the tactical execution of airpower.

Chapter 7

Moving toward Counterinsurgency

Lt Gen Jouke L. H. Eikelboom, RNLAF, Retired

ISAF Director, Air Coordination Element (ACE)
February–November 2008

Under NATO's so-called flags-to-post job assignment process, the Netherlands was asked to fill the position of director of the air coordination element (director ACE) in ISAF headquarters beginning in early 2008. I had been the Dutch national detachment commander there in 2005, and during my assignment as director of operations in the Ministry of Defense (MoD) in The Hague, I visited Afghanistan frequently. So when I was asked to take the job as director ACE, I felt I knew largely what it would entail. I accepted.

I arrived in Kabul in January 2008. It was a crisp, clear day, –16° C, and with the unmistakable "atmosphere" of Kabul that I would become familiar with in the ensuing months. Kabul is not a particularly pleasant place to be in winter, as the often poor Afghan people try to warm their houses by burning anything they can find, including old car tires. Combined with stable weather and often no wind, Kabul Valley during winter has its own distinct smell, and this particular morning was no exception.

My predecessor as ISAF's director ACE, Maj Gen Frederik "Freek" Meulman, was also from the Netherlands. I knew him well from previous encounters, and speaking the same language made the handover quick and efficient. He gave me a run-through of his lessons and perspectives that helped significantly in the starting phase of my new job. Yet my experience in my previous job in The Hague was equally helpful, if not more so, in preparing for this tenure as the senior airman in ISAF HQ.

As a former F-16 pilot, I had experienced many of the challenges facing airmen in the skies over Afghanistan and knew the air force culture relatively well. The director ACE position still provided challenges that went far beyond the tactical scope of airpower. I quickly realized that working in ISAF HQ meant working outside a commonly agreed military strategy—in an environment in which airpower was often an afterthought.

Strategy

As noted, I spent the two years prior to this assignment as director of operations in the Netherlands MoD (November 2005–December 2007). Upon my arrival there, planning was in its final stage for an air and ground task force to be deployed to Uruzgan Province in southern Afghanistan under a new government mandate. As director of operations, I was responsible for all Dutch force operations, but I must admit the Afghanistan mission was, by far, the one that required the most careful and extensive attention. There were numerous challenges. Many perceived that we were going to rebuild Afghanistan. Some believed the conflict was slowly developing into a *counterinsurgency* campaign, but adaptation to this reality was slow and not realized or accepted by many.

This became evident in many discussions in the North Atlantic Council. During my tenure at ISAF HQ, the dialogue illustrated NATO's transition to counterinsurgency. The commander of ISAF from summer 2008 onward, Gen David D. McKiernan, established a foundation for this transition, which I believe has been undercommunicated. The transition to counterinsurgency continued long after my tenure. It was about one year after I left Afghanistan, and after the new Obama administration had taken office, that the so-called Initial Assessment (fall 2009) of the new COMISAF, Gen Stanley A. McChrystal, established a military framework that enabled all the contributing nations to agree to a counterinsurgency strategy.

There was no clear strategy in Afghanistan while I was director ACE. We had a broader direction of our effort. The "Afghanistan Compact" established three lines of operations that guided our effort, of which "security," obviously, was particularly emphasized within ISAF. Our focus and priority increasingly became training the Afghan National Security Forces. Still, it would have been beneficial to have a clearer military strategy at the time. This lack of a clear strategy kept us largely following the same rhythm and path as previous years and left maneuver room for other nations and their PRTs to follow their own senses about operations in their AORs. It made it more difficult to have a long-term cohesive effort.

I would like to point out that even after the Obama administration entered the political arena and the McChrystal era publicly established counterinsurgency as the general "modus operandi," options remained as to what this concept entailed in practical terms. One could argue that, first, the new strategy meant ISAF had to use a lot more troops to cover all the provinces, districts, and villages, emphasizing that our troops were to live side-by-side with our Afghan partners. By sharing the security risks with the Afghan population, we would have a greater chance of winning their "hearts and minds" and thus be better positioned to influence this largely defined "center of gravity" of any counterinsurgency: the trust of the local population. Thus, we would ensure that the insurgents would have a declining base of political, military, logistic, and intelligence support. It meant that we had to provide more training and equipment programs to strengthen the Afghans' capability and capacity to gradually enable them to provide for their own security. This perspective came to be known by many as the "Petraeus Model," based on Gen David H. Petraeus and his experiences in Iraq, as subsequently outlined in the US Army/Marine Corps field manual on counterinsurgency (FM 3-24), which he largely facilitated.

Second, one could argue that this counterinsurgency effort would require a significantly smaller footprint. By establishing fewer but more-robust bases, we could focus more on the counterterrorism portion of the effort. Training and education of the ANSF to gradually enable them to provide for their own security would still be a priority, but fighting the insurgents would be done largely by targeted efforts of airpower and special forces. It would be less focused on transforming the Afghan society and less dependent on large troop numbers. This came to be viewed as the "Biden Model," named after US vice president Joseph R. Biden, who publicly championed this perspective.

In a sense, we never quite decided which model to pursue, even after McChrystal provided his "Initial Assessment" in fall 2009. We ended up doing both. I presume history will inform us about the outcome in Afghanistan and to what degree any of these models were helpful. However, we should remember that even within the concept of counterinsurgency, there are alternatives, options, and nuances in our collective approach to the specific context at hand. It is not like adopting a counterinsurgency strategy means picking out a handbook and implementing it as a theoretical precise piece of science to guide our effort. There are far too many variables at play—in theater, in the wider region, and in the domestic politics of those nations involved. Thus, each counterinsurgency demands its own unique approach and decisions with regard to *how*, *who*, and *what* to influence. Surely influencing and enabling the population, the governmental structures, the bureaucracy, the rule of law, and other basic societal elements must be considered, but to what extent and in what way these dynamics should be influenced have been debated for centuries.

In the end, these choices will be the overarching issues that determine if our effort in Afghanistan is successful or not. A counterinsurgency normally takes years to influence the often deeply ingrained structures one is trying to change. Once we agreed on a counterinsurgency strategy, we put a timeline on our departure. That was very understandable from a political perspective, which always is the most important one, but from a military standpoint, it was not exactly a textbook recipe for a successful counterinsurgency effort. It will be interesting to see how this plays out in the end.

Air-Land Integration

The general feeling among the airmen in ISAF HQ was that the headquarters was dominated by army officers. As the operation gradually evolved into a counterinsurgency, it is understandable that the land component received more attention. Still, there is a fundamental difference between a joint operation with a healthy emphasis on the supported component command versus a top-down army operation with airpower an afterthought that was often simply assumed to be readily available for ground commanders as needed. We never did achieve a fully joint focus within ISAF HQ during my tenure.

I think it is safe to say that in the particularly demanding environment of Afghanistan, airpower was the most critical enabler to extend and execute land operations in areas that would otherwise be off limits. Air support was crucial to these operations. Without it, we would not have been able to conduct many of our land operations, and we would have taken significantly more casualties in the ones we did conduct. Casualties had the potential of directly impacting our own center of gravity, which was defined as continued political/public support for the operation. Thus, airpower was seen as the key asymmetric advantage for ISAF, in that it allowed operations on the ground in Afghanistan to be performed with limited risk for ground forces being overrun by large insurgent forces. The insurgents knew that massing their forces for a coordinated attack on ISAF ground forces would make them a very vulnerable target for air ISR platforms—and subsequent strike missions. Hence they had no choice but to rely on smaller pinprick attacks, suicide bombers, and improvised explosive devices (IED).

One key challenge for us was related to the ground forces mantra of "decentralized planning/decentralized execution." This meant that operations were planned bottom up by the various task forces in theater. With limited emphasis on airpower in general, and limited awareness in terms of what capabilities and effects airpower could bring to the fight, we often saw a lack of jointness that was somewhat disturbing. I would say the situation gradually improved, but it was surprising to see the limitations on our collective effort in this regard.

The area of operation in Afghanistan was divided into five regions, and as director ACE, I had a small air staff element in every regional command operations center, called regional air operations centers or RAOCs. Thus, in terms of air-land integration, the typical flow of events would be as follows: A ground task force in a specific region would plan an operation within its AOR to achieve an effect that typically supported the objective of the regional commander and COMISAF. Based on an instruction from ISAF HQ, a certain risk level was attached to the operation based on, for example, complexity and the predicted/anticipated threat level. The risk level of the operation at hand subsequently had to be approved by the regional command HQ. Based on the nature and size of the operation, the anticipated threat level, and the effects to be achieved, the planners would incorporate airpower into the planning process. Once the necessary air support was determined, they entered the joint tactical air request, or JTAR, process. This was a standardized format for requesting air support in advance of preplanned operations. Every day, a large number of JTARs were received from various task forces in theater. These requests were input to the JTAR matrix processed by my ACE staff in ISAF HQ. This matrix was the most important input to building the air tasking order, the ATO. There were never enough assets to support everyone, and despite often-signaled desires by commanders to have their own assets, we needed to carefully prioritize which operation needed air support the most and simultaneously build in flexibility to quickly support an operation/situation that needed immediate fire support. In effect, we supported all troops-in-contact situations, and the average time from an urgent request for air support to aircraft overhead anywhere in Afghanistan was less than 15 minutes.

Tasks, Responsibilities, and Command and Control

In broad terms, the responsibilities of director ACE in ISAF HQ are described in the operational plan from the commander of JFC Brunssum. This NATO headquarters did the first planning for the ISAF mission back in 2003, which resulted in an operational plan that has been updated regularly based on strategic guidance from the Supreme Allied Commander Europe. Under SACEUR's guidance and the operational authority vested in me by JFC Brunssum, I—as director ACE—was the senior NATO air advisor for COMISAF. Director ACE coordinates and conducts all ISAF air operations in Afghanistan in close coordination with the US deputy CFACC and the US CAOC at Al Udeid, Qatar. On behalf of COMISAF, director ACE also executes command over the NATO airfields in Kabul and Kandahar and is involved in general issues related to other airfields in Afghanistan, such as flight safety, airspace control, and their development in support of ISAF forces. Director ACE also had a responsibility to coordinate and support the development of the Afghan Ministry of Transportation and Civil Aviation, as well as build and improve the partnering effort with the Afghan National Army Air Corps. The latter has since developed into an independent air force. From this perspective you could argue that the director ACE and his team work along the lines of defense, diplomacy, and development—a concept I was familiar with and used in my previous job as director of operations in the MoD when planning for the Dutch deployment to Uruzgan Province. We also used a combination of other analytical approaches to counterinsurgency, for example the "28 articles" provided by Dr. David Kilcullen.[1] Together, this gave a good overview of the military and civilian air issues in Afghanistan, which made this work a profoundly rewarding personal experience.

Air command and control has been a long and rocky road in Afghanistan. I am sure other contributors to this book will emphasize this in their chapters, but I would like to provide my own take on it. At first glance the command and control structure in Afghanistan looked complicated—inside information and experience were required to understand it. That is normally not a particularly good starting point, but in my view, it did provide an effectively networked air C2 capability that delivered the required air support for the Afghanistan mission. It was certainly not designed according to standard NATO doctrine, but as military personnel, we are trained to adapt to local circumstances. Although not perfect, the system was robust, manageable, and adequate. This does not mean that C2 doctrine is not valuable, as it is always a good starting point for providing general reference and direction. It provides a common basic C2 language, a useful framework for exercises/training, and an outline of the general process that in broad terms is useful. This is perhaps particularly important within the airpower community, as these processes are normally executed fairly similarly by various national air staffs. All things considered, it worked very well.

I should point out that NATO's deployable air C2 is largely underdeveloped and has been for years.[2] The opposite is true for the United States, and by the time NATO assumed responsibility for ISAF and was taking over RC-S and RC-E, the US structure was largely already in place. The US C2 resources were a tremendous asset, particularly the C2 hub at CAOC Al Udeid. This air C2 network was well developed when I arrived in ISAF HQ. It was built by dedicated airmen who understood the mission, who worked through communication and information systems (CIS) interoperability problems, and who also somehow managed to work through the "four-eyes" and "US-eyes-only" information sharing problems.

The air team in ISAF HQ generally concentrated on planning with the land forces in the Afghan theater, while the US CAOC at Al Udeid executed the daily ATO in close coordination with the air component coordination element, or ACCE, situated in the combined joint operations center inside ISAF HQ, for last-minute changes and last-minute requests for air support. A small staff element from ISAF was deployed to the US CAOC to make sure that ISAF requirements were included in the tasking. The CAOC's primary focus in 2008 was still on operations in Iraq, so this staff element was critically important in pushing for much-needed US platforms like AWACS, long-range bombers (B-1s), tankers, and ISR platforms that had to be shared between Iraq and Afghanistan. Obviously, there was often a bit of tension in this regard, as the everyday battle for resources to be put on the daily ATO was very important for both theaters of operations. There were only a few times during my tenure in which I had to become personally involved at my level to acquire the right assets to execute the ISAF mission.

Airspace management was a challenge for us in 2008. Shortly after the Taliban regime was removed in late 2001, it became clear that the Afghans did not have any capability to manage their own airspace. An agreement was put in place to have the United States serve as the airspace control authority until the Afghan government was able to fund, build, and maintain these capabilities. This function was mainly executed from the CAOC at Al Udeid. The United States eventually put an airspace management facility at Kabul International Airport that enabled sufficient control to resume civilian airliner overflights en route between Europe and Asia. No radars were available for this mission, so deconfliction was based on procedural control with its distinct inherent limitations. As the ISAF mission was expanding into all regions in Afghanistan, the number of aircraft using the airspace expanded as well. Thus, deconfliction between civil aviation and military aviation needed a great deal of attention. Concerns over deconfliction grew proportionally as more troops and equipment entered the theater, operations increased in scope and frequency, and the number of manned and unmanned military flights steadily grew. Still, the professional staff at KAIA was doing an outstanding job. One critical aspect for the future will be to train Afghans to perform this important task themselves.

Some Observations as Director ACE

A somewhat underappreciated feature of our effort in Afghanistan was related to ISAF/US handling of the various airports there. It is expensive to run airfields, it demands competence, and the logistics involved are so enormous that it can be hard for those not intimately familiar with the requirements for a large, functioning operational air base to fully comprehend. ISAF's biggest air base at Kandahar had only a single runway in 2008, which of course was extremely busy. With 13,000 people on base, a significant number of aircraft cramped into limited tarmac and ramp space, and a large number of units, command elements, logistics, contractors, and so forth, it was a constant "work in progress" to facilitate every need for those resources placed there. It is a side of airpower we hear relatively little about and one often taken for granted. We should have increased the focus on this issue and appreciated the complexity of running these bases, as it is a fundamental basis for our air effort in theater. One of our big concerns was our dependency on the large air bases of Kandahar and Bagram. If for some reason, such as runway repairs, they were to be lost for a significant period of time, we would not have adequate alternatives. Thus, we pushed hard to improve our capacity at the airfields at Mazar-e Sharif and Herat to have the necessary degree of operational flexibility.

Another concern about this operation was related to our structures for sharing intelligence. The national capability and process of collecting, processing, analyzing, and disseminating intelligence are the most delicate and sensitive issues for most nations involved in ongoing military operations. Sharing intelligence information can reveal national structures, platforms, methods, and competence that most nations would prefer to conceal, or at least limit and protect to the largest extent possible. NATO has developed a series of unilateral and multilateral structures for sharing information on the basis of these fears. You have the "six-eyes," the "four-eyes," the "two-eyes," and "national-eyes-only" communities, based on who has the information and which allies they trust to handle this information in a safe and discreet manner. The United States has the greatest resources in this regard and chooses whom to trust to protect its own sources and capabilities—like most other nations. But this issue impacted a multinational organization like ISAF because many very competent officers came from nations that were outside of these limited intelligence-sharing communities, making it very hard for these individuals to be fully informed and make sound decisions on that basis. Furthermore, when you were given only a piece of intelligence and precluded from seeing the process behind or the source that provided this intelligence, you were less prone to accept that intelligence as a basis for important decisions. To be honest, I must say that the quality of our intelligence sometimes could have been better, and as a general observation, intelligence is not the same as facts, and we would be wise to remember that.

The use of ISR increased steadily during 2008, thereby continuing a trend established in the years prior to my arrival. While we increasingly relied on ISR in our operations, we regularly experienced shortages of this capability. As mentioned before, the US assets had to be divided between Iraq and Afghanistan, and Iraq appeared to be the priority. So these resources were scarce at times, which reduced our military potential and output. Still, the availability of ISR became better over time and signified, perhaps, that the Iraq war was slowly winding down.

A favorite whipping post within ISAF was the issue of "caveats." Many nations had national restrictions as to where their forces could be used, in what manner, and under which circumstances. To be fair, this sometimes was a problem, but in my mind not as significant as many proclaimed. The Americans in particular had less patience with this issue and, I believe, exaggerated the problem it presented. Caveats were often a result of logistics support problems and/or intelligence-sharing problems that ended up being the main reason for some nations' reluctance to move their troops to other areas. Caveats are a factor we are unlikely to avoid in limited allied out-of-area operations like Afghanistan. They involve political constraints that enable each nation to participate in a manner consistent with its political leverage. They should be treated more like political enablers than military restrictions, and with sufficient flexibility and organizational skills, this issue can be handled in a manner that does not present significant problems.

The Afghan Ministry of Transport and Civil Aviation represented a huge challenge for us. Not to be unfair, and one must understand that Afghanistan has long been one of the poorest and least developed nations in the world, but the bureaucratic competency of this ministry was extremely limited. I would estimate that about five out of 600 employees had some capability that could be used as a basis for cooperation. Corruption was high, and the most basic processes were slow-moving and incompetent. Thus, our plans for handing over airport and aviation services were moving at an extremely slow pace, a situation I believe persisted for years after I left office. It shows the level of effort and emphasis that must be put into education and development of governmental functionality.

A final emphasis should be placed on collateral damage and civilian casualties (CIVCAS). In 2008 we noticed that CIVCASs were mainly a factor in close air support incidents, when strike aircraft supporting our troops in contact with the enemy had less time and preparation of the battlefield before providing their fire support to save their comrades. This was much less of a problem in deliberate targeting where a target had been planned in advance. With all the procedures in place, target folders established, and eyes on target over time, this was rarely an issue. The tendency to use extensive force—in this case, airpower—when our own ground patrols came under fire was counterproductive, especially in a counterinsurgency environment where it is often hard to define who is the enemy and who is not. We tried to establish a procedure whereby if the ground force and/or the aircrew were unsure who the enemy was, they should retreat rather than request/use extensive CAS. We saw examples of large numbers of bombs dropped on a small number of insurgents, far exceeding established proportionality principles. Not only was this an inefficient use of force that risked the lives of innocent individuals in the area, but it directly undermined the key underlying focus of any counterinsurgency—to gain the trust and confidence of the local population. Gradually, these problems were solved, but they still serve as a reminder to all to be aware of linking means and ends when utilizing military force.

Epilogue

My tenure as director ACE was one of the most rewarding assignments of my career. Looking back, 2008 represented a phase or transition in the ISAF saga in Afghanistan. Although counterinsurgency had always been a part of the strategic mix, by late 2008 our collective effort moved more explicitly in that direction; however, it would take another year until all the nations were ready to officially accept the framework of this concept.

Airpower was a key asymmetric advantage in Afghanistan. It is my hope that the level of joint understanding and appreciation of its role will increase in the future. We come closer to unleashing our full military potential when both air and land work together in a truly joint manner. Hopefully, Afghanistan has taught us a lesson in this regard. I hope that this war has taught us that future education, doctrine, and training should generate officers in both blue and green uniforms who are proud and professional representatives of their respective services but who understand that only by including each other's strengths in cohesive joint planning can we achieve our objectives. Perhaps this chapter and this book can contribute to this end.

Although we lacked a clear military strategy throughout 2008, one should remember that there are always limits to what a military strategy can achieve. In the end it will be up to the Afghan people. They will decide their own path for the future. Setting aside all our mistakes, lost opportunities, and lack of military strategy for years—for the Afghan people to have the opportunity to choose their own way forward is perhaps the greatest legacy of our collective effort in Afghanistan.

If NATO embarks on new operations of a similar nature, it will be wise to deal with intelligence sharing from the outset of its strategic planning. It should focus on establishing a shared network to better enable forces to create the maximum achievable effects and thereby increase the opportunities for success. This will also enable the alliance to fight in a coalition with a minimum of caveats in a more coordinated and cohesive manner.

Notes

1. David Kilcullen, "Twenty-Eight Articles: Fundamentals of Company-Level Counterinsurgency," *Iosphere*, Summer 2006, 29–35, http://www.au.af.mil/info-ops/iosphere/iosphere_summer06_kilcullen.pdf.

2. I believe the reorganization of NATO's C2 capabilities in 2013 and onward will fix some of the underdeveloped air C2 shortfalls within the alliance.

Part III

The Counterinsurgency Debate

Chapter 8

The Shift from Iraq to Afghanistan

Maj Gen Douglas L. Raaberg, USAF, Retired

*US Central Command Deputy Combined
Force Air Component Commander*

June 2008–July 2009

When I was introduced to the FB-111A advanced technology bomber in the mid-1980s, it never occurred to me that I would ever fly this "space-age" flying wing, let alone command the B-2 wing that would penetrate Iraqi defenses 15 years later. It was the Cold War. To me, this bomber was designed for one strategy only: nuclear deterrence. Yet this was an age of enlightenment for the USAF where the application of airpower in Vietnam demanded new thinking, new tactics, and a new way of war for airmen. Lessons of the past provided the foundation to centralize the planning and control of airpower and decentralize its execution. We organized, trained, and equipped to ensure that airpower should and would be the most formidable part of any military strategy—and prove it in battle.

To airpower practitioners, Operation Desert Storm was indisputable in its outcome. It was the most formidable integration of air, space, and cyber operations in the twentieth century. The debut of stealth and precision ushered in an innovative era for the application of airpower. In the end, the operational arts achieved a decisive strategic outcome—removing Iraq's grip on Kuwait. Seizing command of the air was an operational imperative; the Iraqi air and ground forces were decimated from the air. The USAF proved that effects-based airpower would turn the tide of war. A decade later, we were preparing for the next encounter in Iraq. We never expected it would be through neither the back door of a terrorist attack on the United States nor the front door of our battle for control of the Taliban in Afghanistan and the elimination of safe havens of al-Qaeda in the Middle East and Central Asia. A new era of counterterrorism and counterinsurgency clouded the application of airpower in support of operations to rid us of a growing, stateless threat based on an extremist ideology. We were ready to fight Saddam's forces; however, as a coalition of the willing, we were ill prepared for ensuing sectarian strife and burgeoning insurgencies. As the first wave of B-2s launched that first night, I was profoundly struck by the fact that I was confident in our successful outcome and oddly wondering where I'd be years later as a result of Iraq's demise.

The opening air attack in 2003 for Operation Iraqi Freedom was decisive. Our B-2 mission was clear—"Kick the doors down!" As early as May of 2002, we knew our objective was to dismantle Saddam Hussein's regime by attacking the toughest targets—heavily defended redoubts in, around, and beyond Baghdad—undetected. In less than a week, a combined armada of B-2 and F-117 stealth aircraft had accomplished its objective. US and coalition air forces had seized control of all Iraqi airspace in less than a week. A month later, our B-2s were home and back to normal operations. We had been a part of history; we were proud of our contribution, and I felt blessed in having great leaders, team members, and industry partners who made it all a success. No words can describe a wartime command. Relinquishing the flag of the 509th Bomb Wing after two glorious years is equally indescribable. My next challenge was yet to come at the operational level in a combatant command.

When I arrived in Qatar to be the deputy for operations (DJ3) in the forward headquarters of US CENTCOM, our strategic aim focused on fighting counterinsurgency on two fronts. We were now fighting an elusive battle in Iraq with friends and against enemies who had divided loyalties. Support for Afghanistan paled in comparison to Iraq. Less clear were the ends, ways, and means to hand Iraq back to the Iraqis. By 2005, we had framed a new strategy, one that would be a tough road to return sovereignty to Iraq. We embarked on a new plan to embed coalition forces with fledging Iraqi security forces. In some ways the goal was to set the conditions for a sovereign state by training, guiding, and whenever able, relinquishing control of the police, military, and border security to a centralized Iraqi government. For US and coalition military forces, this was an arduous task—overwhelming in most cases.

I left CENTCOM and the desert in the summer of 2006. By then, I had become an expert in organizing, training, and equipping military forces for counterinsurgency. I never imagined that leading operations for Air Combat Command (ACC) would be more difficult than running operations for a combatant command. ACC is responsible to provide strike, ISR, and combat air forces for global combatant command (COCOM) commitments. I spent two years leading efforts to provide combat-ready forces for Iraq and Afghanistan.

Returning to Qatar two years later as the deputy combined air component commander, I knew the CAOC would have to develop a more responsive construct for fighting counterinsurgencies in Iraq and Afghanistan with airpower. The strategy had fundamentally shifted from ousting Saddam's Baathist regime and the Taliban to supporting US and NATO ground forces committed to training Iraqi and Afghan security personnel in air, land, and maritime operations.

With that background, this chapter addresses some of the significant incidents of my tenure that reflect the strategic shift of forces and effort from security in Iraq to combat operations in Afghanistan. Within a month of my arrival at the CAOC, it was clear the fighting season was once again in full swing. It was a difficult summer. For example, on Saturday, 13 July 2008, we were involved in blunting the aftermath of the "Battle of Wanat"—one of the bloodiest battles of the Afghan war. This battle—in a small town east of Kabul and close to the Pakistani border—cost nine US soldiers killed and 27 wounded.[1] A month later, on 18 August, 10 French soldiers were killed and 21 wounded in the Uzbin Valley ambush by the Taliban some 40 miles east of Kabul.[2] Both incidents demonstrated the tenacity of the fighting on the ground and the difficulty of gaining control of the areas that Afghan security forces would eventually occupy. The latter incident was a tragedy for an important ally, France. I remember organizing and providing air coverage and air escort for Pres. Nicolas Sarkozy, who came to escort home the fallen French soldiers from the Uzbin Valley ambush. It was a solemn moment for France and the president and changed the French perspective on the war in Afghanistan.

The Battle of Wanat is significant for two reasons. First, it obviously represented a difficult day for US forces and a real wakeup call. I saw Predator films of the battle, and the US soldiers put up one hell of a fight despite overwhelming odds against them. Within minutes FOB Blessing provided artillery coverage, and we followed up with a B-1 bomber and A-10 and F-15E fighters. We basically mopped up as best we could, but by then things were pretty much over. The second reason I remember this incident particularly well is that while flying a B-1 mission the following week, I saw a very similar situation developing in the same area. However, this time we were prepared. The ground commander saw the Taliban tactic repeating itself, and I became involved in the tactical use of airpower that ensured another insurgent attack was prevented. Between the barrage of artillery and the coverage from our fighters and bombers, the overwhelming use of force made sure that the combat outpost under attack didn't experience a fate similar to Wanat.

I regularly flew 12-hour B-1 combat sorties over Afghanistan during my assignment. From my combat experiences in the air, staff visits throughout the AOR, and COCOM experience, I had a unique perspective on this war from the military strategic level, through operational planning, and down to the tactical execution of airpower. This combination of perspectives became very useful to me. It shaped my view on this war, the utility of airpower, and my dialogue with joint and coalition war fighters in theater.

My 13 months as DCFACC saw a transition of the war in Afghanistan. It was during my tenure that the US political and military focus shifted from Iraq to Afghanistan. In August 2008, the US Navy carrier strike group moved out of the Persian Gulf, and naval air forces were dedicated to operations in support of Afghanistan.

Moving forces from Iraq to Afghanistan would severely alter the dynamics in theater. I met COMISAF, Gen David McKiernan, for the first time in July 2008. Nearly a year later, I met the incoming ISAF commander, Gen Stanley A. McChrystal, whom I had worked with in a prior assignment. In the CAOC, we knew his assignment as COMISAF signaled a more formal transition to counterinsurgency. As such it would become one of the most transitional and formative years of the war in Afghanistan, and the use of airpower would become a key enabler for this transition.

Strategy

My US predecessors are correct that the United States opted for a two-pronged strategy and never quite balanced the campaign between counterterrorism and counterinsurgency. As they have noted, we ended up doing both. Still, let me elaborate a little and expand on their perspectives. There is little doubt that the flow of lessons and perspectives on irregular warfare and nation building was a largely one-way route from Iraq to Afghanistan. Iraq became the model. For years the main emphasis had been on Iraq, which became somewhat of a laboratory for tactics and strategies of irregular warfare and counterinsurgency. We saw the Army and Marine Corps' challenges and their subsequent intellectual and doctrinaire resurrection leading to their counterinsurgency field manual (FM 3-24) published in 2006. I saw this firsthand during my period as DJ3 in CENTCOM working with Gen John Abizaid and with Gen David H. Petraeus when he was a two-star general.

In my view, the grand strategy in Iraq, one that General Petraeus brought to the fore, boiled down to helping the Iraqis help themselves. We acknowledged after a while that if this were to be a nation providing for its own security after the fall of Saddam Hussein, we had to help it strengthen its security forces and government structures. That same strategy shifted over to Afghanistan. Counterinsurgency operations relied on our ability to build security forces, ensure the rule of law, and thereby provide the framework for the Afghan people to make their own destiny. I remember reading in *Seven Pillars of Wisdom* by T. E. Lawrence ("Lawrence of Arabia") that when the Arab revolt captured Damascus, one of the first things the victors had to do was start rebuilding the police. The author pointed to that as an essential first step toward success. In comparison, what did we do a century later in both Iraq and Afghanistan? We started out building the military, or—if you will—the paramilitary forces and concentrated less on the police side. We largely ended up focusing more on general nation building and national military force and less on civil authority. Given the Pashtun tribal affiliation in Afghanistan, I would be remiss to think there is a direct correlation between COIN and change in civil governance. However, I believe this will become the longer line in this debate over the value of applying the same approach as in Iraq: did we focus on the military side to facilitate our ability to do "capture and kill" operations in a counterterrorism context, or was it part of a longer counterinsurgency approach where we genuinely wanted to develop Afghanistan's ability to eventually take charge of its own security?

Our practical strategy was to shift the focus from full involvement in the fighting to more of an advisory role. US CENTCOM wanted to get to a point where the US forces in Iraq could do "strategic overwatch." We sought a transition from "tactical overwatch," which entailed training and equipping Iraqi forces—living with, maneuvering with, and mentoring them—to gradually facilitate their taking over the responsibility of a province, constituting "operational overwatch." Eventually, they would take responsibility for their nation, which would enable us and our allies to reposture to a strategic overwatch of the region. I am talking predominantly Iraq here, but those perspectives were the precursor to what eventually became our approach to Afghanistan. As a basic premise of strategy, I agree with the construct of a counterterrorism versus a counterinsurgency approach, but in Afghanistan, I think the lines blurred fairly rapidly.

There are some longer lines within ISAF that eventually would cross paths in 2008. By 2006, we had largely established agreement on the NATO framework for Afghanistan and the division of the country into regional commands. Late that year, that framework was established but did not have adequate political support to provide actual military fighting forces. COMISAF 2007–08, Gen Dan McNeill, ended up fighting the insurgents with limited resources. When the Marine expeditionary unit (MEU) came with its own indigenous fighting force, that was welcomed by General McNeill. It became his best fighting force.

For his successor, General McKiernan, it was a whole different matter. The dynamic had changed. The emphasis was now on Afghanistan. Gradually, that entailed more of a counterinsurgency approach, but in the beginning it was more about facilitating the large and rapid buildup of forces. McKiernan was now assuming a political and military agenda that had shifted from Iraq to Afghanistan and ISAF. It was around that time we shifted the carrier strike group from Iraqi operations into Afghan operations. General McKiernan's priority had to be to facilitate the rather dramatic increase in ground forces. This entailed a significant increase of the so-called forward operating bases, and with more forces came more troops in contact with the enemy, which in turn led to more casualties. And with a huge increase in the use of force to assist our own troops in contact with the enemy came an increase in both fratricides and civilian casualties. It became a very, very complicated situation. General McKiernan deserves credit for his gradual transition into counterinsurgency by the end of his tenure, but first and foremost, I believe his main legacy was to facilitate the rapid buildup of force that started shortly after he took office.

I think one of the reasons for the somewhat pragmatic strategic approach of gradually helping the Afghans to help themselves was due to our adjusted outlook on counterterrorism. I had dealt intimately with counterterrorism for years and knew we always had a regional outlook on this issue. It was never limited to Afghanistan alone. At some point I think we began to realize the magnitude and the enormity of the situation of dealing with counterterrorism from the Maghreb region of Northwest Africa, through the Horn of Africa, the Middle East, and throughout Central and East Asia. It became a more pervasive problem. Even today it is hard to recognize the impact of an extremist ideology on the battlefield, let alone on a global scale such as al-Qaeda commanded. So I saw counterterrorism more in lieu of the grand strategy that focused on helping Afghanistan to help itself—just as the preceding handling of Iraq had focused on the same issue. Our effort in Afghanistan would become a counterinsurgency. We would focus on building up Afghan forces, mentoring, and going from tactical overwatch to operational overwatch—basically where we are today. Perhaps we may eventually return to a strategic overwatch as force postures are redefined beginning in 2014.

Air Command and Control

It became clear to me after talking to (predominantly) ISAF's director ACE in 2009 and my own forward air component coordination element, or ACCE, that there was a certain degree of confusion as to the most basic premise of air command and control in Afghanistan: who was in charge of the air effort? Who could actually affect a change in a campaign plan? Who should the other commanders in theater turn to if they needed airpower to coordinate their effort? Who would have the decisive voice in the end? In essence, there was a tug between unity of command for C2 of air forces (in the CFACC and ACCE) and the overall command of Afghanistan military operations, where the ISAF commander depended more on his ACE to advise on all matters related to air. It was also a tug on closeness of the relationship: one to a three-star airman (ACCE to CFACC) and the other to a four-star soldier (ACE to ISAF commander). I felt it was difficult to have both an ISAF Air and a forward CFACC ACCE. Which one should I listen to as the primary advisor? Who should sit at the table when important decisions would be made? I think this issue alone created an incredible amount of confusion in theater. In fact, from Kabul it appeared the CAOC was "virtually present" when the ISAF air cell was trying to take charge. I knew that the CFACC's ACCE would ultimately have to be given a greater role and responsibility to command air forces in Afghanistan. Until then, it was a constant strain to hold the relationship between the true command element of air forces in theater—the CAOC—and the commanders in Afghanistan who wanted "organic" and direct control.

Doctrinally, the US ACCE construct was a familiar one in Iraq, where that forward element was put in Baghdad and left no one uncertain of its role and link back to the CFACC/DCFACC. The NATO construct of ISAF Air (ACE) represented a very difficult organizational construct that almost clashed with the overall strategy; rather, it was at least in conflict with our strategy. The CFACC was responsible for the holistic approach to airpower in Afghanistan. He had the bulk of air assets, he had the means to control the air effort, he was responsible for the ATO, and so forth. In effect, the CFACC was technically in charge of the air component of the joint task force commander, which was COMISAF. But this was not recognized in theater. NATO viewed the US CFACC as belonging to the US chain of command, which, technically, was correct. The confusion seemed to stem from the fact that it was the DCFACC who was formally included in the NATO chain of command. So ISAF was formally obliged to adhere to the NATO chain of command, which included me and did not (formally) include my boss, the CFACC.

When I was working as DJ3 at CENTCOM, I had seen the NATO ISAF chain of command built this way to placate command relationships. What I did not anticipate was how it really created difficulty at the leadership level in terms of addressing whom to talk to if you want to change your approach or your plans in theater. In fact, this construct was so delicate it became a centerpiece of my out-brief when I left my position as DCFACC. In my view, until you put full power and authority in the ACCE, you will constantly have an advisor forward who has no voice in the maneuver of air forces, who does not wear any kind of a hat related to the ISAF-NATO partnership, and who is not seen as a partner at the table but rather as a strictly US Air Force CAOC representative. Still, the ACCE, and in many ways the ISAF ACE, were invaluable in terms of really knowing what was going on. By no means do I blame either for this situation. They were up close and personal with the four-star and did their best in working this in accordance with standard US doctrine and NATO standards.

Canadian Forces major general Sullivan was running the limited ISAF Air (ACE) unit. They viewed themselves as the air component of ISAF but were in reality a very small contingent compared to what we were running in theater. ISAF Air was mainly responsible for ISAF/NATO airlift; they had formed an air cell dedicated to this mission. However, the clash of control came in the use of airpower in capture/kill operations or, specifically, the authority to execute kinetic strikes.

The time in which this complex relationship became particularly problematic for me was when ISAF Air suddenly wanted to take responsibility for time-sensitive targeting (TST) by the end of 2008. There was a pervasive feeling in Afghanistan at the time that we were not adequately attuned to the ground commander's need for TST—a responsive action for airpower to emerging or high-value targets. In my view, that was simply incorrect—we had intimate knowledge of how TST was run at CENTCOM and the CAOC, and we had a very good idea of ISAF's lack of capability to perform this task. I felt the demand from Kabul to control and if necessary command sensitive air targeting got out of hand. The ACE was simply not organized, trained, or equipped to handle the complexities of the process or the authority to execute a strike. I was very concerned that ISAF could not adequately follow the ROEs, caveats, and the challenge of processing huge amounts of information in a very limited amount of time. The CAOC, as the epicenter of the theater air control system, planned and executed air operations; it did not abrogate it to a subcell within Afghanistan. This is why we built and dimensioned the C2 infrastructure available at the CAOC. In one visit to Kabul to deal with this emerging problem of wresting air C2 from the CAOC, I had to explicitly explain to a British JTAC officer at ISAF that their operations were well understood at the CAOC when it came to the application of airpower; they did not have the authority to exclude the CFACC in his command responsibility to the CENTCOM and ISAF commanders to prosecute the air campaign. It had gotten to the point that ISAF was marginalizing air control from Qatar in lieu of direct control out of Kabul. At that point I gave ISAF an ultimatum, telling the ACE that we were not going to strike any targets in a time-sensitive manner that excluded the CFACC's authority until they cleaned up their act and obtained all the proper equipment to generate, assist, facilitate, and verify the safe conduct of time-sensitive targeting in theater.

In a sense, the irony of ISAF Air trying to get more responsibility was that it felt it would help get more "unity of command," not realizing that it was actually pulling away from the real unity of command provided by the US CFACC. ISAF wanted control of our assets to gain its version of unity of command, which was impossible for us to allow. Every time I went to ISAF headquarters I stood back and just looked at the facility, the architecture, NATO's ability to command and control air forces. Compared to the CAOC at Al Udeid, it had only a fraction of that capability. General Sullivan had been shaped by the A-10 incident during Operation Medusa prior to his entering theater. I had attended his out-brief of this incident at Air Combat Command, and in fact, several of my staff officers were on his team. I knew that General Sullivan wanted to adhere to the lines of authority for command of airpower through the CFACC; however, he wrestled with how to take that construct and bring it closer to the execution of ground operations in theater. He saw the strong need for unity of command but was challenged in fully translating that at the table with Generals McKiernan and McChrystal, when the CAOC was not represented in the meeting. General Sullivan was a tremendous air leader, but he was dealing with strong ground-centric personalities. I know; I had worked with both of them while in CENTCOM.

It was an unfortunate situation. The US CFACC had the assets, the C2 resources, and the entire infrastructure to be ISAF's CFACC. For political reasons, he was not allowed to assume that role. This created a C2 web that was cumbersome, inefficient, and a continuous source of friction. We found ourselves in numerous discussions with the ACE, who wanted to help the ISAF commander gain control of assets and to assume responsibilities he simply was not fully equipped to handle. It was a continuation of the C2 processes my predecessors had confronted, and like them, I was unable to adequately resolve it.

The Initial Term of General McChrystal

Gen Stanley McChrystal became COMISAF about a month and a half before I left office. During these initial weeks, I worked intimately with him on the use of airpower. His commander's intent differed from his predecessors'. He intended to limit political fallout from any operation that caused unnecessary Afghan deaths, particularly those held "hostage" by the Taliban. It was immediately clear that he was going to focus on minimizing civilian casualties. Although we had focused significantly on this issue before, McChrystal put a particular emphasis on it that ended up having several repercussions in theater. From the outset, General McChrystal held his ground commanders accountable for absolute verification that whatever building they struck and whatever military action they performed, they were sure there were no civilians in the line of fire and only the enemy was being targeted. From the CAOC, it became clear to me there would be a growing tension between the ground commander having the ultimate authority to order airstrikes and the misperception that strike aircraft were the cause of unnecessary civilian deaths. The ROEs were always clear as to the application of airpower. No aircraft could unilaterally drop a weapon without a ground commander's permission. However, we saw a precipitous drop in kinetic strike as General McChrystal began to hold his commanders personally accountable in a way that was somewhat difficult to translate in the field—100 percent certainty that no innocents were in harm's way.

This, logically, became an issue regarding the use of airpower as well. Very unfortunately, in my mind, he started using phrases like "air power contains the seeds of our own destruction if we do not use it responsibly,"[3] as noted earlier in this book's introduction. It created an image that the very nature of airpower was such that it warranted strict control not to become an irresponsible military tool that would undermine our collective effort in Afghanistan. While you can understand the fear and logic underlying this assertion, particularly in a counterinsurgency, the wording created a false impression that airpower was the problem. It was creating mixed signals for how air would support ground maneuver operations. Many casualties were due to artillery strikes and special operations airstrikes that were not fully under the control of the CFACC. However, I explained to McChrystal that the problem of misapplication of airpower by ground commanders in support of ground operations was rooted in their not following his guidance ("Commanders Guidance" and "Tactical Directive") and not in airpower per se. When a JTAC on behalf of a ground commander asked for a bomb on a compound to support our troops in contact, the pilots did not stop to ask for evidence or demand extra verification of that order—they needed to trust the commander on the ground, who had eyes on target and was in the best position to evaluate the potential hazard of civilian casualties and, thus, use airpower judiciously. I saw this at the tactical level while flying combat sorties; ground commanders were dealing with an elusive enemy. They were cautious but not hesitant to ask for air support when it best served their needs in remote locations outside the range of helicopter or artillery support.

In my dialogue with General McChrystal, I felt I had to provide some balance to this issue. I pointed toward the military evolution in

Afghanistan and the historical precedence that had been set from General Richards, to General McNeil, to General McKiernan, and finally to General McChrystal. Over the years, we had developed and refined the capability to be overhead for a TIC engagement in merely minutes, to the degree that air support simply was expected to be available or immediately overhead if a situation occurred and intimately linked to the ground commander, regardless of whether it was a platoon, company-size element, or larger unit. If a ground commander called troops in contact and requested immediate air support, not only were we obligated to respond, but the air component would not be in the business of discerning the commander's intent and evaluation of the situation on the ground. It was the ground commander's call to ask for air support, the strike pilot's responsibility to assure proper execution in the battlespace, and all commanders' responsibility in the chain of command to assure proper authorities in the conduct of war. This well-grounded set of ROEs and command relationships was not adequately reflected in General McChrystal's assertion that "air power contains the seeds of our own destruction if we do not use it responsibly"; rather, the misapplication of any kinetic strike from the ground or air could unhinge his intent to minimize civilian casualties. We had to deal with this. Every strike called for an assessment. I ultimately respect the challenge for General McChrystal to translate his intent into actions on the ground that kept civilians out of harm's way—to set the conditions for a successful counterinsurgency strategy that would give Afghanistan back to the Afghans.

In a meeting on 18 June 2009, General McChrystal pointed out that "when the ground commander orders a strike, Commander ISAF wants a full account within 12 hours. . . . If there is an allegation of a civilian casualty, it automatically calls for an on-ground assessment." Now, if you take this guidance alone, you need to understand the rather dramatic new dynamic he had just created in theater. It meant that regardless of rank or nationality—or whether a fighter aircraft, gunship, helicopter, or artillery was used—ground commanders would have to justify and fully account for their actions to COMISAF. That is an interesting link: from the young captain making decisions under duress at the ground tactical level to the general on the strategic level—all within 12 hours.

General McChrystal had a political and military imperative to safely conduct his strategy—to avoid any form of strategic surprise as a result of unwanted actions on the battlefield. Civilian casualties had been a grave concern for years and were an issue influencing both President Karzai and the domestic public in many of the alliance contributing-member nations. The question is how, as a commander, you articulate and develop procedures to reduce this problem as much as possible. General McChrystal made it a personal responsibility for the ground commanders but also phrased the problem in a way that challenged the airpower community. It generated an uncertainty in terms of who is going to hold whom accountable. Was the airpower community—or rather its pilots—to start questioning the ground commander's decision to drop bombs on a target? It really changed the calculus and in some ways strained the atmosphere in the CAOC–ISAF Air relationship. Now, any weapon on a compound would become a COMISAF "Commander's Critical Information Requirement (CCIR)," which significantly reduced the tactical flexibility in theater. As DCFACC, I had to ask myself how to respond to this: do I change the special instructions (SPINS)? Do I put forward a crew information file change? Should I change the airspace control order (ACO)? How do I operationalize this new process? It was just a new world.

My biggest concern as DCFACC became to impress upon everyone, on a daily basis from the CAOC, that we were supporting the ground commanders and their actions, and that it was not our position as airmen to suddenly start questioning the ground commander's decision.

I should also point out that this shift forced us to take a critical look at our own procedures, which is always useful. We looked at the agility of the system to move ISR to respond to reports of civilian casualties; we started streamlining the process between ISR requests and actual air requests; we put particular emphasis on the system of JTARs; and other actions. There is no doubt that the perception of a bomb on a compound and people picking up the remains of innocent people was and remained an unacceptable outcome. That was one of the reasons I previously had been inflexible in rejecting ISAF and ISAF Air's request to assume responsibility for TST. But there is always a balance between tactical flexibility, the need to save the lives of our troops, time available, and the need for being absolutely sure there are no unforeseen civilian casualties in an often fluctuating, uncertain, and dynamic situation on the ground. Although I fully understood the rationale behind his decisions, General McChrystal's restrictions and additive procedures created uncertainty and confusion in our direct oversight and execution of airpower. All components of air, land, and maritime forces had to adjust to a more restrictive set of rules. Though we felt it, we did not have a good assessment of the inherent risk of this conservative approach.

The Use of Airpower: Some Observations

We had some challenges in theater, as my predecessors have noted. One of them was related to JTACs. I think it is safe to say that NATO JTACs, particularly, came in all flavors. From my own B-1 missions, I knew that if you were called to certain regional commands by a JTAC, chances were you would probably end up not responding with force from the air even though it was called a TIC. Or you ended up talking to a JTAC saying, "I lost my convoy," and you responded, "Well, you called a TIC. . . . Where was the last known contact point and have they already checked in with the forward operating base?" I literally had this one situation in which the individual picking up the phone found out that his team had already returned to base. And this was not only a NATO problem; US forces did similar things. The ISAF director ACE and I had excellent cooperation and understanding of this situation. When JTACs did not perform to standards, we would decertify them. The overall level of competence of the JTAC force of all nationalities was adequate during my tenure. They were professionals!

Excessive use of force occasionally became an issue. I know both General Meulman and General Holland mentioned this factor. For example, the B-1 carries 20 weapons: eight 2,000 lb. bombs and 12,500 lb. bombs with various capabilities. When you carried a lot of weapons, it was likely a "Bone" was called and, in many cases, could get to a TIC faster with range and payload to spare. Ultimately, it could remain overhead a lot longer. The B-1s probably dropped more bombs by virtue of their capability and what they brought to the fight. For years, the B-1s operated from the Indian Ocean, which enabled them to fly at times when the weather and other conditions made it impossible for platforms in theater to fly. There would be days and nights when the only thing flying in Afghanistan was the B-1. So I acknowledge there had been incidents when the B-1 had been involved in excessive bombing, but by my time there, it was not a persistent problem that needed any particular attention. This was by no means a bomber issue vice use of strike aircraft to provide persistent and lethal coverage in what appeared to be benign situations.

The allocation of ISR was an equally contentious issue, especially the use of unmanned systems to support ground operations or the misuse of JSTARS as a primary ISR asset. In some cases, there was a belief that the CAOC controlled the use of RPAs in striking insurgents inside Pakistan's Federally Administered Tribal Areas (FATA). Senior political and military civilian visitors from many nations that came to the CAOC would often ask about CENTCOM's role in these attacks. I reminded them that the CAOC did not have anything to do with activities in the FATA and we predominantly oversaw cargo and personnel airlift to Pakistan. CFACC air assets stayed inside Afghanistan unless we had a preauthorization from Pakistan. Still, the whole emphasis on ISR was interesting. I did not see a fundamental shift in the *use* of RPAs during my tenure—the only fundamental shift in my mind was the continuation of the voracious need for *more* ISR. General McChrystal, based on his previous background with special operations forces, understood the value of unmanned systems to provide full-motion video and the "unblinking eye." I would presume that he contributed to an increased focus on ISR, but I cannot verify that. More RPAs gave you more oversight, which theoretically gave you a little bit more clarity as to what was happening on the ground. I believe General McChrystal wanted to make sure that whatever we were striking in theater had as many "eyes" on it as possible, and RPAs often gave invaluable contributions in this regard. Still, to be honest, the buildup of MQ-1 Predators and MQ-9 Reapers was already in motion and preordained when I arrived. From the CAOC, we apportioned and allocated UAS orbits to support the ground requests and, in turn, executed these systems via the ATO.

The United States suddenly shifted its focus from Iraq to strengthening the effort in Afghanistan. I believe, if you count actual troops on the ground, that the ratio between Iraq and Afghanistan had been a 10:1 ratio in favor of Iraq, perhaps even more. If you look at actual aircraft on the ground, including supporting efforts, the ratio was probably in the range of 3:1 in favor of Iraq. This ratio, however, really started to change in 2008. By the time I left in July 2009, I would estimate the ratio was slightly in favor of Afghanistan, with our numbers in Iraq decreasing rapidly. The process would lead to a complete shift toward Afghanistan. We suddenly had all the air resources we needed, both in and outside of Afghanistan, to handle the demand for air requests.

Air-land integration was also a very contentious issue in theater. A number of observers have noted that airpower became somewhat of a "911 call" for the ground forces. We ended up performing TIC-support to a very large degree, and perhaps should have focused more on operational planning and a more creative process leading to air-power providing broader and more direct support to our overall objectives for the counterinsurgency effort. These are broad questions that seem to consume multiple parts. In fact—from a strategy perspective—air support became the only enabler to the supported land component on the ground. We supported and enabled the overall ground maneuvering units with their indigenous partners to go out and do the counterinsurgency and the nation building that would turn this country around. To provide this support, I focused on ensuring the basic structure of the air operations center and our ability to plan, execute, and measure the effects of air operations at large. I wanted to ensure that airpower was agile enough to deal with large ground battles as well as more-limited operations to sustain the counterinsurgency operation in theater. I wanted to ensure that the air structure—the system—from the ground commander/JTAC all the way to the CAOC at Al Udeid, with all its assets, C2 procedures, and various tools, was able to contribute and generate synergy to our collective effort. In my view, the system we had put in place demonstrated that it could handle the wide range of demands that was requested. It was my conclusion that the CAOC, the theater air control system, and the command structure had adapted well to the ever-changing situation in Iraq and Afghanistan. The air component had adapted well to COIN operations, even when the nexus of countering drugs entered into the equation. From the operational art of air warfare, we had to know whom we were dealing with from the friendly as well as the enemy sides and what each was trying to achieve on the ground.

The way that I, perhaps, did it differently than my predecessors was that I wanted people to understand that we had to know what the different ground commanders were thinking. For example, I would have a weekly conference with the commander of RC-E and his staff. It enabled me to know what they were thinking and what their commanders considered to be the most important issues. In turn, it enabled us to facilitate and be agile to meet their needs and reach out as best we could. This was more difficult in RC-S and with our NATO allies because we did not feel we knew their dynamics and procedures quite as well. We had to go there, sit down, talk to them, and try to learn from each other as much as we could.

The US Air Force recognized and continued to facilitate the airlift requirements for this operation. The effort was not limited to transporting goods and services but also included transporting leadership around to engage with local leaders. Airlift should not be viewed merely as daily movement but rather the fundamental process of ensuring that we got people where they were going. Often we ended up putting this load on a system that was not designed to be an airline, but that happened in large part because this was a critical capability. It was the backbone of our collective effort. While often underappreciated as an integral part of airpower, its fundamental contribution was not lost on those of us who had the opportunity to see the tremendous effort upfront.

In terms of strike capability, it was obvious that supporting troops in contact was of paramount importance. My predecessor, Maj Gen Maury Forsyth, was committed to assuring ISAF of a set response time for a TIC. It was driven from a different dynamic. However, the situation was changing, and I was not ready to set a specific response time; instead, I expected us to evaluate and continuously improve our quality of response. I did not want to contrive a certain time period/response time because I did not want to stimulate a thought process driven by *time*, but rather the *effects* we achieved. If you overfocused on time, you would end up in a situation in which a ground commander started his stopwatch when a TIC commenced, and if air had not shown up within a defined number of minutes, it was faulted as being ineffective. That was not the way this system was built. We had multiple operations going on simultaneously in Afghanistan, and sometimes we needed to prioritize the most important incidents first. I told my ground force colleagues that on average, within (a classified time), you can *plan* on us being there. Still, in some rare situations it might well be 30 minutes until we were overhead, yet in most cases air coverage was almost immediate. I was constantly reviewing whether or not we were truly meeting the maneuver requirements each day for those forces conducting counterinsurgency operations on the ground. Battlefield command detachments in concert with our strategy-to-planning cell ensured that this relationship was working.

Finally, a few words on the air tasking order process. Unlike our predecessors who dealt with thousands of sorties a day in large campaigns such as Allied Force, OIF, or OEF, our ATO reflected a constant battle rhythm of support requests where we provided about the same number of sorties of manned and unmanned capability to the fight each day. That allowed the ATO to be slightly more malleable; we weren't dealing with high tempo battle or ever-changing targets. Iraq and Afghanistan air operations, especially from a strike perspective, called for a routine process of change as ground requests changed hourly in planning and actual execution. As a result, the ATO process became so agile that, in some cases, half of the planned sorties would be changed prior to execution. When the planning cell delivered the ATO in the afternoon, they were still changing the one for the next day. This agility was very important, and that gave me strength in the process and confidence in the execution. We were making those changes to meet the ground commanders' needs for changing their plans due to unforeseen factors that suddenly made a big impact on their plans. We tried to facilitate those changes to the extent possible, while at the same time telling them that there has to be a "good-idea cut-off point." Those changes we did not have time to put into the ATO ended up being solved through the regular and flexible procedures set up for TIC situations.

Epilogue

When I got back to the United States after my tenure as DCFACC, many people asked, "Was there a strategy in Afghanistan?" There was not a short or easy answer to that question. The operational orders that came from the strategic framework were readily available. We understood the end state—return Iraq and Afghanistan to their sovereign status. The ways and means were continuously debated and changed. We continued to relook and revise the joint air operations plan to reflect those changes. If you were to ask whether there was an overarching document which guided clear military strategy agreed to by all players in theater, the answer would be a resounding "no." But if you asked whether by 2009 there was an "end state" to this operation and whether we had in broad terms put together the ways and the means to get there, the answer would probably be "yes." To be clear, the end state technically was—and still is—to give Afghanistan back to the Afghans. Whether or not we have—or will—achieve that is a more open question entailing a discussion that exceeds the scope of this book.

My tenure was marked by the US shift in focus from Iraq to Afghanistan. It was a large logistics demand on the airlift systems to end the surge in Iraq, begin the shift of forces in CENTCOM from Iraq to Afghanistan, and simultaneously prepare the way for a surge and large force buildup in Afghanistan. We were facilitating the move of heavy equipment and forces into theater while conducting daily air ops and building airfield infrastructure from the ground up. Strategic and tactical airlift provided the backbone to ground units' reception, staging, onward movement, and integration (RSOI). It was a key concern of mine. Airpower was a fundamental part of this process, which entailed airlift, ISR, close air support, casualty evacuation, armed overwatch, and so forth. This was almost an all-consuming effort the first part of my tenure.

Gradually, we focused more on strategy. Just as General McKiernan developed the strategy of "shape, clear, hold, build,"[4] the entire focus shifted more toward counterinsurgency, perhaps more so than he has been publicly credited for effecting. This meant that my team focused more on air strategy to fit this new approach in Afghanistan, subsequently ending up with a new JAOP to fit the sign of the times.

My final period was shaped by General McKiernan's transition from ISAF command to the dynamic command under General McChrystal. It was clear from the outset that General McChrystal, who had been intimately involved with Afghanistan and regional issues as commander of the US Joint Special Operations Command (JSOC), would have a different approach to Afghanistan. This approach, as noted previously, would create challenges for the airpower community in the ensuing months. We saw a distinct decrease in the number of air-supported TICs, which in turn generated some friction both with ground forces feeling more vulnerable as well as with airmen who felt more uncertain as to when they legitimately could provide air support. After I left my DCFACC position in late July 2009, Gen Mike Hostage, the incoming CFACC to replace my boss, Gen Gary North, asked me to meet with him on a video teleconference to discuss my impressions of the ISAF and CFACC relationships. In our conversation we discussed the intimate relationship his air representative needed with the ISAF commander to, in effect, have the voice and command to lead airpower from Kabul on behalf of the NATO commander in theater. It was from this discussion and Hostage's perspectives that the ACCE would be given new authorities and responsibilities to lead from Afghanistan. I am therefore looking forward to General Sullivan's and General Hoog's chapters on this period, as they helped transition one combined force air component commander to the next CFACC in a time of dynamic change in the CENTCOM AOR.

Notes

1. See Greg Jaffe, "The Battle of Wanat: Inside the Wire," *Washington Post*, 4 October 2009, http://www.washingtonpost.com/wp-dyn/content/article/2009/10/03/AR2009100303048.html.

2. See Jason Burke, "Ten French Soldiers Killed in Afghanistan as Taliban Attacks Grow More Audacious," *Guardian*, 19 August 2008, http://www.guardian.co.uk/world/2008/aug/20/afghanistan.france.

3. Dexter Filkins, "U.S. Tightens Airstrike Policy in Afghanistan," *New York Times*, 21 June 2009, http://www.nytimes.com/2009/06/22/world/asia/22airstrikes.html?_r=1.

4. See Spencer Ackerman, "McKiernan on Afghanistan," *Washington Independent*, 19 February 2009, http://washingtonindependent.com/30708/mckiernan-on-afghanistan.

Chapter 9

Game-Changing Strategies for Counterinsurgency and Complex Joint Operations

Maj Gen Charles S. "Duff" Sullivan, Canadian Forces, Retired

NATO Air Component Commander to Afghanistan
ISAF Director Air Component Element (ACE)
ISAF Deputy Chief Joint Operations

November 2008–November 2009

Prior to the terrorist attacks on the World Trade Center and Pentagon in September 2001, ordinary citizens paid little attention to al-Qaeda, the Taliban, and the country of Afghanistan. Most would have found it difficult to find Afghanistan on a map of the world, let alone describe its involvement in global terrorism and terrorist training camps. However, within months of 9/11 the international community became transfixed on Osama bin Laden, Mullah Omar, and the Taliban and the need to deliver Afghanistan back to the Afghan people.

Canadians became intensely aware of their country's involvement in Afghanistan in April 2002 when a US F-16 fighter aircraft dropped a 500 lb. laser-guided bomb on a group of Canadian soldiers conducting a live-fire night training exercise at Tarnak Farm near Kandahar Airfield. This tragic friendly fire incident killed four Canadian soldiers and wounded eight others, all from the Third Battalion of Princess Patricia's Canadian Light Infantry. The four fallen soldiers were Canada's first combat losses since the Korean War and the first of 158 Canadian military personnel who would make the ultimate sacrifice for Canada and the Afghan people.

The first significant opportunity I had to focus on Canada's growing interests in Afghanistan was in the spring of 2005 when Chief of Defence Staff (CDS), Gen Rick Hillier, made a short-notice visit to Canadian Forces Base Cold Lake to learn more about Canada's CF-18 fighter community. As the wing and base commander of Cold Lake at that time, I personally briefed General Hillier on the capabilities of our newly modernized fleet of CF-18 Hornets and the fighter community's unmatched expertise in air-land integration and close air support, all of which I trumpeted as an ideal fit for the ISAF coalition and our Canadian task force which would be deploying to Afghanistan in a matter of months. The CDS appreciated what he heard that afternoon and mentioned that a contingent of CF-18s would be on the "A-Team" for Canada's upcoming deployment to Kandahar Province.

Months later I received word from Air Staff headquarters in Ottawa that I would be appointed the next Deputy Commander Air (DCOM-Air) at ISAF headquarters early in 2006. My preparations began immediately; however, three days before I was to depart on a predeployment "recce" visit to Kabul, I was advised that the position had been elevated to the rank of major general and I was no longer eligible. Instead, Maj Gen Angus Watt, who was at the time Assistant Chief of the Air Staff (ACAS) in Ottawa, deployed to Kabul to take the position of NATO's senior airman in Afghanistan and ISAF's DCOM-Air from July 2006 to January 2007.

As discussed in chapter 3, I was dispatched to USCENTCOM in September 2006 to serve as co-president of a Combined Investigation Board convened by Lt Gen Gary North, CENTCOM's CFACC and senior airman, to investigate a friendly fire incident that occurred during Operation Medusa. Shortly after my return to Canada, I was seconded to the Prime Minister of Canada's Privy Council Office (PCO) to serve as senior defence advisor and director of international security. As part of my duties at PCO, I maintained oversight of Canada's security and development missions in Afghanistan. In the spring of 2008, I was advised by Canada's Vice Chief of Defence Staff, Lt Gen Walter Natynczyk, that I would be NATO's next Air Component Commander (previously titled DCOM-Air) at ISAF Headquarters in Kabul, succeeding Maj Gen Jouke Eikelboom of the Royal Netherlands Air Force.

In the few months I had to prepare for my 12-month tour of duty, I spent much of my time reviewing lessons and best practices from various operations. My Afghanistan studies covered several decades, including the country's civil war and its conflict with the Russians; however, my main focus was on the previous eight years under US and then NATO command. An important event in my predeployment training was the opportunity to attend, on the invitation of Lieutenant General North, an intensive three-day programme at the headquarters of Air Forces Central Command at Shaw AFB, South

Carolina, designed to prepare senior US air commanders for their tours of duty in the CENTCOM area of responsibility. My exposure to ISAF's air mission as co-president of the CENTCOM combined investigation board tasked to investigate the friendly fire event during Operation Medusa in 2006 also proved invaluable.

I departed for Afghanistan in mid-October 2008 and spent a few days at NATO's Joint Force Command headquarters in Brunssum, the Netherlands, where I had several consultation sessions with key senior staff, the most valuable of which was with Air Chief Marshal Sir Christopher Moran, deputy commander of JFC Brunssum. My conversations with him were critical in helping me understand key aspects of the role of NATO's senior airman in Afghanistan, most notably how command and control structures had evolved over the previous three years and the professional relationship between the US CFACC organization and ISAF's ACE. His wise counsel on leadership, command, relationship-building, and airpower also helped me get started on what would turn out to be the most extraordinary experience of my career. I had another valuable consultative session with Air Marshal David Walker, deputy commander of NATO's Allied Air Command headquarters in Ramstein, Germany. I was encouraged to know that Air Marshal Walker and his team were postured and eager to provide ongoing support to ISAF's air team in Kabul. Throughout my 12-month tour of duty, I looked forward to my biweekly teleconferences with Air Marshal Walker and our discussions on the key issues and initiatives being shouldered by our collective air team.

Large-scale post–9/11 military and air support operations were first initiated in Afghanistan in March 2002 with Operation Anaconda. However, as I would learn through my predeployment studies, the application of airpower in support of ongoing coalition ground force operations in the years following Anaconda covered the entire spectrum of success and failure. As coalition efforts evolved and became more complex, security, reconstruction, and development efforts— wrapped in counterinsurgency operations—became increasingly more challenging, especially for NATO's airpower experts, as it was not the type of mission the alliance had contemplated during its 60-year history. Fortunately, many coalition partners operating in Afghanistan at that time, which included the British Army and Royal Marines; the US Army, Navy, and Marine Corps; and the Australian Defence Force, had extensive expertise in counterinsurgency warfare and brought to the table tried and tested methodologies that would guide other NATO nations who struggled to deal with a rapidly growing insurgent force.

NATO's highly evolved military doctrine and operating procedures, most of which evolved during the Cold War period, offered few solid lessons to ISAF coalition members as they dispatched their military forces to dirt airstrips and austere expeditionary facilities across a country that little resembled the gold-plated super bases and posh military garrisons of NATO's European theatre of operation. Perhaps more useful were the lessons I learned as a forward air controller and the officer commanding a tactical air control party in NATO's air support mission to the United Nations Protection Force (UNPROFOR) in the Balkans in the 1990s when our air-land integration team, embedded in a ground-force battle group, could, most impressively, dissuade hostile enemy forces with the mere presence of fighter aircraft orbiting overhead. But even the Balkan conflict escalated to the bombing of Bosnian-Serb positions following the fall of Srebrenica, and later, the precision bombing of both military and civilian targets in and around Belgrade following the failure to force a Serb withdrawal from Kosovo in 1999.

Common to both fortress Europe and the historically challenging Balkans was a relatively "linear" battlespace with easily identifiable enemy forces wielding highly anticipated and well-analyzed military capabilities. Thinking that lessons and tactics from previous coalition campaigns could apply to NATO's efforts in Afghanistan might explain why the crude and unsophisticated "search and destroy" tactics of some coalition members ended in defeat at the hands of the Taliban. The tragic failure of Operation Medusa in September 2006, which was touted at the time as the largest ground force operation in NATO history, underscored the difficulties that countries like Canada would experience when trying to draw even the most basic air effects and enablers into their search-and-destroy ground-force operations. Yet, at the other end of the spectrum, joint operations in the 2008–09 time frame in areas of Helmand and Uruzgan Provinces and in several locations across Regional Command East displayed the highest levels of competency in air-land integration and the application of advanced air effects and enablers in complex special forces and conventional force counterinsurgency operations.

Just as coalition ground commanders adapted their methods and tactics to respond to a rapidly evolving Taliban insurgency, so too did

NATO's team of airpower experts as they championed new and, in some cases, game-changing air strategies to support COIN and complex joint operations. In the latter half of 2008, the growing number of civilian causalities that threatened to undermine the central strategic imperative of NATO's counterinsurgency effort—winning the "hearts and minds" of the Afghan population—rested on the shoulders of ISAF's senior leadership team. Led by the COIN vision of COMISAF, Gen David McKiernan, which placed "the safety and security of the Afghan population" above all other priorities, a group of senior land and airpower experts endeavored to set in place new methods and measures that would reshape the way NATO coalition ground commanders would conduct their COIN mission. The protection of Afghan citizens was central to the manner in which "lethal force" would be applied against an adversary that chose to hide itself in the civilian population while conducting its attacks against coalition and Afghan security forces. The central role that airpower was expected to play in supporting security operations, combined with the propensity of ground commanders to call in airstrikes in response to insurgent attacks, meant that NATO's team of airpower experts within the ACE at ISAF HQ would need to do their part in developing unique methods and procedures that would not only ensure the safety and security of the Afghan population, but also allow the Afghan population to place its trust and confidence in NATO's coalition force. This was the vision of its commander in the fall of 2008 as ISAF restructured its headquarters and as the senior leadership team put the final touches on the commander's "tactical directive" and "COIN guidance" for counterinsurgency operations.

The topics and discussion points I have included in this chapter are diverse and cover a broad spectrum. My initial intent was not to touch on many of the points covered by other contributors, but to highlight those areas unique to my 12-month tour as NATO's Air Component Commander, ISAF's Director ACE, and Deputy Chief of Joint Operations. I have also endeavored to include issues related to the realities of leading and managing a 42-member international coalition and, when appropriate, a few related leadership examples. The details included in the various discussion points throughout my chapter are, for the most part, drawn from my recollection of events, activities, and conversations and not from any official diary or military log. When I began to write my account of various events, I was fortunate to have some reference material from Operation Medusa in

2006, the Kunduz airstrike in 2009, and speaking notes and briefing material from the various media events in which I participated as a member of ISAF's senior leadership team. I should also mention that as my two chapters went through various phases of review and revision, I received requests to include greater detail and write on additional areas of interest unique to my perspective and vantage point.

Due to the diversity of the topics, I have divided this chapter into four sections. The first discusses ISAF's air team beginning in 2005, how it evolved, and points related to the challenge of integrating air in land-centric joint and counterinsurgency operations. It also includes discussion points related to managing NATO bases and airfields and, unique to my tour of duty, the 2009 force augmentation effort. Section 2 steps through each of the main "lines of operation" shouldered by ISAF's air team, and highlights, where applicable, the manner in which tactical air activities contributed strategically to ISAF's COIN mission. An important discussion point throughout section 2 is the imperative for coalition partners to contribute full and balanced combat teams and to leave their military politics and national agendas at home. Section 3 focuses on joint operations such as counternarcotics (CN), special forces, and dynamic targeting and highlights the intrinsic nature of airpower in these operations. It also covers a few significant leadership challenges I experienced during my tour of duty. The fourth and final section is my attempt to draw attention to what I believe were the greatest challenges of the ISAF mission in 2009, namely our effort in addressing civilian casualties, the inculcation of General McKiernan's COIN vision, and the change of leadership when he was replaced by Gen Stanley McChrystal. As a concluding discussion point, I summarize our achievements, which, in 2009, helped me be mindful of the contribution ISAF's security mission was able to make in creating the conditions necessary for development, stability, and governance.

Section 1: ISAF's Air Team

I was fortunate to observe firsthand the evolution of ISAF's air team throughout the four-year period 2006–09 from four specific vantage points: namely, as co-president of the combined investigation into Operation Medusa in 2006, from my Director-General position at National Defence Headquarters in 2006–07, from within Canada's Privy

Council Office in Ottawa in 2007–08, and finally, in 2009 as NATO's senior airman at ISAF headquarters in Kabul. A common theme throughout the entire period was the challenge of integrating air in land-centric operations and ISAF's COIN operations in 2009. I also discuss the management of NATO bases and airfields, the extraordinary effort that went into the 2009 force augmentation surge in Regional Command South (RC-S), and the ongoing efforts to provide force protection (FP) to the 42 nations that garrisoned their units and formations on the bases and airfields for which my airfield commanders and I were responsible.

ISAF's "Air Team Forward"

As discussed earlier in the book, NATO's senior airman in Afghanistan was initially established as a post for a one-star general in 2005 but elevated to the two-star rank in early 2006 when NATO's military authority was expanded beyond Kabul to include the five regional commands of ISAF. Consistent with NATO and US airpower doctrine, and not unlike the organizational design of component headquarters across Europe, NATO's air team was, in those early days, "stovepiped" into the ISAF HQ structure alongside various other land-centric roles and functions, and the air staff often found itself challenged to understand the land-centric campaign goals and objectives. Lessons from Anaconda in 2002 and Medusa in 2006 highlight the degree to which air commanders and their staffs struggled in those early days of the Afghanistan mission to understand the goals and objectives of the ground-force commanders they were assigned to support.

Initially tagged as Deputy Commander Air, ISAF's air team was renamed "Air Coordination Element," which caused considerable confusion with the US ACCE which was deployed to the ISAF compound in Kabul in 2007. The ISAF air team was eventually retitled Air "Component" Element following a high-level meeting in October 2008 with the Deputy Commander of NATO's JFC Brunssum, when it was reaffirmed during a conversation with Air Chief Marshal Chris Moran that ISAF's two-star senior airman was, as first established in 2007, NATO's air component commander in Afghanistan with full command authority over NATO airfields and bases and all assigned airpower capabilities, platforms, and air personnel. The role of the US

CFACC at Al Udeid and issues related to unity of command and unity of effort within the ISAF command structure were also vigorously discussed due to problems that had surfaced in the 2005–07 time frame between the US CFACC and ISAF's DCOM-Air in Kabul. NATO's air component commander, who reported directly to ISAF's four-star commander in Kabul on all matters related to the application of airpower in Afghanistan, also wore the hat of director of ISAF's air component element. In addition, he shouldered with his Deputy Director ACE Operations and Deputy Director ACE Plans, one-star generals, the responsibilities associated with the planning, coordination, and execution of all air operations across the coalition theatre of operation. The lack of understanding by COMISAF and the US CFACC over the roles and responsibilities of NATO's senior airman at ISAF headquarters and the manner in which the CENT-COM CFACC was to participate in shaping ISAF air operations in Afghanistan caused problems for the ISAF coalition in the early days of NATO's mission. Those issues have been discussed extensively in earlier chapters and will only be mentioned briefly in the paragraphs that follow.

At the end of 2008, ISAF air operations spanned the entire airpower spectrum to include air medical evacuation (MEDEVAC), intratheatre airlift, armed overwatch and close air support, offensive targeting operations, surveillance and reconnaissance, combat search and rescue, dynamic and time-sensitive targeting, and space-based capabilities. As an integral member of the joint operations team, the ACE ensured that air effects and enablers were not only properly integrated into security operations, but were also standing by to respond at a moment's notice to calls for help from reconstruction, development, and humanitarian teams spread across the country. At the highest level of operational planning, the ACE operations team, led by an RAF one-star general, prioritized and apportioned air resources to NATO task forces and special forces operations based on requests submitted by embedded air planners at regional, task force (TF), and battle group headquarters. The ACE then sent its direction and guidance back to the CAOC in Qatar where ATOs and airspace control orders were disseminated to scores of air bases and flying units in and around the Afghanistan theatre of operation, including to a *Nimitz*-class aircraft carrier in the Arabian Sea.

As discussed with Air Chief Marshal Moran in October 2008, the structure set in place to command and control ISAF's air operations in Afghanistan was unique. Important to note was the decision by ISAF and NATO's JFC HQ not to deploy dedicated air tasking and airspace management teams to Afghanistan. As noted by Air Chief Marshal Moran, these critical processes and functions were delegated to the CENTCOM CAOC at Al Udeid, Qatar, which already had in place robust air C2 planning teams for Iraq, the Horn of Africa, and other US military activities in the AOR. As I was to learn shortly after my arrival at ISAF HQ in October 2008, the fact that critical C2 structures were not deployed forward and collocated with the NATO air team in Kabul did not diminish the role and function of ISAF's senior airman or augment the role that the CFACC played in the Afghan mission. On the contrary, this unique structure helped to draw together the two air component commanders—CENTCOM and NATO—in a manner that would not have otherwise taken place had NATO tried to "go it alone" with its own CAOC organization, which would have included full air tasking, airspace control, and other critical functions and roles. The CAOC in Al Udeid could not do its job without guidance and direction from the ISAF ACE, and we could not accomplish our ISAF goals and objectives without the CAOC shouldering the processes associated with air tasking and airspace management. Of course, having critical C2 roles and functions remotely located at Al Udeid did mean that the quality of the relationship between the two organizations had to be strong and that the double-hatted officer serving as NATO's air component commander and ISAF's Director ACE would need to understand and pay close attention to the air tasking and air management products being produced by the CENTCOM ACC on his behalf. The one-star Deputy ACE Operations general officer played an important role in this area.

To help champion ISAF's direction and guidance in the air tasking and airspace control processes, the ACE had a staff of several air planners and liaison officers permanently based at the CAOC in Qatar. The ISAF ACE coordination cell at the CAOC in Al Udeid was an extension of the Deputy Director ACE Operations team in Kabul, which also directed ISAF's air operations centre, the five regional air operations centres across Afghanistan, and the J3 air planning teams at the five regional command headquarters. Conveniently collocated within the ISAF air operations centre was the Air Support Operations Centre (ASOC), which responded to requests from the RAOCs for armed overwatch and air support in support of ISAF ground commanders. Rigidly adhering to the CAOC's ATO, air assets would launch at their designated time and would be managed by the Theatre Air Control System (TACS), which was responsible for ensuring that air support assets were available when and where air effects and enablers were needed by task force ground commanders. In a 24/7 operation that could not take a break, even when the mountains and valleys of Afghanistan were eerily quiet and coalition forces and insurgents were hunkered down for the night, manned and unmanned aircraft were patrolling overhead watching for insurgent activity and waiting for the ground commander's call for air support. And when the call was made, aircraft watching from above would respond to troops under enemy fire within minutes of the call; MEDEVAC helicopters would rush wounded soldiers to medical facilities; tactical airlift aircraft would deliver personnel and supplies within hours of the request; and threatening Taliban commanders and their forces would be detected, tracked, and then targeted, often in a dynamic and time-sensitive manner by manned and unmanned air platforms and special forces within minutes of establishing positive identification and safe distances from the civilian population.

The numerous remotely piloted vehicles that orbited overhead coalition forces on a continuous basis could also be retasked at a moment's notice on the authority of ISAF's Director ACE or the Chief of Joint Operations through the AOC, ASOC, or Dynamic-Targeting Operations Centre to provide an unblinking and persistent surveillance and reconnaissance over trouble spots, and, if necessary, decisive direct action against Taliban insurgent forces who threaten coalition forces and Afghan civilians. Capping off the impressive array of modern airpower capabilities were countless numbers of US, NATO, and other multinational space-based platforms, which provided intelligence, imagery, navigation, and communications for ISAF operations.

From one rotation to another, ISAF's air team reinvented itself, due in part to the rapid turnover of personnel, but also in response to the challenges of developing viable operational strategies for its security mission. The short tour lengths—some as brief as two months, most three to six—that were preferred by many NATO nations caused problems throughout the ISAF mission. Also problematic was the assignment of personnel to ISAF's air team who were not as skilled or experienced in the application of airpower in combat operations or air-land integration in land-centric joint operations as some would have preferred. The practices of a few NATO nations, including my own, who gave little consideration to the skillsets and expertise needed to shoulder the responsibilities and duties of the deployed ACE and TACS positions was concerning. Most nations acknowledged and understood that community air experts were required in areas such as intratheatre air mobility, combat search and rescue, air medical evacuation, and utility helicopter; however, when considering senior operations staff and key leadership positions at ISAF HQ and in the Air Operations Centre, not all appreciated the fact that complex joint combat operations required highly experienced airpower experts skilled in supporting such operations and air-land integration in land-centric operations. The skills and expertise needed by the ACE could not be learned "on the fly" through on-the-job training while serving at ISAF HQ. Those coalition partners who would carefully select and deploy highly experienced and skilled full-spectrum airpower experts were greatly appreciated. Airpower practitioners who had an understanding of strategic-to-tactical C2 structures, relationships, and processes; force application principles and ROE imperatives; and a crystal-clear understanding of how advanced air effects and enablers could be brought together in exactly the right manner to achieve the theatre commander's strategic goals and objectives infused in their "professional DNA" were most welcomed to the air team. Such were the caliber of air professionals at the CAOC in Al Udeid who were responsible for the application of airpower across CENTCOM's AOR. I was also fortunate during my tour of duty to have a group of senior airpower experts on my ISAF air team, including the CFACC's ACCE, who were, without exception, the most talented and dedicated cadre of airpower professionals I have had the privilege to serve with during my career. Only on a few occasions was I required to deal directly with a coalition member nation, including my own, to ensure the right individuals were selected for the ACE, joint operations, and airfield organizations.

The findings and observations from the CENTCOM investigation into the friendly fire incident during Operation Medusa were concerning to the US CFACC and staff at the CAOC in Al Udeid, which most likely undermined confidence in the ISAF Air organization. During the formal debriefing session on the findings of Operation Medusa in October 2006, General North and his staff at AFCENT headquarters were briefed on concerns regarding the lack of expertise in air-land integration and air support to joint land-centric operations. When an "air component coordination element" was proposed to address the need for air-land integration and airpower expertise, Brig Gen Stanley Clarke, co-president of the joint investigation board, was offered the opportunity to lead the ACCE at ISAF HQ in Kabul. Unfortunately, he had other professional commitments and obligations that would not allow him to accept the position. During the same debriefing session, General North offered me the opportunity to serve as director of the US CAOC at Al Udeid, a position that rotated between US, UK, and Australian one-star officers. General North also offered Canada the opportunity to consider an exchange position at his AFCENT headquarters at Shaw AFB. Both offers were forwarded to the Air Staff at Canada's Department of National Defence in Ottawa; however, neither received consideration, most likely due to the strained professional relationship between the US CFACC and ISAF's Canadian DCOM-Air discussed earlier.[1]

It is difficult to identify all the issues that strain professional relationships between organizations and individuals; however, as with other coalition experiences involving high-functioning "AA-type" personalities, trust and confidence can be undermined by both real and perceived justifications. Issues related to skillsets, experience, expertise, and professional competence, and, as mentioned above, short tour lengths and the rapid turnover of personnel that seemingly undermine any sense of continuity and ownership of the mission were often scrutinized. That is perhaps why NATO and ISAF directed that post-2006, tour lengths for senior members of the ISAF coalition would be six to eight months for lieutenant colonels and colonels, a minimum of 12 months for general officers, and 24 months for COMISAF. Building relationships within the command was important for senior members of ISAF and regional command HQs but also with key leaders of the Afghanistan government and military. Strong relations are developed over time and underpinned by trust and confidence, and whenever possible, close professional and personal contact.

As the senior US airman in the region, the US Air Component Commander at the CAOC at Al Udeid was responsible for the employment of US air assets throughout CENTCOM's AOR, which included ISAF's air mission in Afghanistan. As discussed previously, having the US CFACC in Al Udeid exerting influence over ISAF air operations created problems with respect to ISAF's unity of command and unity of effort in its early days. This became especially concerning when efforts applied by the Deputy CFACC were at odds with NATO's Air Component Commander. The ISAF Director ACE's responsibilities for overseeing the integration of airpower into ISAF's strategic design, operational planning, and tactical execution were sometimes usurped by the Deputy CFACC and CAOC organization. The broad shadow of the US CFACC across Afghanistan and the US government's policy that preferred not to have US military forces serve in combat under the command of non-US military authorities often posed problems for ISAF's unity of command and unity of effort. The air command and control dynamic that eventually settled into place saw the US CAOC produce an ATO and ACO for ISAF based on directions issued by COMISAF, who was also double-hatted as commander of all US forces in Afghanistan. Although it was the ISAF ACE organization that led and was responsible for airpower in ISAF's strategic design, operational planning, and in-theatre tactical execution of the joint mission, the US CFACC had national command and control of US air assets.

Based on the findings and observations from the Operation Medusa friendly fire investigation, the CFACC deployed a cadre of senior US airpower experts to the ISAF compound in Kabul in early 2007, which later became the ACCE. Deploying the ACCE was consistent with the policy and doctrine of the US military, as demonstrated during the Iraq War and as taught in the USAF CFACC course which I had the privilege to attend in the summer of 2006. The purpose of the ACCE was to provide advice and guidance to land-centric staffs and ground commanders on the employment of US air assets, which was exactly what was deemed necessary by the US Air Force in 2006 and early 2007. Somewhat similar to this approach were the practices of other NATO nations (the UK, France, the Netherlands, Germany, Spain, Italy), who also deployed their own national military advisors, sometimes carrying out the role of national "red-card holder,"[2] alongside the NATO command structure to oversee and guide ISAF's employment of their national military forces and to ensure their national "caveats" were respected. Unfortunately, the deployment of the CFACC's airpower experts to the ISAF compound was not well received by ISAF's air team and served to exacerbate an already troubled relationship. ISAF's DCOM-Air organization saw the deployment of US personnel as a further attempt to exert influence on ISAF's air mission. While back in my office in Ottawa in late 2006 and early 2007, I received e-mails and phone calls directly from the USAF colonel tasked to work on behalf of the US CFACC at ISAF HQ. The colonel and his small team were asking for my assistance in dealing with high-ranking Canadian officers at ISAF HQ who opposed US CFACC involvement. Sadly, the poor relationship between the US CFACC and ISAF DCOM-Air persisted into 2007 and affected the development of a collaborative approach that should have otherwise existed for providing air effects and enablers to struggling NATO ground force commanders in the field. The critical role that airpower and integrated air-land operations should have played in supporting joint operations was slow to evolve and sometimes resulted in ground commanders not being as well supported by NATO and US air capabilities as they could have been—an observation offered during investigation interviews of Operation Medusa and follow-on consultation sessions. Beginning in late 2007 and continuing throughout the 2008–09 time frame, the director of the CENTCOM ACCE and his small staff of air experts at ISAF HQ established themselves as trusted colleagues to the ISAF ACE and were regarded by the ACE and me in 2009 as an indispensable part of the overall ISAF air team and a critical strategic asset when dealing with the Deputy CFACC at the CAOC in Qatar and with military headquarters in the United States.

By October 2008, ISAF's air organization was a 120-member multinational air staff, which was most often referred to as the "air team forward," meaning the pointy end of a much larger air community comprised of NATO's air headquarters in Germany and the US CENTCOM CAOC in Qatar. The poor relationship that existed between the US CFACC and ISAF's DCOM-Air in 2006 and 2007 was resolved with the turnover of ISAF personnel. As predicted, the new and improved relations that eventually emerged had a positive effect on the ACE's ability to reach back to NATO air headquarters in Ramstein and the CAOC in Qatar, which became critical to the team's overall success.

The ACE evolved quite dramatically throughout 2008 and 2009 and eventually became fully integrated into ISAF's "joint force" team through a major restructuring of the ISAF headquarters in the fall of 2008. In an unprecedented step in November 2008, General McKiernan appointed me as his newly indoctrinated Director ACE and NATO Air Component Commander to the newly established position of Deputy Chief of Joint Operations (hereafter, Deputy Joint Operations). This appointment meant the Chief of Joint Operations, Maj Gen Mike Tucker, and I would share command responsibilities for joint-force planning and the review and approval of special forces and land-force operations, NATO's support to counternarcotics operations, dynamic and time-sensitive targeting, and ISAF's strike approval authority (SAA). By early 2009, my triple-hatted role as NATO Air Component Commander, Director ACE, and Deputy Joint Operations was playing a key leadership role in the planning and execution of ISAF joint operations while also commanding NATO airfields and bases and shouldering, with my two deputy ACE directors, the planning, coordination, and execution of air, aviation, and air-land integration operations across the full spectrum of security and development activities in Afghanistan.

Throughout 2009, ISAF's joint operations team received positive feedback on how the "air team forward" was contributing to the overall joint operations effort. Different from the NATO and US-styled "air component" approach to war fighting, which typically saw the air component commander and air staff detached and remotely located from the joint force theatre commander and land-centric HQ, NATO's Air Component Commander and ACE were collocated with the land-centric ISAF headquarters and fully integrated and embedded into the joint planning process. As anticipated by General McKiernan and his Chief of Joint Operations, this joint and integrated approach was well received by ISAF's land-centric staffs and regional commanders. It was especially lauded by general officers from the US Army and Marine Corps who often spoke of the dysfunctional relationship they endured with remotely located US Air Force air component commanders. Having NATO's two-star airman and the entire air component element collocated and integrated into the joint HQ structure meant the air team was side-by-side with ISAF and regional staffs and able to fully and actively participate in all phases of the planning, coordination, and execution of ISAF operations. This was regarded throughout 2009 as a welcome sojourn from the traditional dysfunctional "component" war-fighting approach preferred by US CFACCs.

An important mission for air component commanders in major combat theatres of operation such as Iraq and NATO's air war over Serbia-Kosovo was the requirement to conduct counterair operations, both offensive and defensive, including gaining air superiority over enemy territory. However, because NATO's counterinsurgency operations in Afghanistan did not require a counterair campaign, the focus of the air effort was primarily on capabilities for providing air support to ground forces and also for development efforts, which included armed overwatch, close air support, air MEDEVAC, intra-theatre airlift, airspace coordination, offensive strike operations, dynamic and time-sensitive targeting, and ISR capabilities.

As appreciated by NATO staffs in the 2008–09 time frame, the most appropriate location for an air staff charged with delivering these critical air effects, enablers, and capabilities was not thousands of miles away, but collocated and integrated into the joint-force land-centric headquarters. Although the US CFACC and his ISAF-assigned US assets represented the largest contribution and provided stellar support to the ISAF coalition, deep-rooted animosities, most likely from previous experiences in other theatres of operations, served to perpetuate what some have characterized as an institutionalized dysfunctional relationship between US land and air component commanders. An NDU study notes, "Critics suggest that both services [US Army and US Air Force] understandably want to exert control over CAS assets, yet they often have different priorities in mind that can lead to troubled operations."[3] Fortunately, ISAF's working relationship with the CAOC in 2009 was, for the most part, positive and productive, which included my professional relationship with the CFACC himself and most of his senior commanders and staff.

A most rewarding role for NATO's senior airman in Afghanistan was to serve as senior air advisor, mentor, and confidant to Afghanistan's minister of transport and civil aviation (MoTCA). In 2009 the office of Director ACE and the Deputy Director ACE–Plans, Projects, and Partnering enjoyed a very close and personal relationship with the minister, His Excellency Hamidullah Farooqi, and his esteemed deputy, Mr. Alami. Together, the ACE and MoTCA staffs were able to progress on initiatives started by all the previous DCOM-Air and senior NATO airmen, such as planning and support for the annual Hajj pilgrimage, air traffic controller training for Afghan nationals, and management and security of MoTCA airport facilities. Although most military airfields and bases, including KAIA, were under the authority of NATO's air component commander, the approach taken by the ACE was based on a co-authority decision-making arrangement with MoTCA officials whenever possible. Examples of this successful team approach include the decision making that occurred with respect to air traffic and airspace management, traffic flow, ramp space and parking, crash-fire-rescue capabilities, and security at KAIA. Frequent airfield visits by the minister and his staff and, on a few occasions, other key ministers from the Afghanistan government proved successful. Second only to the international community's funding of development and reconstruction projects was the revenue brought into the Afghan government treasury through aircraft landing and overflight fees, which represented a tremendous source of funding for national Afghan programmes.

One disappointing ACE initiative was the effort to establish a ministry development team (MDT) at MoTCA based on establishing senior management and director-level civil servant shadow positions with supporting staffs within the ministry. The purpose of the MDT would be to mentor Afghan public servant staffs in the areas of operations, engineering, HR management, finance, legal issues, communications, corporate services, and so forth. As envisioned, the shadow positions would be sponsored for a three-to-five-year period by a few carefully selected countries that would deploy their senior public servants to champion the MDT. The mandate of the MDT would be to deliver an aeronautics act; an airworthiness framework for operations, technical requirements, and safety; national licensing and standards for Afghan aircrew, aviation technicians, and air traffic controllers; and schools to produce homegrown aviation professionals. Although the initiative was vigorously lobbied by me and my Deputy ACE Plans staff to influential embassy staffs, support was never forthcoming even though the concept was assessed as extremely viable. The method preferred and most often carried out was an ad hoc arrangement that saw, on occasion, senior mentors and advisors deployed into federal ministries with no fixed mandate or commitment. As observed in other civilian development organizations, unity of thought and synchronized effort were rare and bureaucratically constrained. If movement in a preferred direction could be initiated, progress was glacial and fickle. At the end of 2009, a "full-up" and balanced development team for the Ministry of Transport and Civil Aviation remained a feasible, practical notion but without a champion.

ISAF Airfields, Bases, and the 2009 Force Buildup

NATO's air component commander exercised full command authority over the military airfields and bases at Kandahar and Kabul and was responsible for ISAF's operational activities and NATO development efforts at several other military and civilian airfields across the country. As a result of NATO's force expansion in early 2009, the size of Kandahar Airfield (KAF), the largest air base in Afghanistan and the busiest single-runway airfield in the world, was planned to grow to more than 28,000 personnel and 310 permanently based aircraft. The engineering surge to construct support facilities and concrete ramp space at KAF as successive waves of forces arrived in country marked a frenetic pace of military growth unprecedented in the region. Kandahar Airfield eventually became the largest super base not only in all of NATO, but also in CENTCOM's Middle East, North Africa, and Central Asia AOR.

General McKiernan, who was commander of ISAF and US Forces in Afghanistan (USFOR-A) from the summer of 2008 to June 2009, referred to ISAF's Director ACE as his "Air Czar," simply because in addition to leading ISAF's air component and joint force air-land integration team, McKiernan charged the ACE team with masterminding the force flow and beddown of all air assets and ground forces arriving in theatre during the massive 2009 force surge. Leading the entire effort from within the ACE organization was the Deputy Director ACE–Plans, Projects, and Partnering, who, during the first six months of 2009, oversaw the planning of hundreds of strategic airlift flights to ISAF air bases and several hundred follow-on intratheatre shuttle flights to forward operating bases. Bringing order to the three- to fivefold increase of tactical air and aviation activity across RC-S required the ACE's new airspace control plan (ACP), a structure designed to coordinate and synchronize a level of flying activity several times greater than ever imagined in the region.

The force augmentation surge in the spring of 2009 represented an impressive and unprecedented logistics effort for NATO and ISAF. More than 21,000 military personnel with associated support facilities, equipment, aircraft, and combat vehicles flowed into theatre over a three-to-four-month period. Hundreds of strategic airlift aircraft transported personnel and high-value, high-priority, sensitive military equipment to Kandahar, Bagram, Kabul, and other airfields, while the bulk of other support equipment and combat vehicles arrived by sealift from Western Europe and North America to forward staging areas and then on to a port of entry in southern Pakistan near the city of Karachi. From Karachi, convoys of thousands of "jingle trucks" moved by road through Pakistan into Afghanistan through border crossing points and on to coalition bases across Afghanistan.

ISAF understood very well that the logistics convoys flowing through Pakistan to border crossings at Torkham Gate in the northeast and Spin Buldak in the south represented a critical strategic vulnerability to the NATO effort, which could have been a "showstopper" for the entire

2009 surge. Attacks from al-Qaeda and the Taliban could have easily brought the augmentation effort to a halt; however, ISAF's leadership cadre well appreciated that the Taliban recognized that the resupply of NATO forces was "big business" worth tens of millions of dollars to Pakistani and Afghan trucking companies. A failure to deliver supplies and cargo to NATO forces would have resulted in a significant loss of revenue for the entrepreneurs who owned these companies, and more importantly, to their thousands of workers who lived in the towns and villages across southern Pakistan and Afghanistan. A similar Taliban dynamic existed with the development and reconstruction projects funded by Western nations and carried out by local Afghan companies. When Western-funded development projects were supported by local Taliban leaders, the projects progressed successfully and were credited to the Taliban by local Afghans. The commander of RC-S stated at a strategic planning conference in the fall of 2009 that if townspeople and villagers were unhappy with utilities, services, or development projects, they would simply take their complaints to local Taliban leaders, who would then ensure any problems were addressed by civilian authorities and project managers. When power generation failed and the lights went out in towns and villages across southern Afghanistan, the Taliban were the first to be called to fix the problem. Whether dealing with regionally based civilian truckers or local utility and construction companies, it was important to understand that the Taliban and al-Qaeda had significant influence and control over various facets of Afghan life, including Taliban-approved civilian entrepreneurs who benefited from doing business with the ISAF coalition.

The planning effort for the 2009 force augmentation was impressively thorough and rigorous. A "rehearsal of concept" exercise, better known as a ROC drill, was carried out by ISAF's strategic planning staff to replicate in a six-hour period what would occur over three to four months. The drill was conducted in an arena-size logistics warehouse at Kandahar Airfield and was designed to investigate and prove the viability of the proposed sequence of events for the arrival of all military units and equipment and to refine the parallel and sequential timelines and milestones to identify bottlenecks and showstoppers. Once the proposed force augmentation plan had been proved through the ROC drill, the innumerable logistics and force-flow activities were set into motion and carefully coordinated, synchronized, and monitored by the ISAF ACE and KAF operations and planning staffs. Strategic airlift flights were authorized to depart their home bases in the continental United States and Europe only when their final beddown locations were ready to accept inbound personnel and equipment. If units arrived too early, they would need to stay on main operating bases (MOB) until their forward locations were completed by coalition engineering companies. Bottlenecks at border crossing points and MOBs represented significant vulnerabilities to the overall plan, as personnel and equipment would need to be temporarily garrisoned, supported, and secured, which placed tremendous stress on facilities already bursting at the seams.

The ACE's new airspace control plan, which was designed to manage, coordinate, and synchronize the flying activities of the largest and most diverse cadre of manned and unmanned aircraft ever assembled in such a small theatre of operation, was also critical to the force augmentation effort. The unprecedented level of tactical air activity, combined with the seemingly endless stream of strategic airlifters at NATO bases and the tactical airlift operations to support the land-force FOBs, tested ACE and airfield planning teams well beyond all expectations. The risk of midair collisions increased dramatically due to the density of military air traffic, which placed tremendous responsibilities on the ACP and the US AWACS and coalition air traffic control personnel charged with traffic flow, coordination, and deconfliction. The short-term solution to this tactical air coordination challenge was to deploy an additional AWACS aircraft from NATO's fleet in Europe to augment the US AWACS aircraft already in theatre. Of note, the cost of deploying a single NATO AWACS aircraft was estimated in 2008 at $160 million for a 12-month period. The medium- to long-term solution was to install a multilateration surveillance capability,[4] initially around bases and airports but eventually across the entire country for a total estimated cost of $20–30 million. The density of both manned and unmanned aircraft in the low-level airspace structure also had to be carefully managed by ISAF ACE Operations and J3 air teams at the regional commands. The plethora of tactical micro-RPAs in the low-level structure, many of which were rail catapulted or hand launched, were operated autonomously by small land force units and represented a significant safety hazard to tactical helicopter airlift and attack helicopters.[5]

When it was announced in the fall of 2008 that a US Army Combat Aviation Brigade (CAB) and US Marine Expeditionary Brigade (MEB) would deploy to southern Afghanistan in early 2009, the ACE and joint operations team struggled to visualize the luxury of having scores of heavy- and medium-lift helicopters available on a daily basis to transport troops and supplies above the IED-infested roads of RC-S, which was in stark contrast to the deficiencies observed by Canada's Manley Panel 18 months earlier.[6] An MEB of 7,000 troops with its own fleet of fixed-wing and rotary-wing airlift, attack helicopters, fighters, and intratheatre transport aircraft followed the 82nd CAB, with a US Army Stryker-Brigade Combat Team (S-BCT) of 4,000 troops close behind. But the greatest challenge persisted throughout this intense surge period—where to bed down the hundreds of aircraft and thousands of troops that would arrive within a period of a few months. Detailed and coherent commander's priorities were developed by the ACE and joint operations to help define those capabilities and platforms that brought the greatest value to the counterinsurgency effort and those that did not. And if ISAF could only accommodate a finite number of troops and air assets on its limited ramp space and bases across the country, picking the right capabilities and platforms would be of critical importance.

The beddown of forces at Kandahar posed significant challenges in the spring and summer of 2009. Exacerbating an already formidable challenge, a couple of national contingents at KAF behaved as independent fiefdoms, willing to accept orders only from their nations' capitals and expeditionary force headquarters, and often conducting their activities and operations with little regard to the orders and directives of COMISAF and subordinate theatre commanders. It was not unusual for these nations to deploy military units, equipment, and aircraft to Afghanistan without the approval or coordinating actions of NATO and ISAF authorities. Such detachments quickly became problematic when there were fleets of aircraft and equipment that could not safely or effectively operate in Afghanistan or contribute in any significant manner to ongoing security or development operations. In many cases, national military assets and capabilities were deployed to satisfy military and political agendas back home with little consideration given to the goals and objectives of ISAF. The most striking examples included a fleet of fighter aircraft for armed overwatch and CAS operations that lacked the ability to locate and self-designate its intended targets and a fleet of Canadian utility helicopters with such severe operating limitations that they were deemed unsafe and inappropriate for coalition operations. This became more problematic as these less-capable and unsafe aircraft laid claim to valuable ramp space at overcrowded ISAF bases and airfields as more-capable aircraft flowed into theatre. In the interests of coalition cohesion and stability, we decided to manage these challenges as well as possible instead of ordering fleets of unsafe and ineffective aircraft out of theatre.

An enormous challenge for NATO airfield commanders across the country was the protection of personnel, equipment, and aircraft garrisoned on their bases. By far the greatest challenge existed at KAF, where Taliban forces orchestrated rocket attacks several times a week and carried out IED and roadside attacks against the endless stream of operations and logistics convoys coming and going from the base. Also on the shoulders of the commander of Kandahar Airfield (COMKAF), RAF Air Commodore Andy Fryer, and his successor Air Commodore Malcolm Brecht, was the safety and security of the ceaseless tide of VIPs and "internationally protected persons" (IPP) that flowed in and out of theatre to visit their national contingents. These included heads of state, secretaries-general, prime ministers, senators, government ministers, members of Parliament and Congress, chiefs of defence, and scores of senior bureaucrats and politicians, with many of the visits occurring concurrently. Providing protection and security for these VIPs started with a comprehensive assessment of all available intelligence information to characterize the risks and then the orchestration of massive security efforts to secure local airspace, the terrain immediately below aircraft approach paths, ramp and aircraft parking areas, and all planned visit locations and facilities "inside the wire" and at forward operating areas. Entrusted with the Herculean task of defending KAF and everyone on the base was the Royal Air Force (RAF) Regiment, an extraordinary contribution which few other nations could match.

The concept of operations employed by the RAF Regiment for protecting KAF was as comprehensive and robust as any COIN operation conducted by combat task forces or battle groups in RC-S. The regiment's order of battle and FP capabilities incorporated helicopters, remotely piloted vehicles, counterfire artillery radar systems, mortars, snipers, and scores of the best-equipped armored personnel carriers for patrolling forward, outside the wire, to track and interdict hostile forces as they prepared to launch attacks and set IEDs.

Force protection and VIP/IPP security became more difficult when intransigent "tenant-nations" chose not to cooperate with base and command authorities by trying to discreetly slip their visiting nationals in and out of theatre without coordination and authority. One such event occurred when a country's expeditionary force head-quarters back home and its in-theatre task force HQ chose to withhold vital information from COMISAF, NATO's Air Component Commander, and COMKAF regarding the arrival of that nation's most senior government official. The resulting chaos and confusion from this attempt to conduct unilateral and uncoordinated security activities at KAF not only jeopardized the safety of that nation's visiting Prime Minister, but also caused unacceptable risks for the US Secretary of Defence and a high-level member of the Dutch government visiting their national contingents at the same time. Although this unexpected and profound lack of judgment was an isolated incident, it served to highlight the types of challenges that could blindside COMKAF and ISAF command authorities at any time.

The success of COMKAF and the RAF Regiment team in defending and protecting this strategically important centre of gravity in the 2009 time frame was unprecedented. One notable success was the manner in which COMKAF and his staff staved off and eventually eliminated rocket attacks against the airfield for a significant period of time through their proactive and innovative approach to force protection and "community outreach." One night in early 2009 the FP team detected a small group of Afghan teenage males setting up a firing position to launch a time-delayed rocket attack at the air base. They tracked the young Afghans back to their village where they were observed entering a wedding celebration. The young Afghans were taken into custody and screened positive for explosive residue that matched the rockets pointed at KAF. Through COMKAF's outreach programme, a shura was convened with the elders of the village to discuss how the rocket attacks by citizens of the village were undermining the trust and confidence they had been nurturing for the past several months. It was further explained that without this trust and confidence, it would be difficult for KAF to continue employing members of the village in various support positions on the base. The Shura concluded with the elders pledging to accept responsibility for their youth and to reestablish the valued relationship they had been enjoying. The teenagers were released in good faith into the custody of the village elders. The outcome of this effort was the suspension of rocket attacks on the airfield for a significant period of time. Although the attacks eventually resumed, they came from other vulnerable Afghan youths coerced by local Taliban commanders.

COMKAF's leadership challenges in dealing with individual national task force commanders on his base were also quite daunting. Many of the 42 nations in the ISAF coalition had some type of presence at KAF, and trying to deal with independent national contingents—some of which seemed intent on challenging the authority of COMKAF, NATO's ACC, and COMISAF—was burdensome and distracting. Fortunately, leadership incidents were not common occurrences, with one notable example: a national task force commander had to be cautioned for inappropriate comments and behavior toward ISAF's command authority. Dealing with these types of leadership challenges in a strictly national context would have been relatively straightforward. However, to carry out a leadership review on a national task force commander in an international theatre of operation to have him removed from theatre was deemed, at the time, too politically destabilizing for the coalition but even more so for the country involved. Instead, it was decided to manage these situations with the expectation that planned troop rotations would eventually resolve national leadership problems. Offering discreet, confidential comments to the applicable chief of defence during a visit to ISAF headquarters was considered an appropriate way of advancing sensitive leadership issues in a national context; however, such an approach only works when the involved defence chief feels compelled to take necessary action upon return to his national HQ. The turmoil caused by the removal of General McKiernan in May 2009, followed by the firing of General McChrystal a few months later and then the unexpected deployment of General Petraeus from CENTCOM HQ to Kabul to reinstill calm and stability to a troubled ISAF coalition, allowed the serious leadership issue mentioned above to "fall off the radar" of the leadership cadres of ISAF and NATO. The unfortunate result saw disgraceful conduct and behavior go unchallenged and undisciplined, which, in the case alluded to above, emboldened the rogue task force commander and sent a very unfortunate message to other members of his team.

Integrating Air into Joint Operations

ISAF's senior leadership team clearly understood that air-land integration and the *proper* application of air effects and enablers were vital to the success of complex joint operations and ISAF's counterinsurgency mission. Lessons learned from Operations Medusa and Anaconda illustrate maneuvers when the improper application of airpower produced disastrous results on the battlefield. To help underpin this reality, and as noted earlier in this chapter, General McKiernan appointed me to the position of Deputy Joint Operations in December 2008. He explained in very unambiguous terms to his Chief of Joint Operations, at the time Maj Gen Mike Tucker, US Army, and to his new deputy chief that he expected us "to do everything together when it comes to championing ISAF's Joint Operations." "In other words," explained General McKiernan, "I want no space between you guys" when it comes to overseeing the business of ISAF joint operations, which included at that time all major land-force operations, special-forces direct action missions, ISAF support to counternarcotics activities, and dynamic targeting and strike approval of Taliban and al-Qaeda leadership objectives.

General McKiernan's innovative approach to ISAF joint operations set in place a close partnership between General Tucker and me for overseeing and leading the joint planning process, which included J3 Operations, J3-5 Operations Plans, and the J5 Plans processes within the ISAF command structure. The partnership also meant that when either of the joint ops two-star generals travelled away from the HQ to conduct battlefield visits and relationship-building or leadership activities, the other would remain at the HQ—close to the joint operations, air, and dynamic-targeting command centres—to oversee and authorize operational activities. It was quite often a tag-team relationship that saw one of the two-stars in the field with ground force units, special forces, and air commanders in every corner of the theatre of operation. Having a deputy joint operations partner also allowed General Tucker to devote more of his time to the duties of Deputy Commander of USFOR-A, which involved critical national responsibilities related to the rotation, beddown, and support of the 100,000 US personnel in theatre. Hosting and briefing the endless stream of congressional delegations was another of his onerous tasks. Happily, therefore, as his deputy, I was able to focus on the NATO side of the operations equation while General Tucker tried to focus more of his valuable time on shouldering the staggering responsibilities associated with USFOR-A on behalf of the commander of USFOR-A, General McKiernan.

The integration of air and joint operations teams within the ISAF organizational structure brought the amalgamation of the outer offices of the Chief Joint Operations and the Director ACE, which was a logical evolutionary step that achieved phenomenal effectiveness and efficiencies of administration, staff management, and executive assistance to both of the two-star generals. Most notable for the Director ACE team was the outstanding C4 support provided by the US military. As a Canadian two-star general in the Director ACE position, I had not been receiving any support from Canada's Expeditionary Command HQ in Ottawa or its task force HQ in Kandahar. However, once the duties and responsibilities of Deputy Chief Joint Operations were assigned, my office and Canadian staff received overwhelming and generous US support by way of additional administrative staff, SIPRNet accounts and computers, numerous secure telephone means, a secure in-office video teleconference capability, and secure flat-screen monitoring capabilities to oversee dynamic targeting, special forces, and CN operations. Outer-office administrative support and executive assistance virtually tripled overnight, which proved indispensable to my triple-hatted position as NATO's ACC, Deputy Chief Joint Operations, and Director ISAF ACE.

As expected, the unprecedented step of combining the duties of Deputy Joint Operations with those of Director ACE and NATO ACC virtually doubled my portfolio and added to an already striking span of control the shared oversight and command-approval responsibilities of coalition ground force operations, special forces missions, dynamic targeting, strike approval authority, and NATO's support to the counternarcotic mission. The Deputy Joint Operations position also included the responsibility of mentoring senior generals in the Afghanistan National Security Force and meeting with the ANSF operations and planning staffs on a frequent basis. This effort helped to achieve early successes in conducting Afghan-led operations, which began to occur as early as December 2008. This close professional partnership helped to set in place a level of trust and goodwill that underpinned a long and meaningful relationship between ISAF and Afghan senior military leaders.

The roles and functions of my positions as Air Component Commander, Director ACE, and Deputy Chief Joint Operations allowed me to draw together the various aspects of the joint mission. The senior leadership team at ISAF led strategic design for the COIN mission while individual chiefs and their staffs, including the ACE, synchronized and coordinated the necessary operational planning. I could conveniently go from my office to connect, strategize, and plan with the staffs of J2 Intelligence, J3 Operations, J3-5 Operations Plans, J5 Plans, chief of stability, chief of support, special forces, and the commander himself. ISAF's combined joint operations centre, the air operations command centre, the dynamic targeting operations centre (DTOC), and the air support operations centre were also close to my office. If required, I could connect with various teams several times a day, either through formal staff sessions or informal networking, which allowed me to remain fully engaged in the strategy, planning, and execution of the joint mission. It was also rather extraordinary that in addition to my close personal contact with the entire joint operations team on a continuous basis, it was routine for me to have detailed and meaningful conversations with regional commanders and their senior staff on a daily basis. The CAOC at Al Udeid and ISAF's CJOC, AOCC, DTOC, and ASOC in Kabul all shared the same air picture; however, it was ISAF's ACE and the joint ops team that had the full "joint picture" which allowed General Tucker and me to lead strategic design, operational planning, and tactical execution. Fortunately the CAOC in Qatar had a staff of 1,800 air personnel able to shoulder the air tasking and airspace control processes and other supporting activities such as air refueling and AWACS support activities. This alleviated a tremendous C2 administrative responsibility from the ISAF ACE and allowed the ISAF air team to focus on strategic design, operational planning, air integration into land-centric operations, and capability management and tactical execution.

As highlighted above, the opportunity to work as deputy to ISAF's Chief of Joint Operations placed Director ACE at the centre of joint operations and, more importantly, ushered in a truly integrated and joint air-land approach to NATO counterinsurgency and security efforts across ISAF's five regional commands. Having NATO's senior airman as the Deputy Chief of Joint Operations also drew accolades from CENTCOM, the Pentagon, and NATO HQs. Observers from both US and NATO organizations affirmed that with this new relationship, ISAF had achieved "true jointness" in a fully integrated manner. The ISAF operations team itself often remarked that having Director ACE as part of the oversight and approval process for joint operations was "lightning in a bottle" that helped to initiate game-changing results that began to emerge in early 2009. Once the word got out, my triple-hatted position became one of the "must-visit" destinations at ISAF HQ for visiting generals and government and embassy officials.

Integrating the duties of Director ACE with the planning, coordination, and execution of land-centric battle group and brigade-level operations was an effort that would most certainly address the lessons and failures of previous joint force operations such as Anaconda and Medusa. Perhaps most striking was that this rare opportunity had not been previously experienced by any land-force general officer or senior airman. Even so, the challenge that faced the joint operations team in early 2009 was how to operationalize COMISAF's vision of how airpower was intended to influence land-centric operations at the regional command, task force, and battle group levels. The common feeling at the time was that many ground commanders could "wax eloquently" on air-land integration and the employment of various combat effects and enablers; however, the reality was that only an accomplished few could come close to achieving COMISAF's vision. The impediment for many national battle groups was their lack of understanding and inexperience in COIN methods and practices and how to engender the safety and security of the Afghan population as their highest priority while effectively separating Taliban and al-Qaeda insurgents from local Afghan communities.

As a senior leader in ISAF's joint operations division, I had to have a clear understanding of the land-centric world and perfect knowledge of the ISAF commander's goals and objectives. In the early days of introducing a more structured and disciplined approach to joint operations planning, I realized that the definition of air-land integration was often misunderstood by both ground and air commanders within the coalition member-nations operating in Afghanistan. Most understood that flying troops in and out of theatre with strategic lift and then ferrying them around the battlefield with tactical lift and army aviation was the type of air support and mobility a ground commander should normally expect and receive from "supporting" national air wing commanders. However, few understood that air-land integration and the overall air support effort within the joint operations construct were efforts that demanded both air and ground commanders to come together with their collocated and integrated staffs in a joint air-land campaign to consider the full spectrum of capabilities—kinetic and nonkinetic, air and land, space, electronic effects, surveillance and reconnaissance, joint fires, deliberate and dynamic targeting, time-sensitive targeting, force application, Special Forces—and how they could be integrated to achieve the goals and objectives of the theatre and regional commanders' joint air-land campaign. A significant lesson well highlighted from Operation Anaconda stated,

> What cannot be debated is the fact that on the modern battlefield, ground forces must know how to take full advantage of the capabilities of air forces, and air forces must know how to provide a full range of support. At Anaconda, greater inclusion of the air component in early joint planning might have resulted in better air-ground integration during the battle itself and in carrying out the emergency response that was mounted.[7]

Two astute military professionals who understood the exigencies of joint operations and air-land integration were leading some of the toughest COIN operations in Afghanistan in 2009. The commander of RC-S, Maj Gen Mart de Kruif from the Netherlands, and his J3 operations general, Brig David Hook of the British Royal Marines, epitomized ground commanders who embraced joint operations imperatives mentioned above. The Level 2 joint operations proposed by RC-S in Helmand Province throughout 2009, which represented, at the time, the most active and challenging area in the country with respect to large-scale "shape-clear-hold" phases of counterinsurgency operations, were, for the most part, exceptionally well planned and executed. Although a great deal of praise and recognition was owed to the tactical ground commanders and soldiers of the battle groups and task forces in the various districts across Helmand Province, the leadership provided by General de Kruif and Brigadier Hook was key to achieving results that would have not otherwise been possible.

In the early days of the ISAF mission, air effects and enablers were portioned out to ground forces as add-ons, most often as afterthoughts at the end of the planning process, and only after land schemes of maneuver had been established and land-force goals and objectives satisfied from a pure land perspective. By early 2009 the effort of integrating air into joint operations had begun to produce new and positive results within ISAF. However, the challenge that continued to face the joint operations/ACE team was how to institutionalize a formal and permanent planning framework and methodology within the operational land-centric ISAF structure that would eventually extend beyond the integrated operations staffs at ISAF HQ and regional command staffs, down to task force and battle group planning staffs, and down to company and platoon levels.

Many military units in the US Marine Corps and Navy, the British Army and Royal Marines, the Dutch Army, and selected units within the US Army were proficient in air-land integration and applying advanced effects and enablers. However, the impediment to true full-spectrum joint planning for some coalition members was the absence of joint operation and air expertise within their formations and units. A significant challenge that persisted throughout 2009 for the joint operations team was how to assist those national task forces and battle groups that arrived in theatre without the expertise to plan and execute full-spectrum joint operations. There were plenty of lessons from previous operations such as Anaconda and Medusa that identified the difficulties that certain national units and formations had experienced in trying to rally and employ the full range of advanced air effects and enablers, especially in the areas of close air support, ISR, joint fires and precision targeting, electronic enablers and effects, and space capabilities. In December 2008, the joint operations team had been formed, the COIN directives issued, and the relationships across ISAF and regional commands established. Key ISAF and regional command leaders were, at that time, merging on the same page and preparing to champion the COMISAF's vision. Yet the greatest challenge remained—how to draw coalition task forces and battle groups into COMISAF's COIN vision. This is covered in greater detail in sections 3 and 4.

Section 2: ISAF Air Lines of Operation

This section discusses each of the main lines of operation shouldered by ISAF's air team and highlights, where applicable, how tactical air events and activities contributed strategic effects to ISAF's counterinsurgency mission. The lines of operation include air MEDEVAC, intratheatre airlift, armed overwatch and close air support, electronic overwatch, and RPAs.

First, we consider an area that I regarded as one of my highest priorities, flight safety. The loss of personnel and resources through unsafe acts or the employment of unsafe and inappropriate equipment is an anathema to the profession of arms. Although a sad reality of coalition warfare, such events undermined morale and professionalism and posed one of the greatest threats to mission success. This section also highlights the importance for individual nations to contribute, as earnestly as possible, the full range of combat capabilities to the coalition and not ride the coattails of other partners. Nations that showed up in theatre with significant ground forces but without the full range of combat effects and enablers to support operations in their designated area of responsibility placed an unnecessary burden on those countries that diligently deployed their capabilities. Playing military politics in the midst of international coalition operations did not go unnoticed and served to define the lack of professionalism within a country's military leadership and its military force.[8]

Flight Safety

It was not unusual to consider a unit's safety record as one of the assessment factors in the overall mission approval process. Unsafe practices introduced unnecessary risks, which undermined coalition cohesion and effectiveness.

All coalition airfields in Afghanistan were single-runway operations which were required to support 24/7 operations without fail. Some likened this to carrier operations where the flight deck had to remain operational to launch and recover aircraft without interruption. Legendary sea stories of disabled aircraft being pushed over the side during surge operations to clear the deck and keep the operation going would not have been an unlikely scenario at Kandahar. A base where armed RPAs and fighter aircraft, heavy-lift helos, attack helicopters, strategic and tactical airlift aircraft, and civilian aircraft all operated together day and night in all weather conditions represented a most intense and complex flying operation. On one occasion, locally based KAF aircraft were authorized to continue takeoffs and landings on one side of the runway while recovery action took place on the other side to remove an armed fighter that crashed on landing and had come to rest on the edge of the runway. The runway at Bagram Air Base was closed for a couple of days after the crew of a C-17 strategic airlift aircraft landed gear-up. This created a significant disruption to air operations in the northern half of the country.

Kandahar would support 5,500 movements per week—or 800 to 1,000 takeoffs and landings each 24-hour period—on a continuous basis, which made it the busiest single-strip airfield in the world. The importance of KAF to the coalition effort made it a vital strategic centre of gravity for security operations in the southern half of Afghanistan. Even before augmentation forces started arriving in spring of 2009, COMKAF anticipated there would be insufficient ramp space and parking spots for the soon-to-be several hundred locally based aircraft. Add the scores of strategic airlifters that needed to flow in and out of theatre on a daily basis to deliver the millions of tons of equipment and supplies, and one would soon surmise that there was no room for suboptimal fleets of aircraft and equipment.

Runway safety was a critical element to efficient and effective operations at KAF. A significant safety issue that COMKAF and the ACE team had to address was the number of unintended and uncoordinated incursions on the runway and taxiways of the airfield. At the heart of the problem were the 29 access control points (ACP) that allowed a steady flow of military pedestrians and vehicles to travel down taxiways and cross the runway on a 24/7 basis. The control measures at these ACPs were so relaxed that ordinary military vehicles and personnel would use the taxiways and runway to move from one end of the base to the other as a main thoroughfare. In one infamous runway incident, a C-17 had to initiate an abrupt pull up just before touchdown to miss a coalition soldier who ran onto the active runway during his early evening jog. The soldier had his earphones plugged in and the volume turned up high and did not notice the C-17 approaching from behind with landing lights on and gear down. COMKAF reduced the number of ACPs from 29 to four and employed airfield security to control access to address runway incursions. The first few weeks of the new access plan proved difficult, as some tenants who were inconvenienced with limited access to *their* airfield chose to simply cut the locks and chains and proceed onto the airfield. However, with a concerted effort, COMKAF's new ACP plan eventually became the new normal for airfield operations. A long-standing safety hazard was successfully addressed on the busiest single-runway airfield in the world.

Early in the force augmentation planning effort, attention quickly turned to ground equipment and aircraft deemed unsafe for the demanding conditions of southern Afghanistan and inappropriate for combat operations. Less-capable and unsafe aircraft were quickly identified as liabilities that consumed valuable resources and scarce ramp space. Yet, it was a potentially explosive political issue to order less-capable aircraft and equipment out of theatre to make room for more-valuable platforms soon to arrive. In the interest of coalition cohesion and unity, the ACE would manage and mitigate, in coordination with airfield commanders, problematic fleets as effectively as possible. Unfortunately, it was not always possible to influence national military agendas, priorities, and decision making, which resulted in aircraft operating in Afghanistan even though they were deemed unsuitable and, in one case, unsafe for coalition operations. In the case of the utility helicopters mentioned earlier, a tragic accident occurred at an FOB in the summer of 2009 when one of the helicopters crashed, caught fire, and killed the three passengers on board. The deployment of these helicopters was approved by that country's Chief of Defence on the recommendations of his top air force generals and senior community advisors. They were permitted to continue flying in Kandahar Province even after the risks and deficiencies associated with their performance were discovered to be far more serious than portrayed in predeployment decision briefs presented months earlier. Once he learned of these new critical deficiencies, the national air wing commander briefed me and my staff in June 2009, and we decided that the helicopters would not be called upon to support coalition operations due to safety concerns. I passed these concerns directly to the country's Chief of Defence during his next visit to ISAF HQ; however, the fleet remained in theatre and continued to fly in support of national operations even after the identification of severe performance deficiencies and a tragic accident that resulted in the loss of life.

Flight safety was a top-priority briefing item at the ISAF commander's and Director ACE's daily briefs and a key consideration in the mission approval process. Units that displayed a lack of concern for safety or a poor sense of urgency in responding to safety issues were given the opportunity to address their safety deficiencies in an appropriate manner or face being grounded until the issue could be resolved by their national military authority. Concerns with safety, professionalism, and quality of deployed forces could often be traced to the leadership of senior advisors and decision makers in national headquarters. National units that wore their safety record on their sleeve as a "badge of competency" typically excelled in combat operations, whereas units that chose to ignore the warrior's aphorism "fight like you train" were relegated to the category of unacceptable risk, less capable, and undesirable.

Air Medical Evacuation

The depth and quality of a nation's military competence is often characterized by those essential war-fighting capabilities that it is capable of fielding. Major troop-contributing nations (TCN) in the

ISAF coalition understood what capabilities were required to support their operations, and almost all major TCNs were willing and able to deploy those capabilities. A unit's ability to employ advanced effects and enablers and its level of excellence across the airpower spectrum were the hallmark of the most-capable military units. As with air support effects and enablers, essential capabilities such as air MEDEVAC and combat search and rescue also distinguished militaries with depth and quality.

Early in 2009 a command initiative from General McKiernan established ISAF's MEDEVAC capability as a go/no-go factor in the mission approval process. The command imperative to have a MEDEVAC umbrella overhead applied not only to ISAF COIN operations and security patrols, but also to logistics convoys and activities undertaken by PRTs. General McKiernan's initiative also set in place a 60-minute MEDEVAC timeline, which meant that a wounded soldier had to be delivered to a Role-3 medical facility within one hour (the "golden hour"), which translated into a 30-minute response bubble in most areas of the country. This initiative resulted in a requirement for significantly more helo MEDEVAC assets—initially, from 28 to 45 platforms in 2009, with a follow-on requirement to expand to 60 aircraft as the ISAF mission spread across the country. Unfortunately, not all nations that sent military forces to Afghanistan had MEDEVAC capabilities. One would think that countries that relied on this essential capability the most would be most willing to contribute, but this was not the case. The foundation of the helo MEDEVAC capability in 2009 was championed by the US military with impressive contributions from the British, Germans, French, Spanish, and Norwegians. Sweden also contributed a C-130 Hercules aircraft capable of responding to mass casualty MEDEVAC scenarios.

It was not unusual to see 20–30 MEDEVAC missions flown by ISAF helicopters on a daily basis, 50 percent of which were used to airlift Afghan civilians to ISAF medical facilities. The ISAF ACE tracked each event, noting response and delivery times and the status of the wounded passengers on arrival at medical facilities. Updates on the status of wounded soldiers and civilians were often passed to ISAF's command group. Any MEDEVAC mission that failed to deliver its wounded passengers within the "golden hour" would be immediately reviewed and then briefed to ISAF's chief of logistics, Director ACE, and COMISAF. When supporting large military operations in places such as Nad Ali, Kajaki, Musa Qala, Farah, Marjah, and Lashkar Gah, it was not unusual to see individual MEDEVAC helo crews fly 4–6 sorties in a 24-hour period, often in combat conditions. Considering that half of the daily MEDEVACs were responding to civilian casualties, many of which were women and children, the value of this essential capability was deeply appreciated by NATO forces and Afghan civilian authorities. Young children transported to ISAF medical facilities would often be accompanied by their grandfathers, who would not leave the bedside of the injured children until they were well enough to return to their village. On one well-known MEDEVAC event, a US UH-60 helicopter was completely reconfigured in a couple of hours to accommodate a special burn litter unit to transport a young child who had been severely scalded with boiling hot milk over most of his body. These types of events occurred on a regular basis, and the news of these humanitarian missions quickly spread across the countryside and served to foster bonds of trust and goodwill in a very significant manner. Here was one of the best examples of tactical-level events with strategic effect. General McKiernan and his senior leadership cadre understood the COIN philosophy and the need to ensure that these essential capabilities were not compromised.

Intratheatre Airlift

A critical capability for the coalition was the intratheatre airlift system. ISAF's ACE typically had 12–14 tactical airlift aircraft on its airlift tasking roster, which included C-27J Spartans, C-160 Transalls, and C-130 Hercules. The ACE could also call on strategic airlift assets from the US military at a moment's notice. The ITAS fleet of "flying Clydesdales" accomplished astonishing feats of air mobility on a 24/7 basis, which never failed to impress even the most discerning critics. Around the clock, this extraordinary multinational capability resupplied troops in the field; dispatched rapid-reaction forces with little notice; conducted humanitarian airdrops to coalition units and Afghan military and civilian populations; carried wounded and sick personnel, both military and civilian, to medical facilities; and transported thousands of ISAF and Afghan soldiers to various locations around the theatre of operation.

The majority of the nations that contributed to ISAF's intratheatre airlift capability excelled in meeting their stated commitment, many of which exceeded their pledged quotas of sorties and flying hours.

The most dependable countries became well known across the coalition and were the "go-to favorites" of the ACE's tasking authority. Disappointingly, a couple of contributing nations were notorious for withdrawing their committed national assets from the ISAF airlift programme, often with little warning, to conduct their own "national missions." One country in particular was so unreliable that when it did decide to support ITAS assigned tasks, it would typically fly with only partial loads due to coalition partners refusing to book their personnel and cargo on its frequently cancelled flights. To deal with troublesome national agendas, I found it necessary to offer truant nations the opportunity to honour their commitment or withdraw their airlift asset from theatre to make room for more eager, committed, and dependable coalition partners. This, of course, caused great concern for these truant nations as they would no longer have an airlift asset in theatre to support their national tasks. Although it was quite acceptable for all ITAS nations to fly missions in support of national priorities, conscientious and committed nations would meet or exceed their ISAF commitment before undertaking national flights. The truant nations eventually ended up supporting the ITAS mission, not because they were committed to this vital ISAF role, but so they could keep their asset in theatre to support their own national agendas.

ISAF's intratheatre airlift capability was routinely called upon to support President Karzai's visits, which typically required 8–10 flights to transport the presidential entourage, armored vehicles, and security personnel. It was not unusual to see two of these events each month, and the ISAF ACE would liaise directly with the director of security at the presidential palace to coordinate these extremely high-profile, high-risk activities. A very impressive development related to airlift capabilities in Afghanistan was the standup of the Afghan Air Force. Several decades earlier, before the Soviet invasion and the Afghan civil war, the Afghan Air Force was a respected military capability in the region. In 2009, as a revival of former times, Afghan pilots were flying fixed- and rotary-wing airlift aircraft and carrying out security operations with armed helicopters. Their conduct of national airlift missions, which included both humanitarian and military operations, was most impressive. They also routinely supported ISAF's airlift programme and were, on many occasions, able to move hundreds of their own troops when required. Their programme was regarded as a professional and reliable operation by me and my ACE staff, and it wasn't unusual for me to hop aboard an Afghan aircraft to fly from Kabul to Kandahar and return.

Land aviation and heavy helo airlift were traditionally under the direct tasking authority of respective regional command HQs, with oversight and coordination from ISAF J3 Operations. However, with the appointment of Director ACE to the position of Deputy Joint Operations in the fall of 2008, it was a natural fit for the ACE to play an oversight role in managing this critical combat enabler. On behalf of COMISAF, General Tucker and I were responsible for reviewing and approving Level 2 special forces and ground force operations, which included the command prerogative to allocate or reassign support enablers. Land aviation was one such capability that would be reassigned from one regional command to another based on the requirements identified in mission-approval decision briefs. Medium- and heavy-lift helicopters were always in high demand to transport troops above the IED-infested roads and highways, and the arrival of the 82nd Combat Aviation Brigade in spring 2009 at Kandahar saw this critical tactical lift capability added to RC-S's repertoire of essential go/no-go combat enablers.

Armed Overwatch and Close Air Support

For most coalition units operating in Afghanistan, armed overwatch and close air support were decisive game changers for counterinsurgency efforts, but only by those nations adept in this highly specialized discipline. The number of fighter aircraft assigned to support ISAF's counterinsurgency mission in 2009 often exceeded 100 platforms; however, there was always the need for more. On a 24/7 basis, the ACE would have 4–6 armed fighters airborne conducting armed overwatch, with another 4–6 fighters on ground alert ready to go at a moment's notice. In addition, high-priority Level 2 land force, special forces, and counternarcotics operations would receive their own dedicated armed overwatch and air support assets. The performance metric for this critical capability was based on the time it would take fighters to arrive overhead friendly ground forces after the call for help from embedded FACs and JTACs. The standard was to have fighter aircraft overhead friendly forces within 8–12 minutes of the initial request for support. The request for air support would be sent by the JTACs to their respective regional air operations command centres and then relayed to the ASOC at ISAF's air operations centre in Kabul. Within a couple of minutes, fighter aircraft would be dispatched to support the ground force commander. As the fighter aircraft approached the friendly force TIC location, they would employ their onboard targeting pods and sensors to downlink streaming video, which would provide precise information on the disposition of hostile forces to the FAC and affected ground commander. Fighters could provide instant SA to friendly ground force commanders from several miles away, which allowed them to start maneuvering their force to counter the enemy attack. Not surprisingly, many task force commanders, who knew how to properly employ air effects and enablers, would declare armed overwatch a go/no-go showstopper for their operations.

The US military shouldered the main fighter-force effort for air support operations, which included assets from the US Air Force, US Navy, US Marine Corps, and US Army, as well as impressive support from the United Kingdom, the Netherlands, France, Spain, Italy, and Germany. The contribution from a US Navy *Nimitz*-class aircraft carrier stationed in the Arabian Sea just south of Pakistan was also impressive. In addition to the squadrons of F/A-18 Super Hornets, the US Navy operated EA-6B Prowlers from Bagram Air Base in northern Afghanistan. Land-based fighters such as A-10s, F/A-18s, F-15s, F-16s, GR-1s, Mirages, Harriers, and B-1B bombers provided the main effort for armed overwatch, close air support, dynamic targeting, and joint prioritized effects list (JPEL)/special forces operations. The AC-130 Spectre gunship was reserved for special and elite forces. This formidable air support asset could employ its 105 mm howitzer, 40 mm rapid-fire cannon, or 20 mm Gatling gun. The US Navy's EA-18G Growlers and EA-6B Prowlers championed the highly advanced and game-changing mission elements related to electronic attack, "comms herding," specialized EW missions, and predetonation burn missions to electronically clear radio-detonated IEDs ahead of advancing logistics convoys and ground force patrols.

As discussed earlier, the ability to employ advanced air effects and enablers and conduct effective joint operations often defined the depth and quality of national military battle groups. One need only consider the lessons from the Zhari, Panjwayi, and Arghandab districts in August and September of 2006 when the absence of air-land integration expertise during preplanned offensive ground operations produced tragic results on the battlefield. Although the CENTCOM report on Operation Medusa and its 500 pages of interview transcripts was not released to the public, what was abundantly clear to the investigating team in the fall of 2006 was that the defeat of the Canadian army and the subsequent friendly fire incident was directly related to the decision to cancel the three-day air phase and the inability of the Canadian battle group to effectively employ air effects and enablers. A general officer who served as commander of Canada's task force in Afghanistan years later dismissed the severity of the event as "just another bad day for the battle group." Sadly, with five soldiers dead and another 50 wounded, many critically, it is difficult to accept such an offhanded and unprofessional characterization.

In large multinational coalition efforts such as ISAF, each major TCN contributes the capabilities and enablers needed to underpin joint air-land operations—capabilities such as helicopters for air MEDEVAC, forward air controllers, dedicated air-land integration planners, tactical airlift, and perhaps most importantly, attack helicopters, ISR, and fighter aircraft with precision targeting and EW capabilities. The ACE noted that rarely did they see nations with significant ground forces in theatre that were involved in meaningful joint operations exclude these critical capabilities from their deployed formations. Smaller countries with less robust military forces would quite understandably count on the effects and enablers of major TCNs when conducting their joint operations.

When it came to contributing as much as a country draws from a coalition, the Dutch military was often cited as the example for other nations to follow in the 2008–09 time frame. With a total deployed force of approximately 2,300 personnel in and around Uruzgan Province, the Dutch government deployed the full spectrum of capabilities needed for joint operations including AH-64 attack helicopters, F-16 fighter aircraft with precision targeting capability, RPAs for surveillance and reconnaissance, contracted tactical airlift, and Chinook and Super Puma heavy-lift helicopters. In 2006, and later in the spring and summer of 2009, discussions with US CENTCOM and NATO JFC HQ communicated that other nations needed to help shoulder the armed overwatch and CAS missions. Other NATO countries deployed their fighter fleets to support their deployed ground troops.

It may not be surprising to those familiar with Operation Medusa and the challenges experienced by the Canadian army in Kandahar Province from 2005 to 2010 that Canada remained the only major

TCN in the ISAF coalition (ranked fifth of 42 nations) that chose not to deploy its fighter force, a well-appreciated contribution that should have also included air-land integration and full-spectrum airpower experts to rally and employ air effects and enablers that were so noticeably absent from Canadian land-force operations. Instead, the main focus of Canada's military leadership in the wake of Operation Medusa was to deploy a fleet of Leopard battle tanks.

To be fair, the deployment of Leopard tanks was, in part, an effort to mitigate losses from roadside bombs and IEDs but also to demonstrate support for the Canadian soldiers who had just come through Operation Medusa. Canadian forces in Afghanistan in 2006 had no medium- or heavy-lift helicopters of their own or heavy armoured personnel carriers to move their troops around the battlefield. Perhaps most problematic was the absence of a champion in any of the senior leadership positions in Canada's air force headquarters or Expeditionary Force Command with airpower and air-land integration expertise who could speak convincingly and with authority on the critical importance of having a robust and balanced joint force combat team on the ground in Kandahar Province. The air generals in Ottawa and Winnipeg charged with running Canada's air force during the 2005–10 time period were very well versed on domestic peacetime activities and NORAD, but lacked the expertise, knowledge, and experience in air-land integration and the effective application of air effects and enablers in combat operations. These deficiencies meant that Canada's army in Kandahar Province would struggle to effectively employ the combat effects and enablers needed to underpin success in COIN and complex joint operations.

Much to the chagrin of Canada's army in late fall of 2006, the newly appointed Dutch two-star commander of RC-S (Kandahar and Helmand Provinces) would not support the employment of its recently deployed squadron of Leopard II tanks in NATO's counterinsurgency mission. The Canadian army was eventually permitted to deploy its battle tanks to its FOBs in and around the approaches to Kandahar City and to employ them in selected operations; however, the "knock-on effects" of having 60-ton battle tanks rumbling across the countryside were most unfortunate. Counterinsurgency operations were all about "hearts and minds" and trust and confidence of the local population; however, the manner in which the Canadian tanks were tearing up roads and ditches, crushing irrigation culverts and small bridges in Afghanistan's agriculture heartland, and damaging the hardened earth walls of Afghan compounds as they traversed around and through towns and villages did not inspire much goodwill with the local Afghan population.

The Taliban's efforts to destroy a Canadian tank were also concerning. To achieve this goal, IEDs would need to be several times more powerful than what was being employed to take out lighter armored personnel carriers and convoy vehicles. The knock-on effect of having tank-grade IEDs along the roads and highways of Kandahar Province was devastating for both military vehicles and the civilian population and introduced a level of lethality that was difficult to defend against. A point sometimes raised by interested observers related to why other coalition partners had not deployed their tanks to Afghanistan—partners such as the United States, the British army, and the Dutch, who had some of the largest tank forces in NATO and were conducting joint operations in the same areas of RC-S. The answer often centered on the fact that most coalition partners were equipped with medium- and heavy-lift helicopters and heavier armored personnel carriers to transport their soldiers. Also, battle tanks were not considered appropriate for counterinsurgency operations. It is difficult to be seen as living alongside the local population when you're hunkered down in FOBs and driving around in tanks. During a teleconference with Dr. David Kilcullen in 2009,[9] these types of coalition partners were characterized as "FOB-ites" and unhelpful in advancing the COIN mission in Afghanistan.

In an effort to have Canada consider the deployment of its fighter aircraft to Afghanistan, I passed messages directly from Lt Gen Gary North (US CFACC) to Canada's Air Staff HQ in 2006 and 2007 and again in 2009 from ISAF joint operations and the ACE to Canada's Chief of Defence staff. The message was always the same: that a contingent of Canadian F-18s with supporting TACPs, JTACs, and air planners was needed to help shoulder the international community's effort in providing CAS, armed overwatch, and air-land integration to ISAF's coalition force. The staff also noted that the US Air Force needed assistance from all coalition members, but Canada in particular, who had not yet contributed a fighter contingent to help shoulder the massive effort that US fighter pilots were providing throughout the CENTCOM AOR, including Afghanistan. A contingent of CF-18s in Kandahar able to provide armed overwatch and CAS to coalition forces would have allowed the US military to reassign some of its fighter forces to support other hot spots in the region.

Although many interested observers from within the coalition surmised that it was the Canadian government that opposed the deployment of a fighter contingent, I learned through my conversations with the chief of Canada's defence staff that it was the military itself, and most notably Canada's air force, that chose not to support the deployment of CF-18s. Canada's Minister of Defence stated during his visit to Kabul in 2009 that he was ready to give the order to deploy a contingent of CF-18s to Kandahar on the recommendation of his chief of defence and Air Staff in Ottawa; however, the recommendation was never made. Canada's government-imposed personnel cap and its army's unwillingness to give up boots on the ground or any of its deployed Leopard tank personnel in exchange for the 200–300 air force personnel that would have been needed to support a deployed CF-18 fighter contingent also influenced the issue. The Canadian army had only a fraction of the forces it needed to cover its assigned AOR in Kandahar Province, and giving up boots on the ground in exchange for a fighter force contingent was not, and quite understandably, an option for Canada's land-centric military leadership in Ottawa. Interestingly, some opined that Canada should have deployed its fighter force post-2011, after the withdrawal of its ground troops. No doubt, many coalition partners would have found it interesting that Canada would deploy a 3,000-strong ground force without critical air support capabilities and enablers but then offer its fighter force after its ground forces had been withdrawn from combat operations.

Notwithstanding the interesting mind-set of certain coalition partners and their senior decision makers, progress was made throughout ISAF by 2009 on both the *air* and *land* sides of air-land integration. ISAF and its regional commands developed a more robust and capable air support structure and theatre air control system for air support operations. To ensure that operational competence and expertise were achieved and maintained, the ACE focused on maintaining close and continuous oversight of the entire air support structure—from the ASOC and RAOCs down to the TACPs and the more than 300 FACs and TACPs deployed across the country. Due to lessons from Operation Medusa in 2006, regional task forces started receiving fully trained, qualified, and equipped FACs and JTACs, which played a key role in rallying and employing air effects and enablers to guarantee success for land force security and complex COIN operations.

A critical pillar in ISAF's air support and armed overwatch mission was the JTAC/FAC community. Often regarded as the "druids" of air-land integration and joint fires, these highly skilled warriors operated in the field at the pointiest end of the theatre air control system (TACS). As mentioned above, ISAF had more than 300 NATO-accredited JTACs and FACs in 2009 working alongside and often embedded in ground force battle groups, companies, and platoons. Although most coalition partners produced their own FACs at their national air-ground operations schools back home, each FAC and JTAC deployed to Afghanistan was required to undergo a NATO accreditation process, which included a written exam on air-land integration and air support procedures, rules of engagement, and Director ACE's "air tactical directive." The accreditation check also included an in-field practical assessment to confirm skill sets, competence, and minimum equipment list (MEL) requirements. Although JTACs worked for and reported to their respective national ground force commanders when supporting field operations, whenever they sent up a request for air support and transmitted on their FAC radio to coordinate armed overwatch and CAS, they immediately came under the command authority of NATO's ACC and Director ACE to execute their air support mission.

"Electronic" Overwatch

For centuries, tactical commanders on Afghanistan battlefields employed visual signaling techniques to order their fighters to advance, maneuver, attack, and retreat. Even in recent times it was not unusual to see kites, flags, mirrors, and even runners employed to pass critical information across their ranks. However, in a relatively short time, the Taliban developed the ability to employ more-advanced electronic enablers to command and control their operations. Although cell phones had been used extensively for domestic communications, the employment of wireless handheld devices, press-to-talk walkie talkies and short-range radios, and battery-powered "repeater panels" to extend transmission ranges elevated Taliban battlefield activities to a new level of sophistication.

As expected, it did not take long for the ACE operations team to analyze new techniques being used on the battlefield and to identify and exploit the vulnerabilities associated with insurgency methodologies. Indeed, drawing together signal and electronic intelligence effects and enablers, interpreters and translators, and the highly unique capabilities resident with US Navy Super Hornets, EA-18Gs, and EA-6Bs, the ACE brought to bear an innovative "electronic overwatch" battlefield technique that was highly effective in thwarting Taliban operations. The game-changing nature of this new approach saw a dramatic decrease in the employment of heavy weapons to protect coalition forces from Taliban attacks, which in turn dramatically decreased the risk of civilian casualties. This new approach was so effective that many ISAF battle groups and combat units—primarily US, Dutch, Australian, and British in southern and eastern Afghanistan—would declare the electronic overwatch capability a go/no-go advanced enabler for many of their convoys, patrols, maneuvers, and COIN shape-and-clear operations.

The basic concept of employment for the electronic overwatch started with detecting when an insurgent force was about to initiate a maneuver against a coalition formation and then control and deny the Taliban commander's use of his tactical communications network. As a coalition formation began its advance, whether a convoy, patrol, or shaping maneuver, electronic overwatch assets prepositioned overhead would monitor the area of interest and listen for insurgent "chatter." With the aid of translators and interpreters, intelligence analysts would determine the intentions of the insurgent force and pass that information to the overhead air commander and the FAC embedded with the ground force. Using a combination of "comms herding,"[10] jamming, and electronic attack (EA), the network would be disrupted and then shut down at exactly the right moment to introduce confusion and uncertainty across insurgents' ranks. The end result was to delay or halt enemy action, and in some cases, force an enemy withdrawal. Most frequently, insurgent commanders and their subordinate forces regarded electronic attacks and barrage jamming as "harbingers of doom" which would, when required, lead to a show of presence, a show of force, and, as a final effort to protect the coalition force should the enemy attack continue, a full and decisive application of lethal force. Insurgents soon learned not to press on with their attacks in the presence of electronic overwatch measures.

As decisive and successful as this game-changing strategy was, not all battle groups had the ability to employ such advanced air effects and enablers. One disappointing operation in RC-S near Kandahar City resulted in air support being suspended by ACE Operations shortly after the operation was initiated because the ground commander and his FAC employed 14 2,000 lb. and 500 lb. HE bombs during a shaping operation to target Taliban C2 network repeater panels rather than control and disrupt the enemy's communications network through electronic means. More exasperating, after being denied air support by me, Joint Operations, and the regional commander, the national task force commander chose to call in his own long-range heavy artillery to target the same locations. As expected, frustration and disappointment were shared across ISAF and regional command leadership cadres. Fortunately, most other ISAF battle groups were accomplished in the application of advanced effects and enablers, which made electronic overwatch an appreciated game-changing capability that gave coalition forces a new and distinctive advantage in complex joint operations against insurgent forces.

Complementing the ACE's "Electron Overwatch" was another game-changing strategy that elevated many battle group operations to a whole new level. Early in 2009 a senior member of the CFACC's ACCE at the ISAF compound in Kabul carried out an in-depth and detailed analysis on how the monthly lunar cycle influenced insurgent activity. The study analyzed data from the previous three years and plotted insurgent movements, ambushes, complex IED and rocket attacks, cross-border events, and sniper activity against the luminosity of moonlight. The conclusions were astonishing. This critical analysis, combined with the plotting of well-known cultural and religious events, allowed ISAF's air team to predict with extraordinary accuracy when insurgent activity would be at its peak and, conversely, when the Taliban would not be in the field in any great numbers. This gave the ACE the ability to posture airpower capabilities to match insurgent activities and to plan the rotation of critical assets such as the US Navy's aircraft carrier in the Arabian Sea.

This approach was quickly institutionalized in the joint operations risk assessment and mission approval process for Level 2 operations and, on occasion, saw major operations advanced or delayed by days or even weeks to mitigate the insurgents' ability to move around the battlefield at night and target coalition forces under the glow of moonlight. The execution of large troop rotations and major logistics convoys benefited greatly from the ACCE's lunar analysis, and it was not unusual for the deputy of joint operations to challenge the briefing officers from regional commands, special forces, and counternarcotics teams on the timing of their missions with respect to the lunar cycle. This type of game-changing strategy, combined with electronic and armed overwatch, show of presence, show of force, and escalation of force, achieved a significant "tipping point" regarding how airpower could positively change the way ISAF joint operations would unfold.

Remotely Piloted Aircraft

COMISAF's fleet of RPAs championed a critical capability. Although extensively employed in the intelligence role, they were frequently called upon to respond to TICs when manned fighter aircraft were not available or close enough to respond in time. As with manned aircraft, RPAs also provided instant situational awareness and a kinetic response when necessary. The Predator RPAs typically carried two Hellfire missiles and the Reapers four Hellfires and two 500 lb. PGMs. ISAF intelligence and joint ops divisions maintained several RPA orbits continuously across the country to "layer and soak" potential JPEL and insurgent C2 nodes and provide persistent, unblinking coverage over areas of high interest.

Many coalition partners had their own RPA platforms to support national operations; however, the "Clydesdales" of the RPA capability were the US Predator and Reaper fleets. A standard lament around ISAF headquarters was the shortage of RPAs in Afghanistan to support planned operations, while Iraq had more than needed. Perhaps most interesting were the Reaper RPAs that remained in their shipping containers on the ramp in Kandahar because there was simply not enough bandwidth available to fly the platforms or download streaming video and high-fidelity imagery they were employed to provide. Also not widely appreciated were the employment limitations of these platforms. Several times a year strong winds and icing conditions would keep RPA fleets across the country on the ground for several days at a time. During these challenging inclement weather periods, manned fighters would shoulder the highest ISR priorities while still providing armed overwatch and CAS to ground forces. Of course, this would place even greater pressure on ISAF's fighter fleet and those few stalwart nations who continued to provide the aircraft, aircrews, and ground crew so that coalition partners would have this vital capability. Also noteworthy were the challenges of employing RPAs instead of fighters for armed overwatch missions. In addition to being affected by strong winds, clouds, and icing, RPAs were relatively slow and unable to cover large distances quickly. They were also unable to provide effective show of presence, show of force, and escalation of force maneuvers, which were critical elements to COMISAF's and Director-ACE's COIN and force application strategies.

Section 3: Joint Operations

This section focuses on joint operations that relied on advanced air effects and enablers to accomplish their goals and objectives. I've chosen to highlight ISAF's dynamic and time-sensitive targeting capability, the government of Afghanistan's counternarcotics interdiction (CNI) mission, and special forces operations. Of interest, General McKiernan had delegated his commander's review and approval authority for these three joint operations to the Chief of Joint Operations and Director ACE, which represented an unprecedented opportunity for me, as NATO's senior airman, to play a leadership role in operations and activities normally reserved for land-force general officers.

Dynamic and Time-Sensitive Targeting

An important task awarded to the Director ACE and Joint Operations teams late in 2008 was to establish a fully functioning Dynamic Targeting Operations Centre (DTOC) at ISAF HQ. Dynamic targeting (DT) missions and joint prioritized effects list objectives fell under the authority of COMISAF; however, prior to February 2009, each DT mission was facilitated through CENTCOM and orchestrated by its CAOC at Al Udeid. In consultation with the commander of CENTCOM, who was at that time Gen David Petraeus, COMISAF received CENTCOM's full support to move all DT mission elements into a new DTOC at ISAF HQ in Kabul. This would not be an easy task to complete as ISAF would need to acquire and train additional intelligence resources, imagery analysts, targeting and joint-fires experts, and other operations personnel to support the DT process. Critical elements within the DT process were the highly specialized functions of establishing positive identification (PID) of insurgent leadership objectives, pattern of life (PoL) in the immediate vicinity of the objective, and the completion of collateral damage estimates. The final steps in the process were to coordinate strike asset designation and weapons release authority through the CAOC and, as the last command imperative in the process, Strike Approval Authority from either Chief Joint Operations or Director ACE, one of whom would be present in the DTOC for each mission.

The purpose of the DTOC was to support the targeting of Taliban and al-Qaeda leadership objectives and to also oversee special forces missions, CN operations, and offensive preplanned targeting operations. Regarding leadership objectives, ISAF's JPEL was an intelligence-generated roster of various leaders and senior members of the Taliban, al-Qaeda, and other terrorist organizations. COMISAF approved each JPEL objective personally, with the joint operations division responsible for carrying out targeting operations against the objectives. Potential JPEL objectives were recommended to COMISAF for consideration based on a formal intelligence-gathering process and assessment. Placing a terrorist objective on the JPEL roster was, in itself, declaring the objective "hostile." The objective could be engaged by the ISAF coalition without the need for a hostile act or demonstration of hostile intent. NATO rules of engagement were such that conventional forces could apply lethal force against a hostile enemy only in a self-defence situation, when the Taliban had committed a hostile act, or when hostile intent was clearly demonstrated. Different from a self-defence situation, preplanned offensive operations, which included Level 2 land force operations, special forces, counternarcotics, and offensive targeting operations, using air-delivered weapons and long-range artillery, including rockets, required COMISAF approval. The review and approval authority for offensive direct-action missions was delegated to and carried out by the Chief of Joint Operations and his deputy, the Director ACE. COMISAF and his two joint operations two-star generals were ISAF's strike approval authorities for missions that targeted JPEL objectives in a dynamic and time sensitive manner.

The main challenge in standing up a full DT operation at ISAF arose when the Deputy CFACC at Al Udeid expressed opposition to the initiative. Although efforts progressed rapidly to acquire the necessary resources for ISAF's new DT capability, the CFACC and his deputy continued to voice their opposition. The CFACC's opposition was based, in part, on his assertion that the conduct of DT missions, which included the selection of the most appropriate strike asset and the actual order to employ the weapon of choice, was doctrinally part of the US CFACC's mandate. Also influencing the situation was, undoubtedly, a confidence issue related to ISAF's previous track record on employing basic air effects and enablers in support of joint operations. Also problematic was the "four-eyes" intelligence issue, which meant only US, British, Australian, and Canadian personnel could be involved in this highly classified intelligence-led operation. The four-eyes issue created significant tension and acrimony for NATO partners, not just because of the manner in which it played out on the DT issue, but because anytime intelligence was being used to lead ISAF operations, "non-four-eyes" nations would be excluded from briefings and dossiers. This was a particularly sensitive issue for Dutch, German, French, and Italian members of ISAF HQ.

Despite these challenges, the ISAF team persevered in championing General McKiernan's DT vision, and with support from CENTCOM and NATO, the new capability was formally evaluated in February 2009 and declared fully operational and combat ready. Without delay, the DTOC went into high gear and started shouldering a level of targeting activity not previously seen or anticipated. The new DTOC rapidly became a centre of excellence for all direct action and offensive ISAF targeting activities, which included JPEL objectives, special forces missions, CN operations, and offensive-strike operations against Taliban C2 complexes, trenches, bunkers, and weapons caches. The operational tempo supported by the DTOC often saw 2–3 special forces missions per night, 2–3 CN operations per week, and sometimes as many as three JPEL objectives per week. On one occasion, I was required to review and approve eight SOF missions, three JPEL objectives, and one CN mission all in one evening. Demanding for the joint operations team, the Chief of Joint Operations or the deputy (Director ACE) was required to review and approve each mission and then attend the DTOC while the mission was being conducted in order to approve PID, PoL, CDE, and most importantly, strike approval authority at the appropriate moment. Also part of the review and approval process were the assignment and reallocation of critical assets as operations unfolded. On regular occasions, special forces missions and JPEL targeting opportunities would be initiated with little lead time, based on rapidly emerging intelligence information, which frequently required short-notice, middle-of-the-night decision briefs followed by approval and execution. Each and every mission had to be reviewed and approved by the Chief of Joint Operations or Director ACE, which would include at the end of each mission brief the most somber moment when the signature of the approving general officer was placed on the mission execution order. These documents remain in NATO's archives in perpetuity and are the official records of the details approved by NATO's command authority in Afghanistan.

Special Forces

Within ISAF's HQ command structure in Kabul were three formal senior command positions, namely, COMISAF, commander of NATO's air component, and ISAF's commander of special forces. The ACC and SOF commander, as well as the five regional commanders reported directly to COMISAF on all matters relating to ISAF coalition operations. A significant function within the command responsibilities of COMISAF was to review and approve all Level 2 ground force, special forces, and counternarcotics operations. Level 2 operations were often characterized as preplanned, offensive, direct-action missions that required special consideration for troop employment and coordination, support capabilities, apportioned effects and enablers, ROEs, compliance with the commander's tactical COIN directive, and mitigation measures for high-risk operations. The high-profile operations involving brigade-level efforts and priority-one JPEL objectives were sometimes reviewed and approved by COMISAF himself with joint operations advisors alongside, and in consultation with regional commanders, whenever required. However, most Level 2 operations were reviewed and approved by General Tucker and me whereas Level 0 and Level 1 task force operations were reviewed and approved by regional commanders and their J3 operations staffs.

Regarding special forces operations, SOF units under ISAF authority in 2009 reported directly to ISAF's SOF commander, who was responsible for the planning, coordination, and execution of all SOF missions. Members of the ISAF special and elite forces cadre included the US Combined Joint Special Operations Task Force (CJSOTF), several British, French, Dutch, Australian, German, and Norwegian SOF units, and a few countries that can't be mentioned in this unclassified publication. Canadian special forces operated under the command authority of the US CJSOTF. Routine and lower-risk activities could typically be authorized by the ISAF SOF commander; however, as mentioned above, Level 2 operations required authorization from either General Tucker or me. The review and approval process for these operations was based primarily on decision briefs that provided a detailed overview of each mission phase, a phase-by-phase risk assessment, and an in-depth examination of each of the critical high-risk assessment factors. If the risk in any one area was assessed as too high for the mission objective, the Chief of Joint Operations or Director ACE had the authority to allocate or reallocate resources from within the theatre of operation to mitigate risks to acceptable levels and to award special ROEs normally reserved for the highest-profile, highest-risk missions. Generally speaking, SOF missions were intelligence-led operations that focused primarily on counterterrorism and relied almost exclusively on highly specialized airpower assets and capabilities permanently based in theatre. The air assets ISAF had to support our SOF operations included Predator and Reaper RPAs, C-130 Specter gunships, heavy- and medium-lift tactical aviation, and an impressive lineup of fighter aircraft and space-based platforms.

An interesting addition to the lineup of measures and mitigations that joint operations could apply to high-risk missions was the application of no-strip criteria. "No-strip" meant that supporting effects, enablers, and critical capabilities allocated by ISAF joint operations, such as armed RPAs, armed overwatch, gunships, joints fires, and others could not be "stripped" away from a designated high-profile SOF mission to support nearby TIC events. Instead, the ASOC, which was charged with coordinating air support for TICs, would first try to find supporting capabilities from other neighboring operations before requesting to strip assets away from the designated SOF mission. If a strip action was required, the chief or deputy of joint operations overseeing the operation from the DTOC could approve the request within seconds, if and when required. An added responsibility for General Tucker was to provide command oversight of US "black operations," which were typically US-eyes-only but required coordination with Director ACE for obvious reasons.

A welcomed activity related to the interaction with SOF personnel and units was the office calls with new incoming SOF unit commanders and liaison officers and the much-anticipated joint ops field visits with SOF units. It was not unusual for COMISAF or his two-star joint ops generals to deploy to the field to participate in actual special forces and CN missions. Such opportunities allowed ISAF's senior leadership to experience firsthand the professionalism and dedication of these extraordinary military units. Of course, the presence of a general officer on special forces or counternarcotics missions was not made known until after the mission was completed, which allowed the SOF soldiers to focus on the mission at hand and not on the two-, three-, or four-star general maneuvering with the force.

Counternarcotics Interdiction Mission

As the deputy of joint operations and Director ACE, I was tasked by COMISAF to oversee ISAF's support to Afghanistan's counternarcotics mission. With the majority of the world's opium supply coming from Afghanistan and the revenues directly funding the Taliban insurgency, counternarcotic interdiction, better known as CNI, quickly became a vitally important strategic mission that gained visibility and support from across NATO and the international community. The critical elements of this Afghan-led law enforcement programme were the government of Afghanistan's National Interdiction Unit and the Afghan Narcotics Force, both of which were Afghan units but closely mentored and enabled by US and UK special counternarcotics units in theatre. Underpinning the entire in-theatre CNI mission were the stellar efforts of the US Drug Enforcement Administration (DEA) and the US-led Interagency Operations Coordination Center collocated with ISAF HQ in Kabul. The IOCC employed multiagency intelligence sources and analysts to identify potential interdiction opportunities for the Afghan government to undertake, but also provided a rare and highly specialized intelligence capability for select individuals in critical leadership positions in ISAF. Problematic was the fact that IOCC intelligence could not be shared outside of the four-eyes community and was often restricted to US-eyes-only.

An important part of the CN mission for ISAF was to understand the manner in which opium was inextricably linked to the Afghan culture. As discussed in some forums, "110 percent" of the world's opium supply came from Afghanistan, with the majority of the product making its way to the Middle East and across Central and Southeast Asia. But this was the enterprise of the Taliban, narco-drug lords, and organized crime bosses. The Taliban insurgency needed funding, and the opium trade was one of the most effective methods for financing their operations. From an Afghan cultural perspective, the poppy plants were a part of most Afghan household gardens. Considered by some as "weeds" that could grow in the harshest of conditions, poppy plants required very little moisture and could grow successfully without fertilizers, pesticides, and herbicides to support production quotas. In many parts of the country, opium was the local currency and an economic pillar in the local economy. According to Afghan culture, opium was administered for medicinal purposes, not unlike the manner in which Western countries consume acetaminophen and ibuprofen for pain control and to alleviate the symptoms of cold and flu. It was not unusual for Afghan mothers to rub small quantities of opium on the gums of infants and young children cutting new teeth. Just as Western cultures were addicted to pain-control medications, so too were many Afghans addicted to opium to help relieve the aches and pains of daily life. The intent of ISAF was not to deny Afghans an important medicinal staple of their daily life, but to interdict stockpiles of Taliban opium and destroy their narcotics production facilities.

The military capabilities of only a select few coalition partners were called upon to support CNI missions, which typically included surveillance and reconnaissance capabilities; SOF and conventional land forces for cordon and site security; airlift for CNI personnel; and FACs, armed fighters, and RPAs for armed overwatch and CAS should the CNI law enforcement team come under attack by Taliban insurgents or narco-drug lords. CNI missions quite often saw the arrest of narco-drug lords and their underlings and the destruction of large caches of narcotics, production equipment, and facilities.

Each CNI mission was mentored and facilitated by the IOCC from the Kabul compound. The IOCC would do the heavy lifting with respect to intelligence and mission preparation and then brief the Afghans' national interdiction unit on proposed missions. As a major supporting partner and stakeholder in CNI operations, I was routinely briefed on the hundreds of active narcotics processing labs across the country and the ones that were next on the list to take down. CNI decision briefs and risk assessments were similar to JPEL and special forces operations briefs and allowed me to assign ISAF capabilities according to the exigencies of the mission. The CNI ground force would employ Russian Mi-17 Hip helicopters to ingress into the mission area, usually just before dawn. Mission areas typically included several opium processing labs and large stockpiles of narcotics that were similar to a morphine-cake product. It was often necessary to track down and arrest the narco-drug lords and their lab workers and transport them back to Kabul. Once the production facilities and laboratories were cleared of all personnel and narcotics, they were usually destroyed with hand-placed C4 explosives and, in some cases, depending on their size and proximity to civilian populations, by employing precision-guided air munitions delivered by fighter aircraft in highly controlled and precision weapons delivery procedures. It was difficult to completely destroy large narcotics facilities using C4 explosives, and these attempts often saw the facilities back in operation within a few days. However, the employment of air munitions against cleared facilities was highly effective and, more importantly, safer than transporting large quantities of C4 explosives by helicopter and ground forces into remote locations.

In battling the illicit narcotics industry in their country, the government of Afghanistan also championed—with the help of the international community and the United Nations—programmes to eradicate poppy crops and focus on alternative livelihoods for poppy farmers. The international community, led by Britain and the United States, was also involved in setting in place a fully functioning federal ministry and judicial architecture in Kabul that oversaw all CN efforts in the country. ISAF's mandate was to provide security to government-led eradication efforts and directly support the government's CNI mission. After a slow start, the strategic importance of CNI was eventually embraced, and in the April 2009 time frame, a single day's CNI effort interdicted 3,000 kilograms of processed morphine-based narcotics, which denied Taliban insurgents tens of millions of dollars of funding. With a renewed level of support from ISAF, the first three months of 2009 yielded more CNI successes than the previous three years combined. Most notable was the fact that the overall CNI effort had just started to gain momentum. As anxious as ISAF and Afghan government agencies were to go into high gear, ISAF was required to wait for regional command CNI campaign plans and individual responses from coalition member nations to confirm that their in-theatre forces could be authorized to support Afghan-led and ISAF-enabled CNI operations. Although the main focus was to deny funding to the insurgency, I should emphasize that the CNI effort was also removing narcotics from the streets and schoolyards of our own cities and towns back home, which made the overall CNI effort tremendously satisfying and enormously worthwhile.

The counternarcotics mission was often politically charged and often saw the international community divided over strategies for eradication, alternative livelihoods for farmers, and interdiction operations. Perhaps the most controversial topic was discussed behind closed doors in hushed tones and involved the targeting of fully operating narcotic processing facilities, which would have included local Afghans working in the facility. Pressure from NATO and a few coalition member nations was applied on the ISAF leadership cadre to consider the targeting of fully operating narcotics labs based on the assertion that anyone involved in the production of illicit narcotics could be legally classified as part of the insurgency and, therefore, a legal and legitimate military target. ISAF explained to NATO that most of these narcotics labs—and there were hundreds spread across the country—were employing local Afghan civilians from nearby towns and villages, including women and children to provide firewood and water for the production process and food for facility workers. Targeting these labs while in full operation would most certainly result in civilian deaths. Returning messages reinforced the assertion that narcotics labs should be placed on the JPEL targeting list, which should also include facility workers. Local workers in direct support of illicit narcotics production could therefore be legally targeted by NATO forces. Needless to say, the position being championed by those in favor of targeting "hot labs" was deeply troubling to those ISAF leaders responsible for the CNI mission. To purposefully target narcotics labs knowing that civilian workers would be killed was profoundly disturbing from an ethical and moral perspective, not to mention the legal implications as they related to international law and the Law of Armed Conflict (LOAC). As the discussion evolved and clearer perspectives were made known, I found it necessary to express my own professional and personal feelings on the issue, at which time I indicated that it would not be possible for me to continue serving in Afghanistan should direction be given for the joint operations division and Director ACE to start targeting fully operating narcotics labs with civilian workers on site. Fortunately, I received assurances that Generals McKiernan and Tucker were of the same mind and would also not support any move toward targeting operating narcotics labs.

The type of challenge that confronted ISAF regarding the targeting of narcotics labs was an age-old problem that military commanders have wrestled with, which is how to translate political goals and objectives into legal and legitimate military missions without disrespecting international conventions, UNSC resolutions, international laws, and the LOAC. The outcome desired by NATO was to eliminate a major source of funding for the Taliban. However, it is very unsettling to political authorities who appoint military commanders and expect them to follow their orders to receive word that the mission cannot be carried out as directed by the political authority. Most pleasing to some political authorities are those eager-to-please military commanders who are willing to go beyond the legal and valid constraints and limitations of international laws and UNSC resolutions to achieve the goals and objectives of their political master. The elimination of the Taliban's narcotics production capability was a strategic goal for the government of Afghanistan and ISAF; however, the targeting of narcotics labs with civilian workers on-site represented an ethical and moral issue that could not be dismissed or ignored. Moreover, such an action would have been, in my mind, a clear violation of the LOAC.

Translating the goals and objectives of political authorities into a legal and legitimate military mission is not always possible, which means military commanders must be ready to make difficult decisions and step forward with difficult and unpopular recommendations. What must remain inviolate is every military commander's respect for international laws, conventions, and resolutions that have been set in place to define the manner in which commanders are to apply military force and execute their military operations. The LOAC is the business of military commanders and their military legal advisors. Political authorities, whether they are national or alliance based, must be carefully advised by theatre commanders on proper, legal, and legitimate courses of action and, most importantly, when their political goals and objectives cannot be achieved through military means.

Section 4: Counterinsurgency

This final section focuses on civilian casualties, General McKiernan's counterinsurgency vision, and the change of leadership that saw General McKiernan replaced by General McChrystal. As a concluding discussion point, I have included a summary of successes and achievements, which in 2009 helped to remind us of the contribution ISAF's security mission made in creating the conditions necessary for development, reconstruction, stability, governance, and rule of law.

Civilian Casualties

Of all the tough issues that faced COMISAF and the ACE in any day's work, few ranked higher or proved more difficult than the challenges associated with civilian casualties—those tragic events where Afghan civilians are injured or killed by Taliban, al-Qaeda, or coalition forces as a result of the fighting in their own country. Of critical importance was the intense focus of ISAF's leadership cadre on this strategic issue and the declaration that there was no higher priority for ISAF coalition forces than avoiding civilian casualties. And championing this strategic imperative from the very front was COMISAF himself, who communicated his intent regarding the avoidance of civilian casualties through his tactical directive, published in December 2008, and his COIN guidance released in March 2009. At the heart of these two documents was the safety and security of the Afghan population and the commander's overarching imperative of respect for the Afghan people and their culture. This was the guiding principle for all security and counterinsurgency operations and activities. To ensure the air team would be fully compliant with the spirit and intent of COMISAF's tactical directive and COIN guidance, the ACE published its own air guidance document, which mirrored and echoed COMISAF's direction and guidance. At the centre of Director ACE force-application guidance was a methodical and highly disciplined checklist approach for the use of lethal force when coalition forces came into contact with insurgents and terrorists.

To the senior leadership cadre of ISAF, General McKiernan's COIN vision was clear and unambiguous and, most importantly, needed to be implemented without delay. This sense of urgency was related to the numerous CIVCAS incidents that had occurred during the previous months and the growing concern over counterterrorism tactics being carried out by certain special forces and a couple of conventional-force national task forces. Also of concern was the practice of purposefully advancing toward known Taliban positions for the sole purpose of provoking a TIC, which would then allow ground commanders to engage Taliban positions. As discussed earlier, counterterrorism tactics focus on the enemy, whereas counterinsurgency place the safety and security of the civilian population as the top priority. The practice of "advance to contact, close to kill, blow through, and pursue" had caused several CIVCAS incidents, many of which included the inappropriate application of force where escalation of force and proportionality imperatives were disregarded by ground commanders and their FACs in the interest of hunting down and killing enemy fighters. In November and December of 2008, force application violations had become so egregious that General McKiernan placed restrictions on US Special Forces operating in Afghanistan under Operation Enduring Freedom and called upon the commander of US Joint Special Operations Command to address mounting CIVCAS events. General Tucker and I were often called into the commander's officer during this period to discuss such issues.

The Director ACE guidance issued to ISAF's air team across the country, including the commander of ISAF special forces and the five regional commands, demanded that JTACs, FACs, and ground commanders must have, first and foremost, a clear pattern of life with respect to the presence of civilians and a positive identification of hostile forces before the targeting of insurgent positions could be considered. Consistent with COMISAF's tactical directive, if PoL and PID were uncertain, ground commanders were to consider disengaging, repositioning, or even withdrawing their troops to deescalate intense standoff situations. If withdrawing were not a viable option and force had to be used in self-defence to protect coalition soldiers, then the principles of proportionality and escalation of force had to be honoured. A show of presence or show of force, which involved fighter aircraft flying low over insurgent positions, was a warning maneuver to compel insurgents to cease their attack and withdraw lest they be targeted by coalition aircraft. If the insurgents continued their attack, then appropriate force could be applied, exercising proportionality and escalation of force until insurgents were no longer a threat to friendly forces or the civilian population.

The practice of patrolling forward with conventional forces for the purpose of provoking a TIC and then calling in air support to target Taliban positions was often unsuccessful. Frequently, the patrol would strike an IED on its advance, which was synchronized with an ambush that employed multiple firing positions. These desperate situations would invariably result in friendly force casualties. The ground commander would declare a TIC and then call for air support to assist in protecting and, in many cases, extracting the friendly force. In the middle of all this exchange of fire, civilians were often wounded or killed by both coalition and enemy forces. However, the introduction of a structured, methodical, and disciplined application of force was designed to honour COMISAF's tactical directive and COIN guidance and reduced the CIVCAS incidents caused by conventional ISAF units.

Posing the greatest challenge for coalition forces was the Taliban's abhorrent tactic of setting up ambushes with multiple firing positions in the midst of the civilian population to use civilians as human shields and to create civilian casualties when it became necessary for coalition forces to provide cover fire in self-defence situations. Demonstrating a flagrant disregard for the safety and security of Afghan civilians, Taliban insurgents were even known to hold civilians as hostages at their firing positions to orchestrate CIVCASs. But knowing this to be their tactic of choice, ISAF's leadership cadre realized that it was better to pull back and withdraw, whenever possible, than risk the lives of innocent civilians. Unfortunately, insurgent ambushes, which often included IEDs and a complex enemy attack with multiple firing positions, placed friendly forces in life-and-death self-defence situations, which demanded that friendly forces provide their own cover fire to protect themselves as they attempted to extract their soldiers, often wounded, from life-threatening situations. Most regrettably, this cover fire routinely injured or killed civilians, which was exactly what the insurgents wanted to achieve.

Throughout the 2008–09 time frame, the media often used the term *airstrikes* and made general characterizations that created the impression that armed fighter aircraft were patrolling the skies of Afghanistan looking to bomb insurgent targets of opportunity. This portrayal could not have been more misleading. In reality, there were, indeed, armed overwatch fighter aircraft and RPAs above coalition and Afghan forces 24/7, ready to provide help when the call was made. However, air effects and precision air munitions could only be employed when the on-scene ground commander directly ordered and authorized them and when the assigned FACs or JTACs had confirmed PID of enemy insurgents and, most importantly, that there were no civilians in the target area (PoL). It is important to note that fighter aircraft and armed RPAs could only release their munitions on ground targets when explicitly directed by a ground commander and when authorized and facilitated by an ISAF-accredited FAC. Sadly, the most tragic CIVCAS events in the 2008–09 time frame resulted from coalition ground forces engaging enemy insurgents with a confirmed PID on Taliban positions to guide their attack but without applying the same rigor with regard to the pattern of life of civilians in the immediate engagement area. Directing and authorizing the bombing of enemy positions without a clear PoL of civilians was a direct violation of COMISAF's tactical directive and COIN guidance and counter to the most important imperative of counterinsurgency operations—protecting the civilian population and strengthening its trust and confidence in coalition forces. Unfortunately, not all coalition units were capable of applying air effects and enablers in a precise, disciplined, and expert manner, which caused no end of grief for the ISAF command group and the regional commanders.

An important part of ISAF's effort to identify situations when civilians may have been unintentionally injured in airstrikes and kinetic events was the ACE initiative introduced in November 2008 known as "First with the Truth," which involved the close examination and review of each and every kinetic event where air munitions had been employed against insurgent forces. This effort was later expanded to include the full spectrum of joint fires, which included land-force artillery. The purpose of this initiative was not only to verify the appropriate application of force, but also to identify at the earliest possible time when a kinetic event may have caused unintended damage to civilian property or injuries to civilians. Once a kinetic event had been flagged, Director ACE was able to order a battle damage assessment by the responsible regional command. Within a matter of hours, the ACE was then able to bring forward to COMISAF and President Karzai, and shortly thereafter, into the public domain, details of kinetic events that may have caused harm to civilians. Being first with the truth and quick with the details denied the insurgents the opportunity to fabricate and promulgate their own outrageous allegations against coalition forces and allowed ISAF the opportunity to conduct follow-on joint investigations with Afghan authorities in a rapid and thorough manner.

The practice of reviewing the previous 24 hour's kinetic events on a daily basis was successful in exposing several events when there had been inappropriate applications of force by national task forces, which regional commanders were able to investigate and act on. The daily review also allowed the ACE team to uncover an illegal dynamic targeting operation being carried out by a national task force commander in RC-S. The Tactical Operations Centre (TOC) of the national task force was employing its own national RPA assets to locate groups of Afghans and then call in regionally based attack helicopters which could then be tasked at the national task force commander level. When the rogue operation was discovered by the ACE, it was referred to the regional commander, who took immediate action to terminate the illegal activity and strip rules of engagement away from the national task force commander. Critical to these types of targeting activities were ROEs that would, under clearly defined tactical situations and conditions, allow the engagement of hostile forces once positive identification had been established and local PoL and CDE completed. Comments from personnel familiar with these national operations stated that insurgent body count was the focus of the task force commander and that members of the task force with the highest number of dead insurgents to their credit would be publicly commended by their commander.

As expected, some commanders rejected a structured and disciplined approach to the application of force during COIN operations. Those most opposed were typically from units that caused the greatest harm to the Afghan population, and, in return, received the most harm back on their own coalition soldiers. The first-with-the-truth initiative championed by ISAF's ACE, combined with the methodical and disciplined approach to force application, was eventually institutionalized at ISAF HQ. This approach, in concert with the commander's tactical directive and COIN guidance and the Director ACE's force application guidance had tremendous positive effects on reducing the number of airstrikes and kinetic events and, more importantly, the number of civilian casualties. The most compelling testimony on the success of ISAF's air team forward was from COMISAF himself, Gen Stanley McChrystal, when he wrote to ADM Mike Mullin, Chairman of the Joint Chiefs, immediately following Afghanistan's national election in August 2009:

> In the days leading up to the election we hit record numbers of TICs supported by air, going from a daily average of 20 TICs to 35, 50, then 80+ on election day, which represents over four times the normal volume. These levels rival the height of operations in Iraq during the surge of 2007 and are particularly noteworthy when one considers the force structure we have in place today. What I am most impressed with is the true Joint, Coalition teamwork that it took to achieve this level of activity while maintaining a very low level of kinetics. Crews from the USS *Ronald Reagan* extended their duty day, landing at Bagram and Kandahar, and hot-pitting to provide extra coverage. Coalition crews used Full Motion Video with ROVER downlinks to provide Armed Overwatch and situational awareness to ground forces, extending coverage and supporting more TICs—up to 20 taking place at one time. Joint EW crews also extended their flying days providing critical non-lethal support to operations, possibly

one of my most valuable COIN capabilities. The CAOC leaned forward diverting tankers to the fight and proactively pushing air effects to my ground commanders, dynamically managing reach back of assets flown from the AOR and locations back in the states.

For air to be employed correctly, it must have an effective interface and teamwork with ground commanders, which is exactly what we demonstrated these past few days. From the TACs system at the ground commander level, to the ISAF [ACE] here at ISAF, to the CAOC at Al Udeid, the C2 demonstrated that air-land integration and teamwork at every level creates success on the battlefield. This teamwork extended to the Afghans as well, as we were able to quickly respond with Air to their "high interest" situations often without a JTAC and sometimes with only a map grid location providing shows of force and ECAS.

In the 72 hours surrounding the election, we supported 164 TICs, with only 12% delivering weapons. In effect, 88% were able to diffuse TIC situations without kinetics. Zero TICs were unsupported by air, all were supported by ISR and most importantly, there were no Air CIVCAS events. As we well know, Air is our strategic advantage but can become a strategic vulnerability if not employed with restraint and precision; as the past few days have shown, when employed professionally it can significantly impact the ground commander's fight.

Unfortunately, there were some isolated events when ground commanders found it difficult to conduct their operations in accordance with the guidance and direction outlined in COMISAF's tactical directive and COIN guidance. One of the greatest losses of civilian Afghan lives was in the north of the country in September 2009 and involved the targeting of a large group of Afghan civilians attempting to remove fuel from two stolen fuel tankers. Characterized as "a tragic event where a ground commander thought he was attacking insurgents as a target of opportunity," the investigation established that the commander did not follow applicable ISAF processes and procedures and relied on a single SOF intelligence source to establish PID of an estimated 140 Afghans in a complex target area, all of whom came from several different villages and towns across the local district. Very troubling was the ground commander's declaration of "imminent threat" and a TIC situation even though the situation on the ground did not support such a declaration. Perhaps most troubling of all was the commander's rejection of several recommendations from the involved aircrew to conduct "show of force" maneuvers to disperse the large group of Afghans in the target area before striking the stolen fuel trucks. The aircrew also recommended coordination with higher headquarters, which would have been appropriate for the tactical situation; however, authorization for target engagement was declared by the on-scene ground commander, which demonstrated a lack of understanding of proper engagement processes and targeting procedures. The fighter crews ultimately released their weapons on the target area based on the ground commander's declaration that there was an imminent threat of a probable attack on the nearby military installation. However, the investigation team was unable to find any information to support this declaration. Unfortunately, all the measures, safeguards, and directives set in place to guide ground commanders in the appropriate application of force could not prevent one of the most tragic CIVCAS events in ISAF history. Following a two-month investigation, the ground commander was returned to his home country where his military and civilian national judicial system processed the case.

ISAF's Counterinsurgency Mission

The responsibilities associated with the positions of Deputy Chief Joint Operations, Director ACE, and NATO Air Component Commander allowed me to travel extensively throughout the theatre and permitted up-close and personal contact with coalition battle groups and their operations. These visits aided me in developing a clear understanding of the different approaches used by various nations in advancing their security, governance, reconstruction, and development strategies within the districts and provinces. As different as the districts were from one another with respect to culture, ethnic affiliations, tribal politics, and security, a common challenge for ISAF coalition commanders was the integration of governance, reconstruction, and development efforts into security and counterinsurgency operations. For obvious reasons, most development and aid agencies preferred to conduct their activities in safe and secure areas. Most striking was the observation that even when their projects were in close proximity to ISAF security operations, nongovernment organizations, aid agencies, and the civilian cadre of PRTs preferred to keep their distance from ISAF military activities and were reluctant to align their efforts too closely, if at all, with ISAF security efforts. This uneasy relationship made an interesting challenge for ISAF insofar as successful COIN operations needed effective development and governance, and conversely, governance, reconstruction, and development were difficult to champion in unsecured areas. The challenge that persisted for ISAF was how to draw development and governance into security operations in some of the most unsecured parts of the country. The one critical activity that was common to all missions and operations, without exception, was provided by ISAF's air component element.

ISAF's counterinsurgency formula was championed through General McKiernan's tactical directive and COIN guidance documents. It was characterized as a simple yet visionary approach which was designed to draw security, governance, reconstruction, and development stakeholders together. Based on the COIN formula of "shape-clear-hold-build" (SCHB), COMISAF's vision demanded that regional and task force commanders must include as part of their shaping and clearing operations, detailed and purposeful plans to *hold* the ground once it had been cleared and to then *build* and *develop* the communities through reconstruction and development programmes once the hold phase had been set in place. As enforced by General Tucker and myself through ISAF joint operations, task force shaping and clearing operations would not be approved unless they included well-planned and robust holding and building phases as part of the overall concept of operation. The SCHB formula was not meant to be a one-size-fits-all or a cookie-cutter approach to COIN operations, but was meant to provide a framework to guide task force commanders in designing their COIN missions. It was well understood by ISAF and regional commanders that each community was unique, and each village was different from the other village two valleys over. Accordingly, each COIN operation needed to be tailored to meet the unique exigencies of each community.

The shape phase would typically begin with a district development assessment, which was designed to define the counterinsurgency effort needed within a specific district area, including all follow-on reconstruction and development that would take place based on the expressed desires of the local population. This assessment identified the security and threat situation and the type and size of coalition force needed, which included both Afghan National Security Forces and ISAF, to separate insurgents from the population and to hold the ground once insurgents and criminal elements had been cleared from the area. Key to shaping was relationship building and connecting with village leaders, which took place through shuras (relationship-building meetings), and focused on winning the community's support for the upcoming SCHB operation. Through these shuras, village leaders would come to understand the manner in which their community would benefit once the Taliban and criminal networks had been cleared from their villages. They would also learn how their community police force, which represented the first tier of local governance, would provide law enforcement, backed by nearby ANSF and ISAF forces if necessary to guarantee the safety of the community. Finally, local leaders would learn all about how humanitarian and development efforts, which were specifically tailored to meet the needs of their community and would commence as soon as the community was safe enough for aid workers, development agencies, and PRTs to begin their reconstruction and development projects.

Once the shaping phase was completed, the clearing phase would be initiated and would see ANSF and ISAF coalition forces conducting joint and combined military operations to clear and secure the village area. The clearing phase typically included route clearance, cordon and search, security check points, and the destruction of IEDs, weapons, and ammunition cashes. In an attempt to counter coalition force clearing efforts, the Taliban would employ its tactic of choice—the IED ambush with coordinated multiple firing positions. Sadly, these types of indiscriminate IED attacks injured, maimed, and killed far more civilians than coalition forces. But when faced with overwhelming coalition forces, insurgents would seldom take a conventional stand as they did during Operation Medusa, but instead would evade and run to their safe havens to avoid fighting and capture. The strategy of communicating coalition intentions and then arraying the coalition force was sometimes all that was necessary to clear insurgents from a community. Once insurgent strong points and firing positions were located and identified using surveillance and reconnaissance capabilities, the full repertoire of air effects and enablers would be applied to force an insurgent withdrawal. In the event of an insurgent attack, the ACE would be standing by to apply its entire lineup of advanced air effects and enablers. If force application would come into effect as a final decisive act, all while ensuring collateral-damage safe distances from civilian populations were respected. Once the cordon and search phase neared completion, the village would be cleared of insurgents and IEDs, which could take several weeks and sometimes months. The ANSF and ISAF would establish holding positions throughout the community, which also involved the new community police force taking control of law enforcement and neighborhood security activities in the village proper. As "clear" transitioned to "hold," large convoys of humanitarian aid would flow into the local area to deliver food, water, blankets, beds, medical supplies, cooking pots and utensils, power generators, small appliances, furniture, and other items that families might need. Community police would continue to carry out law enforcement and security operations in the village area while nearby ANSF and ISAF forces would remain ready to support holding operations, as required. It must be emphasized that the lines of operation in the SCHB often had significant overlap and would even see considerable concurrent activity rather than a sequential approach. Throughout the SCHB phases of the counterinsurgency effort, intelligence-led special and elite force operations and dynamic targeting missions would be applied as required to ensure insurgent leadership objectives were eliminated from the battlefield.

The build phase, which would commence as soon as possible following the establishment of a secure village area, would see concurrent ongoing holding operations and include projects related to the steady and dependable supply of clean water, local medical facilities, refurbishment or construction of religious centres and mosques, and establishment of new community police stations. It might be necessary to rebuild new sections of road to reconnect parts of the community. With shaping and clearing phases leading the COIN effort, it was important that the hold phase create a sense of safety and security for the community, and that any reemergence of insurgent activity was quickly countered by local community police and the ANSF, and, if necessary, ISAF coalition forces who remained part of the COIN from beginning to end. The local population had to know and understand that ANSF and ISAF coalition forces were there to stay and to support the community for as long it would take to deliver it back into the hands of the Afghan people.

A most celebrated and defining tipping point would occur when the local community would start to feel empowered to take security into its own hands and begin assisting in finding and turning in IEDs and signaling to local police when criminals and insurgents had reentered the community. The three lines of COIN—security, governance, and reconstruction and development—would then be methodically expanded to include larger-signature projects from the provincial and federal levels such as electric power production, schools and training facilities, hospitals, large-scale agriculture and irrigation projects, and major transportation projects. Other tipping points which indicated that security and development were having their intended effect included the opening of schools, the inclusion of girls in school programmes, and the meeting of community councils to discuss and plan local economic and security initiatives. When local trade and commerce finally returned to the shops, bazaars, and market places of villages and towns, nearby and outlying areas would begin to see what Afghan life could become in a safe and secure Taliban-free community.

The most critical aspect of the COIN effort is the ability to connect with the local community and to develop a relationship that leads to its participation in keeping insurgents and criminals separated from it. This relationship had to be nurtured and developed throughout each phase of the SCHB process until irreversible momentum was established. The greatest challenge for the Afghan government and ISAF was related to the training and fielding of sufficient police forces to effectively hold and secure local communities, and in drawing from the international community the civilian development teams and financial resources to directly support the COIN efforts at the village and community level. The Afghan government's local initiative in 2009 in Wardak Province just to the west of Kabul, known as the Afghan Public Protection Programme (AP3), saw unprecedented success in generating and deploying local community police forces to champion the hold phase of the COIN operations. It was anticipated at the time that similar efforts might emerge in other parts of the country.

COMISAF's COIN formula offered an approach to those commanders and national PRTs whose success in complex COIN operations remained out of reach. In the southern part of the country where one would find the home of Mullah Omar, the cradle of the Afghan Taliban insurgency, and the insurgency's agricultural centre for opium production, the situation remained stalemated after years of military operations. The lack of progress was due in part to the efforts of the Taliban in thwarting coalition progress, but was more the result of coalition forces too thinly spread over too large an area and conducting counterterrorism search-and-destroy operations in the same districts month after month and year after year without the resources to hold the ground or to build and develop the ground that had been cleared at the community level. Exacerbating this lack of progress in achieving the desired tipping points was the situation where millions of dollars of aid and development funding which had

been pumped into certain districts for several years by sponsor countries served to reinforce the dysfunctional situation where districts
dominated and controlled by the Taliban could receive and benefit
from national-level development projects even though security wors-
ened and IED and insurgent attacks escalated unabated. In many of
these areas, especially in and around Kandahar City, the four-year
period of 2005–09 saw each successive year 40 percent worse than the
previous year with respect to IEDs and insurgent attacks. Yet repeti-
tive military search, destroy, and disrupt efforts continued in the
same valleys and districts month after month and uncoordinated
with and disconnected from reconstruction and development activities, signature projects, and job-creation programmes.

Fortunately, successful COIN examples in other parts of the country offered solutions for those areas that remained stalemated. In areas
such as Sangin and Gareshk in Helmand Province, Tarin Kowt in Uruzgan, and all across Regional Command East, coalition forces were
successful in holding and developing Afghan villages and communities in the heartland of the Taliban insurgency. Although it was recognized that many of these areas were, in some cases, small microcosms
of successful governance, development, and reconstruction, the Afghans outside of these areas looking in, those right next door in the
neighboring district who continued to be dominated by the Taliban,
clearly saw how safe, secure, and prosperous a community could become once insurgents were separated from the population and aid
and development agencies were allowed to come in.

COMISAF's COIN academy at Camp Julian just outside of Kabul
was led by the US Army and well supported by the US Marines, the
British Army and Royal Marines, and the Australian Defence Force,
and highlighted to its apprentices the COIN strategies that worked
and those that didn't. Of note were two examples referred to as the
"Kandahar examples" that were touted as being how *not* to go about
COIN and development. In 2009, Canada's army was invited to attend ISAF's COIN academy in hopes that the experience might lead
Canada to start following COMISAF's tactical directive and COIN
guidance with respect to introducing counterinsurgency methodologies and practices in and around Kandahar City. Sadly, the commandant of the academy advised me that Canada had declined the invitation citing that the counterinsurgency approach, which they placed
under the umbrella of nation building, was not a mission practiced and
espoused by Canada's army.

COMISAF's COIN approach, which represented the collective wisdom and tried-and-tested best practices of those who had gone before, offered an approach where security, community development, and local governance stakeholders could successfully coordinate, synchronize, and focus their efforts in building irreversible momentum toward greater stability. Many villages, communities, and districts across Afghanistan achieved their tipping points and witnessed Afghans declaring that they did not want to go back to Taliban control. This irreversible momentum started with connecting with the local community;[11] it progressed to clearing, holding, and building, and then arrived at the tipping points where local villages felt empowered to take their future into their own hands. Local communities rejected Taliban insurgents when they started to believe that ISAF and Afghan security forces were there to stay and to guarantee their safety. Across RC-S, it became evident that clearing and holding operations would gain in frequency and intensity throughout 2009 and 2010 as the US Army deployed its combat brigade teams into the region. What was not so certain was the manner in which the UN's Assistance Mission Afghanistan and the international community would be able to rally their civilian cadre and financial resources to make "build and develop" a successful part of the COIN formula throughout the region.

Unexpected Change of Leadership

The sudden removal of General McKiernan as commander of ISAF and US Forces–Afghanistan in May 2009 shook the ISAF leadership cadre to its core. However, as discussed earlier, it truly was about the political goals and objectives of the *administration* of the day, which defines the timeline and milestones of military operations and campaigns, including the termination of the mission and the withdrawal of military forces regardless of conditions on the ground.

General McKiernan's visit to Washington in the spring of 2009 was intended to update the Pentagon and key US security officials on ISAF's way forward in the coming months and years. However, the president's security advisors were not happy with McKiernan's plan and perhaps the manner in which it was delivered. Shortly after his return to Kabul, General McKiernan was called by ADM Mike Mullen and asked to voluntarily step down. McKiernan's response was something like "you'll have to fire me if you're not happy with my leadership." Days later Admiral Mullen flew to Kabul to advise General McKiernan in person that he would be relieved of command. Not surprising, General McKiernan went back to Germany for a few days where his family was stationed and then returned to break the news to a small group at ISAF headquarters. It is difficult to describe the effect that this event had on the morale and esprit de corps of the leadership cadre at ISAF HQ and across the regional commands. The situation seemed to worsen when it was announced *why* General McKiernan was relieved and *why* Gen Stanley McChrystal had been appointed the new ISAF commander.

Across ISAF and Afghanistan, General McKiernan was regarded as a balanced, measured, and unpretentious military leader who understood the team he was leading, the country he was helping, and the enemy he was defeating. A very modest and humble gentleman, he was respectful and kind to most people but bristled at extreme views and never suffered fools gladly. He understood COIN and the Afghan people and rolled out a vision that was embraced by coalition and Afghan leaders without exception. For the first time in the ISAF mission, the coalition had a strategy that was not just working well, but was delivering results that exceeded expectations. Tragically, politics trumped military vision and brilliance. General McKiernan's timeline for success did not match the one the White House was demanding—to be out of Afghanistan sooner. Unwilling to accept a shorter timeline with more ambitious and perhaps unrealistic milestones, Washington saw Gen Stanley McChrystal as one who could deliver a US withdrawal sooner. Within hours of the announcement that McChrystal would replace McKiernan, sound bites started flowing out of Washington that indicted that the ISAF coalition was broken and the escalating CIVCAS events were symptomatic of what was wrong. The new ISAF commander's mantra became "we need to do things differently . . . and fast!" which undoubtedly pleased Washington security advisors.

Within hours of General McKiernan's departure, waves of colonels and generals started arriving at ISAF to commence work on General McChrystal's new strategy. The influx of new advisors, strategists, and action officers tripled the headquarters' headcount in a matter of days, and it was very quickly made known that they were on a short timeline to turn things around. Frustrating for those of us who had to keep the operation going in the midst of the turmoil and angst, the tsunami of new staff officers seemed oblivious to the fact that ISAF was in the middle of a force augmentation surge that involved the arrival and beddown of 21,000 combat troops and airmen and that the entire theatre of operation was focused on the Afghan national election that was only two months away. All this, plus the highest number of COIN operations that the command had seen to date, meant that there was plenty to keep the joint operations division and the ACE fully engaged and focused.

By the time General McChrystal arrived in Kabul, the HQ staff was well briefed on what the new commander wanted to achieve. The problem was that it didn't seem all that different from what was already taking place. On his third day on the ground, General Tucker and I, along with key members of the ISAF ACE, US ACCE, and joint operations team, went behind closed doors with General McChrystal in my office and stepped through the most important issues being shouldered by the command at the time. Briefing items included force augmentation efforts, the upcoming national election, counternarcotics missions, and many of the COIN operations that were ongoing at various locations across the country. The most difficult discussion point to cover that morning was related to CIVCAS and the approach being championed by ISAF. The message delivered to General McChrystal was one that his Washington staff had neglected to include, which was that CIVCAS was not a problem for ISAF conventional forces as it had been 6–12 months earlier but continued to challenge US special forces, who were responsible for 80 percent of the civilian casualties incurred in the previous 12-month period. We emphasized that General McKiernan's tactical directive and COIN guidance, which focused on the Afghan population instead of the enemy, combined with the ACE guidance and the "first with the truth, fast with the details" initiative, had been successful in addressing the CIVCAS problem for ISAF conventional forces. We also emphasized that the disciplined approach being employed by JTACs, FACs, and most ground commanders had dramatically reduced the number and intensity of airstrikes and kinetic events across the country, which had an astonishing positive effect on reducing the number of CIVCASs. Somewhat pleased with the CIVCAS news, General McChrystal soon thereafter directed that all land force operations that targeted insurgents in or near civilian compounds would be investigated in the same manner the ACE was investigating air kinetic events in close proximity to built-up and populated areas.

The agreement set in place by the Pentagon and the White House with General McChrystal as he took command of ISAF and US Forces–Afghanistan was that he would provide a 60-day assessment that would outline the changes that were needed to fix the ISAF coalition and to deliver on the president's timeline and milestones for withdrawal. A special working group was formed, which was led by General McChrystal's newly installed strategists and analysts and included support from the ISAF headquarters staff. Each division and group from within the HQ contributed members of its team to assist in carrying out a comprehensive analysis on how best to accomplish the ISAF mission in accordance with the direction that arrived in theatre with General McChrystal. Not surprising to the HQ staff that served under General McKiernan, the findings and recommendations of the working group reported that no significant changes were required other than ISAF needed additional coalition forces to shoulder COIN operations already set in place and that a significantly greater number of Afghan security forces needed to be trained faster. The working group's final assessment confirmed that the various strategies and approaches being championed by ISAF joint operations, ACE, and the chiefs of ISAF support and stability were not just working well, but were highly effective. No changes in strategy were required other than to train more Afghans faster.

To say that General McChrystal was very unhappy and frustrated with the findings and recommendations of his working group would be an understatement. As he took the stage in the ISAF theatre to address the assembled group of senior leaders immediately following the working group's presentation, the tension was palpable. He had been on the ground in Afghanistan for three months, and his 60-day assessment that Washington was waiting for was late. What he had just heard from his working group was not what he had been communicating since the removal of General McKiernan. As he stated to the group assembled in the ISAF theatre that afternoon, he needed something to fix, and he just needed to figure out what needed fixing. Much to the relief of the working group, the commander's 60-day assessment would focus on Afghan training. Perhaps the greatest change that emerged from the various assessments in the early days of General McChrystal's tenure was the deployment of V Corps from Germany to form a new operational-level joint command headquarters to manage the five regional commands.

Within months of General McChrystal's report arriving in Washington, ISAF started receiving additional forces, the new ISAF joint command took over NATO's base at Kabul International Airport and started commanding the regional commands, and the ISAF training command went into high gear with the ANSF to recruit and train new Afghan soldiers. General McChrystal continued to shape the ISAF coalition into something he felt more comfortable with, which included shutting down morale and welfare facilities, closing stores, kiosks, and restaurants on coalition bases, and banning the consumption of alcohol. A difficult conversation I had with General McChrystal's new command chief warrant officer was related to the importance of the Tim Hortons coffee and doughnut kiosk on the boardwalk in Kandahar, and the ball-hockey pad that was used extensively by Canadian soldiers and anyone else who dared pick up a hockey stick and strap on the pads in the 45° C (113° F) weather. Few other coalition partners understood the iconic importance of Tim Hortons coffee and doughnuts and ball hockey to Canadian morale. I actually invited the chief to a game of ball hockey and to experience the magic of a "Timmy's large double-double" (large coffee with two creams and two sugars), which seemed to have had its intended effect, as the kiosk was still open and doing great business when I left the theatre in November of 2009.

With respect to strategy and momentum, the vision that General McKiernan rolled out while he commanded the ISAF coalition continued to guide operations years after he departed. In the winter and spring of 2009, as we were championing the 21,000 force augmentation and building new bases and support facilities across the country, ISAF's joint operations team (ACE and ACCE included) and the regional commands were applying General McKiernan's COIN guidance and tactical directive as we went about planning COIN operations in almost every region and district of the country. Initiatives related to CIVCAS, force application strategies, and, perhaps most importantly, General McKiernan's COIN philosophy had been institutionalized, which allowed follow-on troops to arrive in theatre and start their COIN activities right from day one working off the same page as the previous rotation.

The game-changing strategies introduced by ISAF joint operations, ACE, and the CFACC's ACCE in the 2008–09 time frame were tailor-made for General McKiernan's COIN vision and strategy and allowed coalition forces to shape-clear-hold-build communities across Afghanistan while successfully separating, isolating, and containing insurgent forces. The new approach to force application saw a dramatic reduction in the frequency and intensity of airstrikes and air kinetic events, which had an astonishing positive effect on reducing civilian casualties.

End State

The commander's morning update brief in early 2009 often included headlines from all corners of the world and perspectives and views from national capitals on Afghanistan-related issues such as exit strategies, troop contributions, and timelines and milestones for mission success. To be expected, there was no shortage of observations from national spokespersons on how well their national campaign was progressing with respect to defeating the insurgency or winning the war on terror.

Interestingly, it was not as easy to find opinion editorials that spoke clearly on the goals and objectives of the current strategy or recognized established milestones against which progress was measured. Some opined that NATO's coalition force was in Afghanistan to kill insurgents and defeat the Taliban as quickly as possible while rebuilding as it fights. Others were more seized with trying to find a common purpose among the aid and development agencies—a purpose that would build consensus on development and governance and a coherent strategy for the allocation of human and financial resources. There were those, however, who understood that progress and mission success were condition-based; that governance, development, and reconstruction could be better achieved within a safe and secure environment; and that championing security and freedom of movement in key parts of the country was the much-needed nationwide effort that would allow the growth and development of the Afghan National Security Forces, Army, and Police so that someday, in the not too distant future, Afghans would be able to defend their own communities and guarantee a safe and secure environment for their citizens.

This had always been at the centre of ISAF's strategy—to hand over responsibility to Afghan authorities when their security forces were ready to take the lead and for ISAF to mentor the ANSF in General McKiernan's COIN formula so they would be able to continue the effort of separating and isolating the insurgency from their communities. As part of this strategy, and as articulated in early 2009, the Afghan National Army would need to grow quickly to 134,000 soldiers by 2011 with measured and steady growth in the years following. The Afghan National Police would need to reach 80,000 by 2010 and, with continued support from international partners and stakeholders, would also need to see steady growth. But in 2009, ISAF's strategy recognized that the ANSF needed time to grow and time to learn from the best in the business on how to conduct COIN operations against a fierce and determined Taliban insurgency. Without security, governance, development, and reconstruction would be difficult. What was required in the years ahead was the continued commitment of ISAF coalition nations to clear and hold the ground that had been shaped and to maintain security and freedom of movement across the country, which would allow aid agencies to continue their development work and the ANSF to develop and grow.

In October 2009, as I was nearing the end of my 12-month tour of duty, I saw many who stood ready to highlight what they perceived as ISAF's lack of progress and only a very few who kept a running tally on our successes and achievements. I kept my own running tally, which I often used to remind myself exactly what we had achieved. My 2009 list was not exhaustive but touched on areas that I thought important at that time, most notably:

- coalition security efforts had enabled millions of Afghan refugees to return to their country to seek a better life;

- 80 percent of Afghans had access to basic health care (as compared to 9 percent in 2003);

- more than 13,000 km of roads had been built, paved, and rehabilitated since 2003, which improved freedom of movement and economic prosperity for all Afghans;

- more than three million Afghans had benefited from clean water and sanitation projects;

- more than 15.5 million Afghans had registered to vote in the 2009 elections;

- women were able to appear in public, run for public office, go to school, and work as professionals in their own communities;

- thousands of markets and bazaars were open in hundreds of villages and towns across the country after ANSF and coalition forces successfully separated insurgents and criminals from the civilian population;

- public parks and soccer fields were being used for sporting and recreation activities instead of public executions by the Taliban; and

- perhaps most importantly, almost eight million children were attending school, compared to fewer than one million in 2001, and 35 percent were girls.

The accomplishments I've mentioned above, plus the successes achieved following my tour of duty, were only possible in secure and safe environments created by ISAF's counterinsurgency effort.

A Final Word

I had the privilege to serve my country in Afghanistan for almost 15 months, most of which was focused on trying to create a safer and more secure country for the Afghan people. During my time as a member of ISAF's senior leadership team in Kabul I gathered many solemn memories of the soldiers and civilians that were wounded and killed on my watch and the scores of insurgents and terrorists we were required to target and remove from the battlefield in order to protect coalition soldiers, civilian aid workers, and Afghan civilians. As I came to know, being so close to the loss of human life, regardless of what side of truth one may stand, helps to better understand oneself and to hold tight the values and beliefs that guide us through difficult and challenging times. Also revealed to me was how a mere 12 months on the ground in Afghanistan can add so many years to one's life as the transforming nature of command, leadership, and sacrifice acts as a refiner's fire to inspire insight, knowledge, and wisdom. Of special significance to me and those with whom I worked so closely was the manner in which we were able to shoulder Gen David McKiernan's visionary strategy and prove how air effects and enablers, when applied effectively and in well-structured and disciplined air-land integrated operations, could have such a transformational effect on ISAF's joint operations and its counterinsurgency mission across Afghanistan.

To all the families back home, from the 42 nations that made up our ISAF coalition who came to know the painful and heartbreaking experience of losing a member of their family while they served their country in a far off land, I can offer my personal assurance that those who served and those who made the ultimate sacrifice truly did make a difference that will have a lasting effect for the people of Afghanistan. And creating "a more secure Afghanistan" has contributed to safer environments elsewhere in the world including in our own neighbourhoods and communities back home. And I know most assuredly that all of our citizens who offered a silent prayer during the countless "moments-of-silence," who lined our "highway of heroes," who stood shoulder to shoulder on bridges and overpasses, standing at attention, saluting, and holding tightly our nation's flag as our fallen soldiers, sailors, and airmen made their final journey home— our citizens came forward to honour our wounded and fallen military members and their families, and to say "thank you, we deeply appreciate and respect, more than words can express, your dedication, commitment, and sacrifice." As I came to know, the Afghan people are a very proud, honourable, and grateful people who knew that we were there to help them stand tall against a formidable foe and to help deliver their villages, towns, and communities back into their eager and most capable hands.

Special Thanks

I would like to end my chapter by giving special thanks to Dr. Dag Henriksen of the Royal Norwegian Air Force Academy, Trondheim; Dr. Alan English of Queen's University, Kingston, Ontario; Dr. Randall Wakelam of the Royal Military College of Canada, Kingston, Ontario; and Dr. Daniel Mortensen of the US Air Force Research Institute, Montgomery, Alabama.

Notes

1. As noted, Canada had senior officers in the DCOM-Air organization in 2006 and during Operation Medusa who may have experienced the poor relationship with the US CFACC organization.

2. "Red card holder" refers to a national representative responsible for approving the employment of national assets and resources in a coalition theatre of operation.

Several NATO nations placed caveats on the employment of their national military assets to restrict participation.

3. Richard L. Kugler, Michael Baranick, and Hans Binnendijk, *Operation Anaconda: Lessons for Joint Operations* (Washington, DC: Center for Technology and National Security Policy, National Defense University, 2009), 24.

4. Multilateration—network of ground-based sensors able to detect the transponders of aircraft.

5. RPAs operate under visual flight rules (VFR), which means the principle rule for traffic deconfliction is based on "see and avoid." However, RPAs do not have the ability to scan the local airspace to visually detect and acquire nearby aircraft. Moreover, RPAs are extremely difficult to spot—especially micro-RPAs—by pilots flying fixed- and rotary-wing aircraft. The risk of collision between RPAs and manned aircraft increases dramatically due to the volume of aircraft, manned and unmanned, flying in such close proximity but unable to visually acquire each other.

6. The Manley Panel was a task force of bureaucrats and ex-politicians commissioned by the government of Canada in 2008 to review Canada's mission in Afghanistan and identify the conditions under which the mission could continue and the resources needed to support the mission. The task force was led by John Manley, former deputy prime minister of Canada. A significant observation made by the panel was the lack of heavy- and medium-lift helicopters.

7. Ibid.; and Kugler, Baranick, and Binnendijk, *Operation Anaconda.*

8. I should mention that in the interests of keeping this chapter to a reasonable size, much of the discussion in sections two and three represents a "wave-top pass" over a number of air-related topics. Consequently, I have saved specific details and information related to actual operational missions, events, and activities, especially special forces, dynamic targeting, and COIN missions, for other publications and presentations. I have also reserved the majority of my personal leadership, command, and coalition experiences to small-group public speaking engagements where I am able to tailor content and detail to meet the specific interests of the group.

9. David Kilcullen is the founding president and CEO of Caerus Associates LLC, a strategic design consultancy with a focus on the overlapping problems of conflict, climate change, energy, health, and governance. Dr. Kilcullen also serves as an advisor to NATO and a consultant to the US and allied governments, international institutions, industry, and NGOs on conflict and postconflict environments and the developing world. He is also an adjunct professor at the School of Advanced International Studies, Johns Hopkins University.

10. *Comms herding* refers to a technique where enemy-force communication frequencies and networks are disrupted to force the enemy to use a single frequency monitored and controlled by friendly forces. At exactly the right moment, the frequency can be shut down.

11. *Irreversible momentum* was a term used by General McKiernan to describe the positive progress achieved by coalition ground commanders.

Chapter 10

Airpower over Afghanistan: Observation and Adaptation for the COIN Fight

Lt Gen Stephen L. Hoog, USAF

US Central Command Deputy Combined Force Air Component Commander

July 2009–August 2010

I began my tour as DCFACC with a perspective already shaped by my previous experience from Iraq as the air component coordination element (ACCE) in Baghdad as well as commanding general of a coalition air force transition team in 2006–07. During that time I had the extraordinary opportunity to work with many superb airmen and watched when Gen David H. Petraeus replaced Gen George W. Casey Jr. as commander, Multinational Force Iraq (MNFI) in 2007. From the newly published COIN doctrine to the "surge," it was a time of adaptation as the United States and its allies sought to change the tone and vector of the conflict. As we look back, some would say the strategic die was cast—in Iraq as well as in Afghanistan—within the first 12–18 months. Historians will spend most of their time on the policy formulation, national objectives, and strategic implementation in both theaters. Decision points such as the removal of former Sunni government employees, the partition of Afghanistan into regional commands, the effectiveness of the two surges, and underlying causes and effects will be studied for years to come.

This chapter, however, focuses on pragmatic aspects of airpower in support of our national objectives and the interaction with our ground forces and coalition partners. It begins with an assessment of airpower's integration in the overall Afghanistan effort, including the growing impact of RPA operations across the theater. Then a review of command and control of air assets—both US and coalition—highlights the constraints that defined the overall construct. Subsequent sections illustrate various adaptations during the 2009–10 time frame, to include General McChrsytal's impact from the highest levels of command to frontline troops displaying "tactical patience." His renewed focus on reducing civilian casualties set a new standard for operations across Afghanistan in which the air component made several significant changes to normal CAS procedures. Adaptations in both airlift and ISR provide examples of evolving capabilities and how sometimes as airmen we can do everything right but still get "dinged" by failing at the "optical level" in the joint fight. Finally, a quick discussion highlights some key evolutions of the theater air control system.

Many issues have clear parallels in Iraq and Afghanistan. In a sense it was encouraging to see how many problems from Iraq had been addressed during my two years stateside between AOR tours, yet disheartening to see that some of the same issues remained unresolved. In what has become the longest war in US history, the main effort clearly came through the use of ground forces along with a much greater use of the whole-of-government approach. It is my conviction, however, that airpower played an essential role across both theaters and influenced more aspects of the overall campaign than is commonly understood.

The Role of Airpower

When the local ground commander can drive up to a village, have tea with the elders, order MQ-1 Predator surveillance of the area overnight, and then in the morning either draft a contract for a new water system or order the demolition of a particular house, it is clear that OEF in Afghanistan is a fundamentally different kind of war. As the lines of operations came to be measured in terms of the population's security, hours of electricity, or number of operational schools, airpower's role evolved to meet the unique requirements of the theater. Ground commanders needed different tools to conduct operations, including the ability to expand their influence beyond the limits of available manpower. Provincial reconstruction teams represent a prime example of increasing our sphere of influence across the battlespace. The time and space challenge presented by having PRTs or SOF elements dispersed across the country is one key area where airpower was able to work in conjunction with ground forces to provide options for meeting joint force commander objectives.

First, we had to ensure we could work with these various teams if the situation required. Most forces were set in positions that allowed mutual support from nearby artillery or other forward operating bases. In addition, Army aviation assets, such as attack or scout helicopters, were positioned across the battlespace in large numbers wherever possible. Troop insertion was a combination of ground and air, depending on the range and terrain in the local area. Fixed-wing air operations were always an option—and in some cases the only quick option due to distances across the battlespace.

In 2009–10, the average response time for a "troops in contact (TIC)" request for air to come to the rescue was about 10–12 minutes—a number I believe is down to about 8–10 minutes today. It is understood that airpower, whether fixed or rotary, has the ability to change the correlation of force in near real time in TIC situations. What perhaps is not as widely acknowledged is just how critical this quick change in correlation of force is in a widely dispersed COIN fight when commanders make risk decisions on troop locations and potential operations across the Afghanistan AOR.

Likewise, the continued advance of airborne ISR has changed the level of impact and awareness of the battlespace. Capability that used to be measured in photographic resolution is now measured by the number of full motion video (FMV) combat air patrols (CAP) we have providing constant overhead surveillance of key potential targets or preoperational ISR "soaking" to understand pattern of life. No amount of coverage can eliminate uncertainty across the battlespace, but with the available ISR from both organic resources and those tasked to cover the regions by the CAOC in accordance with ISAF priorities, commanders are better able to mitigate risk across their operating areas. This combination of increased ISR (from all sources) and rapid air capability fundamentally expanded the operational calculus across the Afghanistan AOR. Essentially, it expands the amount of battlespace a ground commander can potentially influence with available forces by not only increasing their survivability, but their overall effectiveness as well. Combine this with a superb MEDEVAC system, aerial delivery systems capable of resupplying remote outposts across the theater, and strike assets able to attack with precision—it equals enormous flexibility for JFCs.

This flexibility has essentially become assumed after years of operations and planning across Afghanistan. When asked how airpower influences strategy, my response is that it is a fundamental underpinning at the operational and tactical level. If you take overall airpower contributions off the table, the basic operational strategy employed in

Afghanistan—with the limitations of boots on the ground across a vast country—would not have been executable as designed. In short, airpower was an integral element of the campaign plan, and there is a fundamental assumption that it will just be there when needed.

However, a strategic second-order-effect issue inherent in the nature of airpower in wars like Afghanistan and Iraq has not been sufficiently discussed. If you interviewed Hamid Karzai about the use of airpower to fight insurgents in his nation, he would no doubt have a lot to say regarding the strengths and weaknesses of this particular military tool. But we often forget that, at the root level, foreign airpower over a nation represents a very visible sharing of national sovereignty. This perhaps seems an odd observation when we have so many ground troops throughout the country. However, airstrikes are probably the quintessential example of independent application of force or decision since direct control of airstrikes is not in the hands of the local government. This may seem like an obvious assertion, but in terms of influence and perception it is not. On the ground in Iraq or Afghanistan, our ground forces partner with local ground forces. They share facilities, go on exercises, and engage in firefights together. But when you look up into the sky, almost everything you see represents NATO or the United States of America. It is a daily noisy reminder of the sharing of sovereignty. When civilian casualties resulting from airstrikes are figured into that dynamic—even though significantly fewer than civilian casualties as a result of ground operations—it becomes a perceived issue. There is a certain mystique, or perhaps a feeling of helplessness, in being attacked from the air. The amount of ordnance coming from ground-based field artillery much exceeds that coming from aircraft. Yet air attack has a disproportionate impact on the perceived sovereignty of a nation like Afghanistan. We would be wise to remember that when applying this instrument of war. With the increasing debate concerning "drone" operations, this topic will only become more important in the future.

Air Command and Control

The C2 issues in Afghanistan are regularly discussed and debated in theater as well as in this book. On the air side, the debate often relates to a national mandate, authority, and construct of ISAF Air versus the US Combined Force Air Component Commander (CFACC) and the CENTCOM air component. Several key factors constrained or put practical limits on the various C2 arrangement options, but while often acknowledged, those factors seemed to be overlooked at times when specific staff planners sought to modify the structure to solve either real or perceived problems. The most basic difference between the NATO/ISAF mission and the OEF mission is that US forces had a specific mandate to conduct counterterrorism when necessary in support of US national objectives. US forces were conducting increasing counterterrorism and special operations in Afghanistan, and while the detailed shared intelligence data generated often spanned the ISAF mission, many unique objectives and targeting efforts became a US-only effort. This meant that from the boots on the ground, to the various dedicated ISR assets, to the rotary-wing and fixed-wing air capability overhead, all had to have a clear US chain of command to execute the counterterrorism mission in accordance with US national laws.

We had very specific rules of engagement and caveats in theater to ensure each nation's political boundaries were not breached. There were NATO/ISAF ROEs, US-only OEF ROEs, and often additional national caveats. Several nations had dedicated legal representation, as did the United States, located in the CAOC or downrange to ensure their forces were operating within their given mandates. There was a US lawyer on duty in the CAOC battle cab every day to help sort these things out. One enduring lesson from the CAOC is that having a legal team that understands not only the ROE, but also the inherent capabilities and limitations of your force quickly becomes a force multiplier. Given the increasing worldwide visibility of all military operations, especially airstrikes, having near-real-time legal review available is almost a requirement in a COIN environment. By understanding these aspects, a skilled lawyer can often provide options to meet the air commander's requirements while still conforming to national policy.

It is well known that ISAF often wanted to assume greater command responsibility for airpower in Afghanistan. What is often not communicated is that if ISAF were to receive what NATO calls "operational command," or OPCOM, of US air forces based in Afghanistan, those forces would not be able to work with US Special Forces conducting dedicated OEF missions. So when we scheduled an F-15E out of Bagram Air Base to support a US JTAC as part of the SOF mission, we needed to have operational control (OPCON) and a national chain of command to legally execute that mission. And that, by definition, took an ISAF-based C2 structure out of the hunt for our air assets. That does not mean that the same US F-15s could not take off the next morning to support a German PRT in the north, but it absolutely meant that German or Italian fighter aircraft could not take off to support a kinetic strike for a US SOF mission. So we needed to have a separate legal chain of authority at all times, and this dynamic drove the fundamental structure in command and control of air assets.

It is important to note that this does not mean we cannot have unity of effort during air operations; it just explains why ISAF Air could not assume OPCOM of those US air assets supporting the relatively large US SOF contribution in theater. As a practical matter, the unity of effort continued to improve during my tenure, building on the gains started before with greater cooperation between ISAF's DCOM-Air and the CFACC's CAOC team. Lt Gen Mike Hostage, the CFACC, built upon previous commanders' efforts across AFCENT and made it clear to all that our job was to support the ISAF commander's strategy within Afghanistan. We would develop the master air attack plan (MAAP) for CAS and JTARs trying to match the priorities given by the various regions and the DCOM-Air's weekly guidance. Relative weight of effort was shifted between various regions based on current operations and their priority within the theater as passed by the DCOM-Air. There was often debate on the various MAAP strategies: Do you optimize for number of JTARs supported or minimize CAS TIC reaction time? How do you best support remote PRT-type locations—with a long-endurance Reaper that could switch from ISR to kinetic attack quickly or several pairs of CAS assets nearby during key vulnerable periods? We had operations analysis teams studying the data to attempt to quantify the effectiveness of the various approaches. As always, even in this COIN fight with literally hundreds of hours of FMV, there were not enough assets to cover all the requests—the line had to be drawn somewhere.

Production of the daily ATO was a more contentious issue at times. There were those who thought we should have re-created a CAOC-like capability in Afghanistan to focus purely on that fight. Besides the obvious boots-on-the-ground limitations and potential impacts that were levied later in the campaign, from my point of view it would needlessly complicate a coordinated C2 structure for no gain in effectiveness of the overall campaign strategy. Ours was not a classic air campaign ATO where various enemy capabilities were targeted to achieve air superiority or execute an upcoming line of advance to move the fire support coordination line (FSCL) forward. There were no "air-only targets" to be struck. However, like all ATOs, this one started with logistics; the orchestration of assets from literally a half-dozen countries and a carrier battle group when combined with the air mobility division's (AMD) efforts presented a daily logistical and time/space challenge. With the ASOC forward in country to provide real-time prioritization of assets and the other liaison officers (LNO) embedded within each region, the CAOC ATO process did a more than reasonable job of executing the ISAF commander's intent. In effect, that was my primary job—as assigned by General Hostage—to ensure that the task of generating combat airpower met the ISAF commander's intent on a daily basis.

The *optical level* is simply a term I learned from one of the wing commanders in Afghanistan. It basically defines the difference between what was requested by the local commander (either ground or air) versus what was actually provided. Most of the time the air action provided matched very closely with requested effects, but on occasion we would miss the mark for a variety of reasons. Some examples include additional ROE constraints, theaterwide competing priorities, normal peacetime DOD airlift polices, and access to air planners across the ground force. While some of these can be particularly challenging in a COIN environment, they likely apply to higher-intensity conflicts as well in varying degrees.

We had to be there to understand the conditions in the local headquarters and interface quickly and accurately with the CAOC and AFFOR staffs to solve problems in advance and avoid a conflict in priorities. To be an effective advocate for airpower, you must be available. That is why the Air Force started early on putting the ACCEs forward to local headquarters within Iraq and Afghanistan. Someone has to be at the table representing the Air Force when decisions are being made. These officers should be readily available, know their stuff, and understand all aspects of airpower. If the Army ground commander calls at two o'clock in the morning to figure out how to get something done and your response is that you will have to contact the CDDOC for the C-130 or the AFFOR staff on a manning issue, by the third time they ask and can't get the answer straight from you, then you will have little value anymore, and they will seek their answers elsewhere.

On a larger scale, this became an issue with the ACCE construct. About halfway through my tenure as DCFACC, the ACCE evolved from a strictly liaison element into the 9th Air Expeditionary Task Force (AETF)–Afghanistan. Its commander, a two-star airman, now has limited OPCON/ADCON of the airmen in theater. This was a major change in the evolution of the ACCE construct. As the new CFACC, General Hostage made it clear to everyone that "whatever check the 9th AETF–Afghanistan commander writes, I will cash." We now had a two-star general at the table that could make decisions on behalf of the CFACC. It was a game-changer in terms of the relationships in theater. As a practical matter, for long-term steady-state operations, having an airman commander for all units in the AOR put us at the table at a peer level—face to face—with our counterparts. In the joint fight, an LNO—even at the general-officer level—does not compare to the commanders around the room. In addition, having a single commander for all airmen proved its worth time and time again, from routine ADCON issues to key support for various wings and groups across the Afghanistan AOR. The key issue is that TACON of the air assets still fell under the direction of the CFACC via the CAOC, just as our UK and other allies kept OPCON of their aircraft and personnel and made missions available via TACON and the ATO process. This represents the natural evolution of air operations with several separate supported commanders' joint operating agreements (JOA) across a COCOM. The question is not "if" to move beyond the ACCE construct, but "when" in our future sustained operations. At the "optical level," it made a big difference to the supported commanders in theater.

Commander's Impact—General McChrystal

I watched General McChrystal take over from General McKiernan in Afghanistan and stand up the new operational-level HQ. He received significant media attention and cast a certain narrative for transformative leadership during his time at ISAF. In my view, General McChrystal's work relied heavily on many of the same themes General McKiernan had put in place before him. Real change, such as the standup of ISAF Joint Command (IJC) HQ, which put a new focus on theaterwide coordination and priorities, was a significant evolution. Other initiatives, such as the effort to reduce civilian casualties, were based not just in changes to written guidance, but in the day-to-day forceful interaction between McChrystal and his commanders. As far as I know, most of the key CIVCAS rules that he issued were almost the same ones that McKiernan had in place before him. But from the CAOC view, McChrystal's emphasis on "tactical patience" and daily accountability was different.

A few months into his tenure, McChrystal changed the CIVCAS dynamic within his headquarters. In the middle of the morning update brief, he would interrupt and challenge the regional commander to justify the use of force in an operation if it resulted in a CIVCAS incident. He opted to do that in a public forum, with deliberate detailed questioning, and would challenge both US and NATO general officers in front of their peers. He held people accountable every day, and commanders started responding to it. For example, when RC-E was debriefed on why the local commander asked for a 500 lb. bomb to be put into a building on the outskirts of a village from which he was taking fire, McChrystal would ask, "Could you bypass the area? Was there another way to disengage or involve the local leadership in the attack decision to make sure you fully understood who lives in the house?" In short, the message to ground commanders was to continue the mission and defend their troops but consider overwhelming firepower only as a last-resort option. It was easy enough to tell the difference in firepower options between an enemy attack on a remote FOB or shots being fired in the middle of a small village. Simply put, General McChrystal's emphasis on tactical patience evolved the dynamics within ISAF headquarters.

Here is another small but key example related to battle damage assessment. The normal procedure was for the aircrew to pass initial BDA on the effect of the airstrike. One morning, in the middle of the battle update briefing, McChrystal said, "Stop. The aircrew does not do BDA." In effect, what the aircrew reports for BDA is interesting, but if there is a soldier on the ground, the BDA should come from the team that called in the strike. There was some controversy over this decision, since often ground commanders did not want to put their soldiers at additional risk doing BDA. But McChrystal pointed out that BDA is the ground commanders' business—especially in terms of CIVCAS. If they can do the BDA without excessive risk, then they should. If there are injured civilians, it is far better to provide aid (as they normally did with known civilian injuries) as best we can versus having the local villagers make claims after the fact. That callout in the morning battle update was a big deal. I know our forces did these things before, but his emphasis on the fact that BDA really needs to be validated by ground commanders in the COIN fight evolved their thought processes.

After a month or two in office, General McChrystal hosted a conference for his commanders and staff, and I attended on behalf of the CFACC. He brought along Greg Mortenson, author of the controversial book, *Three Cups of Tea*, which focused on his experiences and perspectives on this war from establishing schools across rural Afghanistan and his interaction with people and communities in the region.[1] The conversation covered a number of issues related to the region and how to succeed in our counterinsurgency effort. As you would expect, when the topic of airpower came up, it immediately turned to CIVCAS; General McChrystal wanted to know what the air component was doing to reduce the number of such events.

The technical solutions were straightforward: smaller and fewer weapons, delayed-impact fusing to reduce blast effects, almost exclusive use of PGMs, double-checked target coordinate generation, more use of ROVER downlink to verify target location, and so forth. Even with all of these efforts, we needed to share lessons quicker between our units—having them learn through shared success and, if necessary, mistakes across the theater. Therefore, in coordination with ISAF and the ACCE, we started having weekly video teleconferences (VTC) with every fixed-wing air unit that flew in Afghanistan. They were hosted by the CFACC, but ISAF Air and the ACCE were cohosts as we reviewed every kinetic drop from the week before. It quickly became a good example of close cooperation between the CFACC and ISAF. During these VTCs, and every time there had been a CIVCAS incident, our team asked three basic questions:

1. Did we hit what we were aiming at?

2. Did we hit what the ground commander wanted us to hit?

3. How did the joint team—air and ground—arrive at that strike decision?

These three questions became instrumental in identifying root causes for any CIVCAS incident at our level. Unfortunately, during my tenure we had a number of such incidents related to air attacks in various regions in Afghanistan. In one of these incidents, a ground commander requested an airstrike on two fuel trucks on a river bank, which resulted in up to 142 people killed or wounded, including a high number of civilians. Analyzing this incident through these three questions identified the weak point in this chain of events fairly quickly:

1. Did we hit what we were aiming at?

   Yes, the weapons hit the desired aim point and functioned properly.

2. Did we hit what the ground commander wanted us to hit?

   Yes, we hit two fuel trucks.

3. How did the joint team—air and ground—arrive at that strike decision?

   The decision to put 2,000 lb. bombs on fuel trucks was based primarily on the ROVER downlink feed and various reports received through local sources. What started as a clear military target—fuel trucks stolen by enemy forces with potential massing of forces—simply evolved over time into a much more complex situation. The local commander's assessment of perceived imminent threat did not measure up against the tactical patience standard General McChrystal was attempting to instill across his forces.

The pattern that emerged after reviewing these events and follow-on meetings was that the strike decision itself was sometimes the key link in the chain. We had the normal share of errant weapons and misguided bombs on the wrong aim point, but this was our first attempt at trying to address the strike decision as a stand-alone factor from the air side.

As we reviewed more CIVCAS incidents, the value of the normal joint air request net (JARN) process became obvious. We found that when the on-scene commander (OSC) requested an air attack, the request normally went through several layers of review to validate the original request. The requests are sent to the "joint fires" cell and then run through the battalion or RC headquarters, which asks several basic questions: Is there ISR that can provide imagery of the situation before we make a decision? Is there artillery that can take it out? Is there organic aviation available that can take it out? Can higher headquarters (HHQ) provide additional forces to change the overall threat to personnel? Personnel involved in this process are trained to quickly assess all these questions to analyze the situation and make careful deliberations on the best solution to the fire support problem. What we found when looking into this issue was that civilian casualties were more likely to happen in operations that did not have this system in place. The problem seemed to accumulate in situations when forces were operating semiautonomously; without the JARN process (and other support options to fall back on), the OSC was often left with the more binary kinetic options. Having the intermediate HHQ to filter, evaluate, prioritize, and validate air support requests offered value in reducing CIVCASs. After the "Kunduz airstrike,"[2] General McChrystal made the point that "if you are not comfortable with the situation as an aircrew—do not drop the bomb." To put it mildly, to suggest that the aircrew would question the ground commander's CAS decision was not particularly welcomed in either Army or Air Force circles. The airmen felt they often had insufficient information available to make the decision. Conversely, the ground commanders, who knew they were typically best positioned to make the call and wanted that responsibility, feared that airmen—wary of the potential confusion—would elect to not drop a bomb in fear of being accused of lacking "tactical patience," thereby further endangering soldiers on the ground. Despite the initial emotional response, the end result was that the aircrew became more of a partner in the team effort. Classic TIC situations or attacks on FOBs were relatively straightforward—deciding what weapons effect would best accomplish the mission while minimizing potential collateral damage. In other cases, timing of the strike request slowed down as the OSC explored other options. We eventually added a requirement to get the ground commander's initials prior to dropping any ordnance. Normally, this was only needed when ordnance was going to be delivered "danger close" to friendly troops. Many ground commanders chaffed with this new guidance, but with so many new sources of information—from ISR feeds, to national assets, to local village elders—McChrystal wanted that final "mental" review before executing an airstrike, because he correctly assessed that the unabated CIVCAS events could turn the tide of the strategic battle at the Afghan national level.

Beyond the JTAC

One thing that started to frustrate me more over time was a phrase I often heard within the Air Force: "Do not tell me how to do it; tell

me what effect you want to achieve." Many airmen were bristling because the ground guys were telling them *how* to do it, including requesting a specific type of aircraft. I could understand the frustration
on both sides of some of these exchanges. There are numerous examples of ground commanders not understanding the full second-
order effects of a specific request. Likewise, some air planners did not
fully appreciate the integration challenge facing ground commanders
as they sought to control effects across the whole-of-government approach—including kinetic and nonkinetic operations. On balance,
however, I felt the problem rested more within the lane of the airman
whose job it was to provide the insights and planning experience to
act as integral elements of the difficult COIN fight. As a result, when
I first came to the CAOC, I had a meeting with the key planners and
reviewed a brief history of COIN operations involving airpower over
the past nine years. My message was simple: if as airmen we did not
yet know how to use our tools of airpower to support the joint commander's COIN scheme of maneuver and convey that information
quickly with local ALOs, JTACs, and air planners—then we were the
core problem.

Part of this issue was simply because we took a while to expand our
skill sets when aligned with our ground forces. It was not until the
2005–06 time frame when we (the joint force) began adding ISR and
EW LNOs to augment the ALO team. Also, whom they worked for
and where they were located within a battalion, brigade, or division
evolved over time. To be clear, we have the best-trained JTACs, ALOs,
and AMLOs (now includes ISR and EW LNOs) in the world; but as
noted earlier, on the kinetic side most of that training begins with an
identified target. In similar fashion, once you move beyond the classic MAAP process, the typical training provided for our air planners
in the CAOC was based on high-end kinetic operations with moving
FSCLs—often not very relevant to an ISR saturation effort over a
small village prior to an upcoming key leader engagement meeting.
Local units (at the ASOC and ASOS level) were taking the lessons
they learned and sharing across the JTAC community. In addition,
the widespread fielding of joint fire observers (JFO) became another
evolution as they were integrated into the battlespace.

The 561st Joint Tactics Squadron was set up at Nellis AFB just a
year earlier to gather, capture, and share lessons between units, both
downrange and for specific Green Flag predeployment training for
combat aviation units. As this model expanded, it included our JTACs

and other airmen assigned to work in conjunction with ground forces capturing the most effective TTPs spread across our Air Force. The tactics developed needed to be included in mission planning, not simply used as a learning point after the fact. Air planners in this fight need to know how to do a nighttime helo insertion to conduct a clear-and-hold mission. They need to know how best to execute an ISR saturation effort with push-to-talk "herding" and exploitation/denial to offer solutions in the planning process versus being added on to the mission after the fact. They cannot simply apply conventional Air Force targeting processes to the COIN fight.

To illustrate just the electronic warfare side: if the insurgents were prone to using the old push-to-talk radio in a certain regional command, what do you do when it is time for the air assault? Do you jam them or do you listen to them? Do you listen to them up to a point, then jam them electronically during the assault, and then stop the electronic jamming to try and triangulate them? What is your best tactic for EW effects to do an air insertion into an insurgent village? Where is this all written down? Does the ALO/EW LNO know how to do that, or is it the Army EW guy who does it? And what organic capabilities should we be partnered with for best effort? Can the EC-130 do that? Can the EA-6 do that? These are the questions we should know the answers to *before* they arrive and bring them into the planning process. If we are not at the table as equal partners during the planning stage, we should not be surprised when we are told "how to do it" after the fact. It might be tactical, in a sense, but I believe it is an enduring lesson on the operational level. After almost 10 years in Afghanistan, many of our airmen still knew more about taking down an SA-6 than working in conjunction with a ground commander to successfully execute a clear-and-hold mission. As an institution, we had a difficult time learning how to fight the war we were in and instead relied on the training we had to fight the war we had been trained to fight.

Evolving COIN ISR—Beyond F2T2EA

When the weight of effort started to swing to Afghanistan, a lot of the initial ISR and its 24-hour FMV went to the SOFs. The Army invested heavily in its own organic ISR platforms in theater, including modified C-12s, RQ-7 Shadows, Aerostats, "Gray Eagle" versions of the MQ-1, handheld RPVs, ROVER feeds, and others. Despite all of these assets, ISR was always in short supply in terms of requests versus available platforms for conventional forces. General McChrystal's senior intelligence commander published an article describing how the SOFs used ISR in their TTP of find, fix, finish, exploit, analyze, and disseminate (F3EAD). This became the "gold standard" of integration between operations and intel. SOFs were conducting operations at 10 o'clock at night in which they would *find, fix,* and *finish* a target; conduct real-time *exploitation*; and then quickly execute another operation two hours later while the information they had gathered was *analyzed* and *disseminated* into the various fusion centers.

This led to essentially two parallel universes in practical terms of ISR resources. The conventional force battalion commanders who were ordered to move a convoy from point A to point B were, in comparison, very limited beyond organic assets. They would put in a JTAR request in accordance with standard procedures but did not know whether their request would be filled until 12–24 hours before ATO execution. Meanwhile, SOFs received 24-hour Predator overwatch with dedicated F-15Es to support them as well as perhaps an EC-130 along with their organic assets. We all understand why SOFs received such a high priority for their operations, but as a result there are two significantly different tempos and levels of air integration. If you are the SOF commander with an MQ-1 ISR, F-15E, and EC-130 readily available in addition to the normal organic assets, your operation is fully integrated. But if you are the battalion commander who is moving a convoy, you need to decide what to do if your air request is denied or whether the air asset that is provided is adequate for your mission. True integration really does create dependency and vice versa. If the SOFs are denied certain capabilities, they will not perform their operation because their integration, procedures, and success depend on it. Conversely, if ground commanders cannot count on air capabilities, they are less likely to integrate them into their plans. The lower the assigned mission priority from HHQ, the lower the odds that nonorganic air capability would be allocated. This reality of available assets simply defines the left and right bounds of integration.

Gen McChrystal's intelligence commander did not simply allocate ISR assets proportionally to the various RC commanders or by national division. He implemented an ISR weight of effort and made sure that high-priority "named" operations received more ISR to do persistent network nodal analysis and intelligence preparation of the battlefield. It may sound trivial, as weighted efforts are not a new invention in military operations, but this was somewhat remarkable at the time. This decision, the real weighting of the ISR effort, was the perfect example of Kabul expanding its influence as an operational headquarters, allocating among the RC commanders who would get the most assets based on overall theater priority strategy.

One evening we received a regular request for air to support a TIC call. When ground commanders call a TIC, the first thing the USAF/coalition air forces do is fly as fast as possible to the "sound of the guns." When this particular request for air support arrived, we had an MQ-1 five minutes away and two F-16s 30 minutes away from the TIC location. Based on the timing response and the ASOC assessment of the situation, the CAOC retasked the MQ-1 Predator to support the troops on the ground involved in the TIC event. This caused the regional intelligence cell to "go through the roof" because the MQ-1 was on a very high-priority effort and the CAOC normally supported the intelligence cell (J2) for priorities. In classic staff fashion, a series of e-mails was launched, escalating up the chain and finding its way to my inbox in short order.

In the ensuing discussion, we showed them CENTCOM's priority list, which is clear on TICs being the number one priority in theater to protect soldiers' lives—thus the decision to retask the MQ-1. The regional G2 said, however, that was not our number one priority in this case. The G2 had been doing surveillance of high-level insurgents at a safe house for more than four days but now had lost contact and had to restart their efforts to locate this key target. He then noted, "And by the way, it was not a *real TIC* anyway." He described the situation as ground forces calling a TIC due to an IED event and said the ground commander called it a TIC because he wanted to get air overwatch quickly on the area to be sure there were no additional enemy forces around the scene—a logical request given the unknowns in the area. Since we are not in the business of determining whether a TIC is "real" or not, we asked if the regional joint operations center could make that distinction. In most regions the JOC knows if the OSC is taking incoming fire, if it is an IED explosion, or whether the OSC is simply not comfortable with the situation and is requesting additional air assets to deter potential attackers or gain SA. We realized we needed to partner to create more flexibility in the system and provide another level of request instead of the current binary TIC "yes or no" construct. After working with both the ISAF DCOM-Air and the ACCE in country, we established three distinct categories: TIC, priority, and normal JTAR support.

The first category was the regular TIC, which would have clear priority—one that airmen were not interested in getting into the business of "grading." The regional JOC floor normally knows what is going on and what other assets it can bring to bear. If it wants to move an MQ-1 Predator because troops are dying, it is going to make that move regardless of what the intelligence cell says are the priorities. We told the ground commander that, in a situation as described above, if he could afford to wait 15 minutes for a new set of fighters, he would have that option. He would then have a lot more firepower from the fixed-wings, and he would let the MQ-1 continue its mission, which could be of paramount importance. We needed CENTCOM approval for this procedure since it deviated from directed priorities, but CENTCOM understood the concept completely and approved it in short order. Now, the RC commanders on the JOC floor, through the normal ASOC process, had the ability to divert the nearest Predator or not, depending on the specific situation. This was a risk they assumed, and it was a risk they were willing to assume because they knew the situation on the ground better than anyone else.

The second category we created was the "priority," which soon became known as a "Pri." A Pri was a request for air overwatch. While the TIC was the 911 call for kinetic CAS, a Pri was in effect the 411 call for ISR overwatch support. A Pri could pull assets off a routine JTAR in situations where they were just orbiting in circumstances deemed of less importance by the ASOC in coordination with the JOC floor. The Pri was basically a request to increase a ground commander's own situational awareness—military forces have always sought the visibility the high ground provides. In the end, we made two key changes: (1) we basically acknowledged that the battlespace commander or regional commander's situational awareness was high enough to prioritize between TICs and critical ISR assets in the COIN fight, and it was his call to assume the risk if it took another 15–20 minutes to get bombs on target; and (2) we added another category called *Pri* that allowed commanders to ask for full motion video for SA without making it a TIC. This did not cost the Air Force much effort, and the results were significant. It was the regional commands who had to go through the agonizing prioritization of resources and move assets back and forth. As airmen, all we wanted was to be in the best possible place to affect the efforts and safety of troops on the ground.

The use of ISR in this manner speaks to the larger issue of cooperation between the current operations community (J3) and the intelligence community (J2)—or the J2-J3 seam. In my view, one aspect that really separates the SOFs from conventional forces is that within the SOF world, the J2 and J3 really become one element. In their world, intelligence drives operations—thus the evolution to the F3EAD construct. In the conventional battalion commander's world, logistics, local area engagement and patrolling, or simple partnering efforts tend to be much more forceful drivers of daily operations. The intelligence piece is not irrelevant but generally not as readily available in time or quantity to affect a plan of attack, as compared to the SOF world, unless planning a major named operation.

Airlift

Airlift is a fundamental part of any major military operation, and it was a critical part of our engagement in Afghanistan. Theaterwide airlift was another case where the Air Force executed a priority system that often generated heartburn at local unit levels. By the time OEF and OIF both became steady-state rotations of forces, it was clear to CENTCOM that it needed a way to balance between the two theaters—from "patch chart" rotations to unit R&R programs, airlift is always a scarce resource. It established the CENTCOM Deployment Distribution Operations Center (CDDOC). The CDDOC published the priorities for airlift across the theater and provided input with the CENTCOM J4 to US Transportation Command (TRANSCOM) on overall theater priorities.

The priorities for intratheater airlift, while logical and consistent, created some very real problems. Without revealing the priorities in detail, it should be clear that emergency supplies, ammunition, MEDEVAC, human remains, and unit rotations were high priorities. Priority number nine was "fresh fruits and vegetables," two places above the transport of one-star generals which was listed as priority number 11. The real issue, though, is that there was an inherent conflict between large-scale unit moves throughout the theater and the needs of regional commanders that might just be looking to move 75 soldiers effectively from one FOB to another. This dynamic between "efficient versus effective" is always present, and where you stand on the issue is usually related to where you sit. At the CDDOC level, tough decisions were being made daily to ensure redeployment dates (RDD) were met, while local commanders disappointed that their requests were not being answered clamored for better, more responsive support. The air mobility division in the COAC attempted to help alleviate this problem with channel missions (regularly flown routes between bases in country), but for a generation of ground officers the lesson came down to organic support as the preferred option; they just knew what they asked for and what they received. When you show them CENTCOM's priority list that says this is why they are not getting a C-130 for the next two days, they do not blame CENTCOM; they blame the airmen, because it is our effect to deliver and we are obviously not meeting it on the timeline requested. It is the quintessential "optical level of war" example where the airman can be meeting all the stats and RDDs while still leaving a company of soldiers stranded at an FOB for a week awaiting the right priority.

Our Air Force airlift system must operate as an enterprise with the efficiency needed to maximize movement across the theater and at the same time be flexible enough to support critical requirements that may not rack and stack within the normal priority framework. One of the approaches we tried to meet this demand was something we called "priority 3B." We worked with CENTCOM and the CDDOC to create a new priority within the current allocation system high enough that it became the highest priority after emergency, ammunition, human remains, and MEDEVAC, and would be supported in the next lift cycle. Gen McChrystal delegated the authority to pull that trigger to the commander of IJC, Lt Gen David M. Rodriguez. This meant he could access a C-130 outside of the normal CENTCOM priority process if the HQ really needed it. Giving the ground forces the ability to reach out and touch a movement and make it a priority fundamentally changed, but did not completely eliminate, the friction between the Army and the Air Force on this issue. Leaders from all services understand logistics and the opportunity cost of shifting a C-130 from the intratheater support flow into a dedicated mission set. As expected, it was used very judiciously since commanders understood the downstream impact cost on other theater movement requirements.

About the same time, Iraq started a test case for what was known as the "C-130 direct support program." A C-130 detachment was placed on an Army-run FOB operating on an old Iraqi airfield to make up for departing CH-47 helicopters. Sorties were flown in accordance with the local Army division's priorities according to a memorandum of understanding (MOU) established between the USAF and US Army at very senior levels. It normally made any left-over space on the aircraft available to cargo waiting to be moved by the normal theaterwide system. As you would expect, the program was viewed as a success by the local division commander—but at the theater level, the relative utilization of the airframe was not as high as those used elsewhere in the system. It was, however, close enough to justify the success of the overall program. As I shared with the division commander, a friend of mine from previous tours, the only way to fail this test was to leave the aircraft sitting on the ground tied to one particular commander or mission set. You really can't surge just airlift; it is the steady day-to-day efficiency over time that makes airlift effective for the JFC. Everything else becomes a tradeoff where competing priorities must be weighed accordingly. This concept is still being discussed between the services and may be useful in future conflicts.

In 2006, Gen David Petraeus was trying to get a number of foreign bankers to fly to Baghdad to discuss opening banks as part of the comprehensive approach to getting Iraq back on its feet. I had to inform the general that we needed to get the State Department to put in a request so that the DOD could get the needed authorization to transport foreign nationals on a DOD airplane without a senior military escort. Needless to say, the general was unimpressed by this answer. His staff just called the Japanese air force and asked if it could take on these passengers, which it had no problem doing immediately to support the meeting in Baghdad. That is a basic example, impacting the highest-ranking commander, where the Air Force was viewed as inflexible and incapable of meeting his demands. We later fixed this issue, but the fact that three years into the war I needed a waiver to transport foreign nationals is hard to understand, and that is why the Air Force sometimes comes with baggage. The USAF reliance on procedures and regulations has led other services to question its ability to cut through red tape and enable practical solutions to practical problems on the tactical level. As airmen it is our responsibility to clear out procedures and devise an organization to facilitate these needs. At the optical level of war, we could not bring those international bankers to Baghdad in a timely fashion, yet the Japanese air force could with relative ease.

Over time the planners within the AMD developed predictable channel missions for routine movement within the AOR. They perfected the "multidrop" C-17 airdrop mission that supported several FOBs on a single sortie, maximizing the amount of supplies that could be delivered on a single mission. The medical system was able to move wounded patients from the AOR to Germany and then to the United States with incredible speed and responsiveness. The new 3B priority, and later both C-130 direct support and SOF-allocated C-130 missions, all attempted to meet the needs of the local commander in terms of responsiveness as well as the overall theater commander force-rotation requirements. In terms of adaptation and evolution, the airlift accomplishments in Iraq and Afghanistan are extraordinary. Theater airlift and airdrop have probably evolved similarly, if not more, than the close air support aspect in this fight.

Conclusion

Airpower is a fundamental part of operations in Afghanistan, integrated into every decision, scheme of maneuver, intelligence-gathering effort, and attack plan. It is available 24/7/365 and provides rapid response, surgical strike, MEDEVAC, resupply, and critical airlift, giving the theater commander operational flexibility rarely enjoyed in previous conflicts. We have continued to evolve as a service with respect to the use of airpower as an integral partner in the joint effort, and while we have made significant strides, often TTP changes came too slowly in the early stages. One of my previous commanders used to say, "It is what you learn after you know it all that counts." As airmen we use terms such as *innovation, flexibility*, and *adaptation*—it all boils down to creating a learning organization that can change not only from top-down directives, but from bottom-up resourcefulness, as airmen figure out how to get the job done.

That learning was critical to our operations and success over the past few years. Changes to command arrangements within the theater had a direct impact on Air Force–sister service component relations. Likewise, focus on CIVCAS and commanders' priorities led to not only modifications of our JARN and CAOC procedures, but also changes in how to integrate and use available 24/7 ISR in new ways across the battlespace. On balance, however, adaptation was slower than it should have been for all the service components in both Iraq and Afghanistan. The major rewrite of ground COIN doctrine is a case in point—institutions produced the new doctrine after the hard lessons of the first several years of conflict. At the tactical level, the learning spread quicker between units as they prepared for the next rotation. At the operational and strategic level, several rotations of leaders were required to generate the momentum for change outlined in the 2006 FM 3-24. When it was published, airpower was an afterthought added as a few pages in an appendix to the overall publication. Within our own service, the 561st Joint Tactics Squadron was stood up "out of hide" to meet the need to capture and share lessons with little higher-level institutional support. We now have a much more robust lessons-learned project being run at the Headquarters Air Force level. However, the challenge of bringing new ideas, equipment, and concepts to fruition will continue to exist in every fight, especially when it competes with the realities of the DOD programming and budgeting process.

As a service we need to advocate for the value of airpower, and educate those who have little or no knowledge of its potential—particularly those in predominantly ground-centric operations whose leadership may not be aware of the options that airpower brings to a joint fight. Each service component and associated forces have advantages and limitations. Airpower is often viewed as highly technological, impersonal, and distant. Those misperceptions can be twisted to negative effect if airpower is used without host nation support of its own air forces. Airpower advantages in a COIN environment can sometimes be misused in a campaign formulated to win "hearts and minds" because that type of campaign is so difficult, especially if not applied with the insights of airmen.

We must also be willing to challenge some of our most fundamental operational command and control assumptions. We have learned in Afghanistan, through ever-increasing efforts to provide maximum effects, that centralized control and decentralized execution do not always provide the flexibility air commanders need. Today we talk in terms of centralized command, distributed control, and decentralized execution across the vast AORs that exist with the current COCOM construct. The creation of the AETF commander in Afghanistan is just one of many examples of this approach. At the same time, the lack of true joint organizations in both Iraq and Afghanistan sometimes contributed to a suboptimization of air that forced workarounds to traditional command relationships.

Finally, as airman we must constantly be aware of the *optical* level of airpower as it relates to mission accomplishment. There are mission sets and processes we need to continue to institutionalize in our Air Force; from TTPs, to organizational constructs, to equipment procurement, we need to keep certain key capabilities as we prepare for the next conflict. However, there is no doubt in my mind that our nation has learned some of the wrong lessons from the past 10 years of conflict. Prior to my departure, we started to see standard procedures from Iraq and Afghanistan being applied to other theater planning efforts that assumed air superiority was simply a given. On balance, airmen must understand the importance of their role in articulating both the value of airpower and what it can and can't do across the entire spectrum of conflict. However, we cannot hesitate in stating the requirements the Air Force will need to ensure that the next generation of joint warriors can operate in the battlespace with the same expectation of airpower effectiveness that the Air Force has provided for over 65 years. We simply have to get that part done right, done quickly, and done in partnership with our treaty allies. Everyone understands the force multiplier effect of the US Air Force—especially our potential adversaries.

Notes

1. Greg Mortenson and David Oliver Relin, *Three Cups of Tea: One Man's Mission to Promote Peace . . . One School at a Time* (New York: Penguin Books, 2007).

2. See, for example, Stephen Farrell and Richard A. Oppel Jr., "NATO Strike Magnifies Divide on Afghan War," *New York Times*, 4 September 2009, http://www.nytimes.com/2009/09/05/world/asia/05afghan.html?pagewanted=all.

Epilogue

Lt Col Dag Henriksen, PhD, RNoAF

Royal Norwegian Air Force Academy

The events of 11 September 2001 would not merely alter the dynamics of international and security politics—they would challenge how the United States and NATO approach war. The US Army and Marine Corps point out that counterinsurgency and irregular warfare were neglected in US military doctrine during the 30 years preceding the war in Afghanistan (and Iraq).[1] Former NATO secretary general Jaap de Hoop Scheffer notes in his foreword to this book: "In the early twenty-first century, NATO forces were not adequately prepared, trained, educated, and equipped to fight a counterinsurgency in mountainous Afghanistan. . . . It had taken years to change our mentality and international structures after the Cold War a decade earlier, and in many ways we were still in that transformational mode when the airplanes hit the Twin Towers and Pentagon." Now, more than a dozen years after the US-led war in Afghanistan started—and a decade after NATO assumed leadership of the ISAF operation—the time has come to address the larger lessons of this war as seen by the generals involved in the day-to-day processes and decisions.

The intent of this book is to describe and explain the actual use of military force in Afghanistan and the context and dynamics that influenced and governed this use of force. More specifically, the book seeks insight and understanding of the processes influencing the cohesion between political goals, military strategy, operational planning, and the actual tactical execution of airpower. The focus is on bringing forward the larger lessons, challenges, and dynamics related to the use of airpower in Afghanistan.

In retrospect, this has become a fascinating journey into the world of alliance/coalition warfare that stretches far beyond the often too narrow scope of airpower literature. For the informed reader, the lack of a clear overarching strategy in Afghanistan for almost the first decade of the war is hardly a surprise. Neither is the lack of cohesion often found at the operational level in terms of agreeing on a common approach in all regional commands and by all contributing nations. But rarely have these perspectives been put on paper with such detail, directly and personally, by a cadre of commanding generals who were intimately involved in these processes. One of the striking features of this book is how closely aligned the air commanders are in their views on this war. Although various challenges were addressed at different times in the evolution of the Afghan war, several common factors in the use of force recur, and I chose to structure this epilogue around these.

The Role of Strategy

The attack on Afghanistan commenced 7 October 2001—less than a month after the 9/11 attacks. As noted in the introduction, this book does not focus on the whys and hows of entering this war, on any normative evaluation of the wisdom behind the decision to go to war, or on the strategy chosen. But it is of interest to discuss the strategy and how it impacted the use of force in Afghanistan. In his memoirs, Pres. George W. Bush outlines the "war plan" for Afghanistan:

> Tommy's [Gen Tommy R. Franks, commander CENTCOM, 2000–03] war plan, later code-named Operation Enduring Freedom, included four phases. The first was to connect the Special Forces with the CIA teams to clear the way for conventional troops to follow. Next we would mount a massive air campaign to take out al Qaeda and Taliban targets, and conduct humanitarian airdrops to deliver relief to the Afghan people. The third phase called for ground troops from both America and coalition partners to enter the country and hunt down remaining Taliban and al Qaeda fighters. Finally, we would stabilize the country and help the Afghan people build a free society.[2]

President Bush describes a meeting in late September 2001 with General Franks, CIA director George Tenet, and a number of key advisors in which "I threw out a question to the team that had been on my mind: 'So, who's going to run the country?'" Perhaps indicative of the thought process at the time, he notes, "There was silence."[3] Looking back, the former US secretary of defense Robert M. Gates says, "I came to realize that in Afghanistan, as in Iraq, having decided to replace the regime, when it came to 'with what?,' the American government had no idea what to follow."[4] He added that "US goals in Afghanistan—a properly sized, competent Afghan national army and police, a working democracy with at least a minimally effective central government—were embarrassingly ambitious (and historically naïve) when compared to the meager human and financial resources committed to the task."[5] I refer to these anecdotes to illustrate a broader point: the challenges encountered in Afghanistan—in part—started with this approach to the war. Having a plan saying you will hunt down the enemy and build a free society without defining the ends, means, and ways to do so is hardly an adequate political objective and surely not a strategy.[6]

Evidence suggests that the multinational force operating in Afghanistan hardly shared a common vision set out by President Bush. In his chapter, General Willemse points out that

> in terms of strategy and a broader, more long-term focus on Afghanistan, I must admit all this was in its infancy in ISAF HQ at the time [2005–06]. . . . We simply did not have a pointed, commonly agreed upon, strategic document or outlook. . . . ISAF consisted of a number of PRTs that, more often than not, were controlled and driven by their respective nations rather than ISAF HQ, thus operating very autonomously instead of as part of a cohesive, long-term effort.

General Meulman similarly asserts that some two years later,

> the fundamental problem for ISAF in early 2007 was that there was no overarching political-military strategic plan for Afghanistan from which operational-tactical campaign plans could be derived. As the in-theater operational-strategic headquarters in Afghanistan, we simply had no long-term vision or focus. Operations were concluded without proper analyses of effects and/or how to build on the operations gains for more long-term stability. The operational tactical scope for ISAF HQ was only a couple of weeks instead of months or years. . . . During my tenure (2007–08), the PRTs were still largely nationally driven. The influence of ISAF HQ increased, but in essence, the guidance and ambitions within each PRT and its area of responsibility were mainly influenced by the nations.[7]

Major General Eikelboom argues that by late 2008, political and strategic cohesion was starting to surface in theater:

> The notion that the conflict gradually had developed into a counterinsurgency was slowly being realized in 2008. This was also evident in the political discussions in the North Atlantic Council. It was only after the so-called Initial Assessment of the new Commander ISAF, Gen Stanley A. McChrystal, in 2009, that the countries involved agreed on a counterinsurgency strategy. Because of this, the strategy in Afghanistan was unclear until the McChrystal period, and even after that there were discussions on how to execute such a strategy.[8]

Thus, ISAF consisted of a number of nations which had their own ambitions and agendas. On the ground in Afghanistan, the perception within ISAF HQ was that the PRTs were operating largely autonomously, receiving their guidance mainly from their respective nations, and that this, in turn, manifested itself in the way each PRT operated. For years, there seemed to be little cohesion at the political level but rather a number of nations with differing political ambitions—perhaps offering some validity to Lord Palmerston's often-paraphrased analysis of international politics: "Britain has no permanent friends, only permanent interests. And so it has been for all nations and alliances."[9]

The lack of sufficient political cohesion made it difficult to carve out a commonly agreed upon strategy for the endeavor, and as the generals cited above point out, there simply was no common strategic outlook. Rather, there were a number of individual differing strategies represented by each contributing nation. This resulted in a compartmentalized approach to the war and huge individual differences with regard to troop contributions, willingness to take risks, and how each opted to operate militarily. The lack of unified and adequate political goals and a clear unified strategy would mark this operation for most of the first decade—a situation that, to a large extent, logically excluded cohesion at the operational level and the actual tactical execution of force. What was supposed to be collectively achieved, and who de facto was giving the orders? Or as Prof. Colin S. Gray sums up the efforts in Iraq and Afghanistan: "strategic function requires a purposeful, mutually enabling marriage among (political) ends, (strategic) ways, and (military and extramilitary) means. When the political ends are absent, unclear, or flatly contradictory, strategy worthy of the name is impossible, and one is reduced to an effort comprising tactics alone."[10]

The lack of a clear strategy in Afghanistan might arguably be linked to a broader problem related to the term itself, its use, and how one approaches war more generally. In a highly recommendable article, "The Lost Meaning of Strategy," Prof. Hew Strachan points out that the word *strategy* has acquired a universality which has robbed it of its meaning and left only banalities.[11] Governments have a "strategy" to tackle housing problems, advertising companies have a "strategy" to sell cosmetics or clothes, and business schools have business "strategies," and so forth. He argues that the term *strategy* "is about war and its conduct, and if we abandon it we surrender the tool that helps us to define war, to shape it and to understand it." The state therefore has an interest in reappropriating the control and direction of war: "That is the purpose of strategy. Strategy is designed to make war usable by the state, so that it can, if need be, use force to fulfill its political objectives."[12] Strachan further argues that today's wars are not like the two world wars, whose scale sparked notions of grand strategy with grand ideas that helped tackle significant problems. Rather, loosely applied concepts today rob more localized wars of both scale and definition:

> The "war on terror" is a case in point. In its understandable shock after 9/11, America maximized the problem, both in terms of the original attack (which could have been treated as a crime, not a war) and in terms of the responses required to deal with the subsequent threat. The United States failed to relate means to aims (in a military sense) and to objectives (in a political sense). It abandoned strategy.[13]

The strategic thinking on the war in Afghanistan was, of course, not illuminated by the war in Iraq, which consumed the lion's share of political and military attention, focus, and resources. Perhaps as candidly as their positions permitted, the US contributors to this book did not elaborate too much on the lack of strategy but merely said it was not entirely clear what the strategy was during their tenure and that it ended up being sort of a combination between "counterinsurgency" and "counterterrorism." For all practical purposes, this meant that for many years, they ended up doing some of both, and as Major General Holland points out in his chapter,

> the US strategy in Iraq and Afghanistan became twofold: one objective aiming to root out insurgents and terrorists in targeted counterterror operations was done largely by special forces and airpower, hence the rationale for Operation Enduring Freedom. The other arm of our strategy became counterinsurgency, which was a completely different approach. It demanded different qualities of our forces and the way they operated. While the former included very familiar elements that the organization was trained and equipped to do, the latter provided huge challenges to the way we normally operate. It took quite some time to understand that.

For NATO/ISAF, which did not sign on to the counterterrorism (OEF) part, there was little political will to collectively define this as a counterinsurgency and provide adequate resources to enable their forces to pursue such a mission. And even if they had, though now a more household concept in military circles, counterinsurgency was hardly a universal concept the first years of the Afghan operation. It was not as though this concept had been thought through and implemented in the organization set to handle this war. As General Willemse points out with regard to ISAF's ability to implement the counterinsurgency approach to the war in Afghanistan in 2005–06,

> In reality, most of what we did in terms of airpower was reactive and ad-hoc operations—we tried to handle problems as they arose. . . . Our mission could

hardly be qualified as "counterterrorism" or "counterinsurgency (COIN)." ISAF was there to assist the government of Afghanistan (GIRoA) with security and reconstruction, but there was far too little coordination and integration of other means of power to deserve a label anything close to COIN. And our focus and resources were certainly not designed to single out and chase al-Qaeda or other terrorists in a coordinated counterterrorism endeavor.

General Meulman asserts in a similar tone when reflecting on the status of the COIN approach during his 2007 tenure:

> Adding to this was the realization that the United States was somewhat pushing us into the counterinsurgency domain. It became obvious that the link between COMISAF and US CENTCOM was very strong and directly influenced the planning and execution of ISAF operations. . . . Suddenly, ISAF was going to conduct an all-out counterinsurgency (COIN) to "defeat the Insurgency." What did that mean? There was no discussion or elaborations on the content. . . . The only reference made was FM 3-24, a US field manual on counterinsurgency that had its origins in the US military experiences in Iraq. Although this field manual has received a lot of attention since, perhaps with the exception of many in the US contingent, hardly anyone in ISAF HQ was familiar with it.

And this was probably even worse for many of the individual nations contributing in the NATO/ISAF chain of command through PRTs. Most people involved knew that the war in Afghanistan was somehow related to, in President Bush's phrasing, "hunt[ing] down remaining Taliban and al Qaeda fighters" and "help[ing] the Afghan people build a free society," but how to do that was elusive to most people involved. What developed as the key vehicle to reach this loosely defined direction—counterinsurgency—was largely an unfamiliar concept with little cohesive or competence depth in theater.

Not until 2008–09 did NATO/ISAF appear to have a better operational grasp of the counterinsurgency concept throughout Afghanistan, which allowed for greater operational cohesion.[14] Several of the contributors point out that, contrary to public perception, the main change came under Gen David McKiernan and not Gen Stanley McChrystal. Rather, General McKiernan's thoughts on counterinsurgency were further developed and refined by General McChrystal. Somewhat ironically, when one finally managed to muster a more cohesive and substantiated emphasis on counterinsurgency, it coincided with the publicly announced decision to withdraw NATO/ISAF and US forces out of Afghanistan by 2014. By 2009–10, it became even clearer that the strategy was to hand over responsibility to the Afghans themselves.

And this should probably be the starting point for evaluating the cohesion among political goals, military strategy, operational planning, and the actual tactical execution of airpower. There was no commonly agreed upon strategy in Afghanistan until the Obama administration and NATO set a fixed timetable for withdrawal—a strategy centered on ensuring that the ANSF were capable of taking responsibility for the security of Afghanistan by the end of 2014.

The Challenges of Operational Cohesion

Without a clear strategy, operational cohesion was difficult to develop. Without adequate strategic guidance, what would the operational direction be? For years, nations appeared content with their individual contributions through their PRTs. The PRT construct ensured their desire for political control and risk management for their military forces. The numerous national "caveats" and often significant national influence made a difficult situation worse; what authority could ISAF HQ exert to influence the largely nationally driven PRTs? Similar structures were established for national contributions within the framework of ISAF's regional commands. General Meulman notes that operations performed by the respective national task forces within the various regional commands often had a predominantly *national* focus and perspective, and it is an open question how much influence ISAF really had in relation to the national perspectives in these operations.[15]

Adding to this problem was the division of Afghanistan into regional commands. Several generals say that for years Afghanistan in reality consisted of several operations with different foci, emphases, and modus operandi. Major General Holland notes in his chapter,

> It is important for the reader to know that by fall 2006, Afghanistan was not one cohesive theater of operations. It was one theater of operations in the east, one theater of operations in the south, and one theater of operations for the rest of the country.... Each of these two theaters [RC-E and RC-S] was organized differently, with different focuses and priorities. In effect, I felt as if I were cooperating and working with two separate and distinct theaters of operations within Afghanistan.

RC-E, driven by the US military, had a more heavy-handed military approach and was more influenced by the counterterrorism effort. Getting RC-E to adapt to a softer ISAF HQ counterinsurgency approach was a challenge. RC-S appeared to have its own take on counterinsurgency, and the relative calm in RC-Capital, RC-West, and RC-North largely allowed them to find their own, and often nationally driven, rhythm within the PRT framework.

The generals indicate that all of these factors—lack of a unified strategy, unilateral national emphasis on the PRT construct, the division of Afghanistan into regional commands with significant autonomy and lead nations in charge, a loosely defined concept (counterinsurgency) that had no universal acceptance, significant limitations in competence within ISAF HQ involving all of the new concepts governing the approach to this war (e.g., counterinsurgency, effects-based approach to operations, and comprehensive approach), lack of resources, and lack of public/political attention during years of televised havoc in Iraq—made the job of generating greater cohesion at the operational level in Afghanistan a Herculean task. Major General Holland describes the lack of cohesion during his tenure:

> To me it was obvious that there was a disconnect in the whole approach of defining a commonly agreed strategy that ensured a cohesive effort in theater. . . . The regional commands had huge leverage in terms of planning and executing combat operations, and with little strategic guidance, they devised their own. I [as DCFACC] was focused on getting the regional commanders to help *me* understand what *their* strategy was, because I felt that, from a tactical standpoint, I was supporting their strategy much more so than the ISAF strategy. There were some attempts to rectify this and have the regions adopt General Richard's vision, but these attempts were rare and inadequate. This resulted in some operations having a counterinsurgency focus and some a counterterrorism focus, and sometimes operations flew in the face of each other.

Adding to the list of problems with operational cohesion in Afghanistan was the military and politically contentious issue of who had "command of the air." When ISAF assumed command of RC-E on 5 October 2006, NATO and ISAF formally assumed the responsibility for the whole of Afghanistan. Other than special forces operations as part of the US-led Operation Enduring Freedom, this meant ISAF was responsible for ground operations in Afghanistan. The matter of who was responsible for air operations in Afghanistan was far more complicated. Should this be a NATO (ISAF) responsibility, or a US (US Air Forces Central) responsibility? With airpower as the number one killer of insurgents in Afghanistan, collateral damage having been a source of political friction for years, and NATO's competence and resources to assume responsibility for air operations in a conflict like Afghanistan being questioned, the issue of who directed and was responsible for air operations in Afghanistan had military and political ramifications that far exceeded this particular theater of war. This was very politically sensitive because NATO did not want to do offensive counterterrorism operations (i.e., OEF). As noted by General Willemse, there was not always a clear-cut or seamless distinction between ISAF and OEF missions: "If you participate in OEF before lunch and ISAF in the afternoon, it reduces the distinction between the operations—a distinction of significant political importance within many NATO countries."

From the USCENTAF perspective, Afghanistan was but one of several hotspots demanding attention. Of course Iraq had been predominant for years, but the Horn of Africa and other areas in CENTCOM's area of responsibility also demanded attention and resources. With centralized control–decentralized execution and unity of command as key formative concepts for organizing its airpower, US reluctance to apportion a large part of its air fleet under ISAF command and control is understandable. It would potentially decrease CENTCOM's flexibility and ability to allocate resources when needed within its AOR.

From ISAF's perspective, it too wanted centralized control–decentralized execution and unity of command within its AOR, which was limited to the Afghan theater of war. But orders from NATO's JFC Brunssum that the senior airman in ISAF would be the NATO combined force air component commander (CFACC) became a difficult balancing act when NATO did not provide adequate resources to support this ambition. Thus, heavy dependence on the USCENTAF hardly matched the desire for centralized control and unity of command within ISAF.

The relationship between ISAF Air and USCENTAF was off to a difficult start immediately after ISAF assumed responsibility for the whole of Afghanistan. Particularly, Operation Medusa in late summer 2006 identified shortcomings that would influence the level of trust between the two organizations. NATO's largest-ever combat operation at the time, according to General Sullivan, proved to be a tragic military failure that involved crude and unsophisticated operations conducted in RC-S and the lack of basic competence and expertise in airpower and air-land integration methods and practices. By late 2006, the command tension between ISAF Air and USCENTAF had deteriorated to a level of personal and institutional distrust. The incoming ISAF DCOM-Air after Operation Medusa, Maj Gen Freek Meulman, argues that Operation Medusa presented a number of shortcomings at ISAF's tactical and operational level, which in turn produced increased strain on an already "troubled" relationship between ISAF and USCENTAF.

The friction between ISAF Air and CENTAF would continue for years. In principle, this issue was never entirely solved, but the procedures, cooperation, and infrastructure were gradually built to provide ISAF more influence. By 2009, the war in Iraq had wound down, huge US resources were reallocated to Afghanistan, and the establishment of the ISAF Joint Command (IJC) further developed the operational cohesion in theater. The US influence on the air side within the ISAF framework became very significant, which certainly helped ease the tension between ISAF and USCENTAF. It was to become a largely US-dominated endeavor that reflected the US resource contribution in theater.

The question of who controls the air is militarily and politically of great significance in any war. For NATO and the United States, the experiences in Afghanistan became particularly troubled, and there is an open question whether NATO nations' political control of air operations were sufficient. The United States has enormous air resources and has gradually built a command and control infrastructure and competence that separate it from other NATO nations by a wide margin. According to General Willemse, the air resources and the operational experience of US air officers are often so overwhelming compared to their allied partners that over the years one has come to rely on them as a basis for almost any NATO military operation. He says the command and control relationship was a "marriage of necessity" or of "realpolitik" rather than an optimal command relationship for NATO, and that the communication relationship between ISAF Air and USCENTAF started out as that of a "mosquito and an elephant."

There is little evidence that this balance will change significantly in the years to come, and NATO should be prepared to face this dilemma once again: either provide air resources and build competence that enables it to assume the command responsibilities of a CFACC, or, if not willing or able to provide this, accept US dominance. In Afghanistan, from a military point of view under those particular circumstances, that would logically include a US CFACC, as argued by the USCENTAF from the outset.

Another contentious issue that reduced operational cohesion was the inadequate joint focus at the operational level in theater. If there is one thing the air commanders agree on—although with different degrees of emphasis and frustration—it is that the war in Afghanistan has been a very land-centric campaign. For a counterinsurgency operation to have a particular emphasis on land operations is natural. What the air commanders contributing to this book argue is that even in a land-centric campaign, one should orchestrate all instruments in a manner that, to the largest extent possible, allows the orchestra to play as one, using the strengths of each individual instrument. If one instead orders one instrument to support another instrument without asking the musician how his or her instrument best can contribute to the collective effort, and, indeed, for years is unable to determine what melody to play—or that various segments of the orchestra play different melodies—the orchestra's cohesion and musical output would leave a great deal to be desired. Based on the cohesive feedback from the air commanders, there seem to be two factors of particular importance that need to be discussed in the years to come.

First is what too often appeared to be an almost fundamental lack of "jointness" in the operational approach to the challenges in Afghanistan. It appeared as if the approach to Afghanistan lacked the fundamental dialogue necessary to facilitate an adequate process to utilize the collective resources available. As noted, once it became a counterinsurgency operation, the fact that this operation would have a predominant role for land forces is logical and acknowledged by most observers, regardless of service or color of uniform. But this time the notion of ground supremacy seems to have become conventional wisdom to the point that it significantly reduced the collective output. It appeared to be generally accepted that airpower, at best, was a tactical instrument in support of land operations—so much so that one rarely managed to establish structures and a dialogue on how best to create a joint force that would utilize the best features of each service to collectively achieve optimal results. As late as in 2007, according to General Meulman, even the most basic fragmentary order planning did not always properly include airpower. The premise of ground supremacy dominated to the degree that a number of ground commanders openly argued for a return to the interwar debates of the 1920s and 1930s in terms of ground commanders having their own allocated aircraft/air forces. Notwithstanding the saddening incompetence in air-land planning displayed in Operation Anaconda

(2002) and Operation Medusa (2006), the most profound and disturbing problem seems to be the largely institutional lack of focus on a joint approach.

Secondly, this puts in question the professional education of officers. General Sullivan described a key lesson for the Canadian army after evaluating its level of training and education prior to Operation Medusa:

> As a result, the training of subsequent army ground commanders resulted in them "not knowing what they didn't know" when it came to the employment of critical effects and enablers in joint war-fighting scenarios. They thought that they were "full-up," "good-to-go," and doing a great job, which seemed to be the sentiment shared at all levels of leadership in the Canadian Army.

The fact that many of the ground units and officers involved did "not know what they didn't know" is hardly a problem isolated to ground forces. Surely, as contributing authors have noted, air force officers have similar challenges of not knowing what they do not know regarding land operations. But if the air commanders are right in their assessment that the sustained and prevailing culture was not a positive invitation to discuss how airpower—together with land and naval forces (carriers)—best could contribute to reach the overall objectives of the campaign but was rather an afterthought that needed to fight its way to even get a seat at the decision table, this indicates a fundamental organizational and educational flaw that is somewhat unacceptable. The logical basic reflex should be to gather all involved services, along with other representatives/sources of power, and have that discussion—and insist that it become a continuous dialogue. This would be the best tool available to ensure that all creative, innovative, and sound ideas on how best to utilize the collective resources become available to the decision makers. For years, according to the air commanders, staffs failed to facilitate this process in a robust and conscious manner, which is perhaps one of the key lessons to learn for future operations.

My final point regarding operational cohesion is related to the airpower community's historical tendency to gravitate toward the tactical level of war rather than operational and strategic thinking, and to what degree the airpower community manages to be a good learning organization on all levels of war. In other words, if you want influence on the operational and strategic levels of war, as in Afghanistan, you should establish structures that ensure your best men and women are trained, educated, and competent to assume influential joint positions.

In the fall of 2012, I attended a lecture by an appointed "mentor" of the US Air Force, retired general Michael C. Short. In front of several hundred students at the Air War College at Maxwell AFB, he expressed his concern that the US Air Force has gradually become less focused on strategy and the operational level of war. He feared that more than a decade in Iraq and Afghanistan has made it more prone to emphasizing the tactical level of war. Among other things, he pointed to what he perceived to be a "losing battle" in the joint community, where particularly the US Army appeared to be more influential, resulting in few important joint positions being held by Air Force officers. The same issue has been debated in the Royal Norwegian Air Force and other European air forces.

While the airpower community's lack of influence on the operational and strategic levels in Afghanistan may be rooted in external factors (as previously noted), there also seems to be a more structural problem within the airpower community and what many believe is a more general lack of enthusiasm for operational and strategic thinking. Prof. Dennis M. Drew argues that

> US airmen have long been known for their fascination with technology and the mental toughness required to press home a bombing attack against fierce resistance or to out-duel an enemy fighter. But they have never been known for their academic inquisitiveness, their devotion to the study of the art of war, or their contributions to the theory of airpower. Instead, American airmen have remained "doers" rather than introspective "thinkers."[16]

I should emphasize that although the quotation focuses on US airmen, there is, arguably, little evidence to support that other parts of the airpower community are much different. Surely it is the case for my own air force. In his recently published *History of Air Warfare*, Dr. John A. Olsen similarly sums up a key feature of the challenges facing the broader airpower community:

> Armed forces and their military institutions tend to concern themselves more with war fighting capabilities, such as weapons systems, high technology and firepower, than with the study of history. Consequently, when examining the enemy, they often concentrate on numeric orders of battle and the comparative performance of military equipment, rather than on exploring the complexities inherent in the nature of war. . . . Air Forces in particular confront an institutional challenge. Airmen are trained to get "bombs on target," and to do so effectively they must think in terms of improving the accuracy and destructive power of those bombs and the speed, range, instrumentation and maneuverability of aircraft. . . .

Perhaps for this reason, of all the military services, air forces, although brilliant at tactics, are probably the least intellectual, insisting as they so often do on technological answers to very complex problems.[17]

If the perspectives of Short, Drew, Olsen, and a number of other authors are true regarding the airpower community's preference for the tactical level of war,[18] they may offer a more structural answer as to why airpower's influence in a joint major combat operation (MCO) like Afghanistan was limited. Air force leaders are recruited from highly technological and specialized communities (historically, predominantly fighter or bomber communities) that often entail flying and being part of the tactical level for the first 20–25 years of one's career and thereafter commanding tactical units within the air force structure. The "academic inquisitiveness, . . . devotion to the study of the art of war, or their contributions to the theory of airpower" within these communities, to quote Dennis Drew, are very limited. Herein lies a structure that challenges the need to get early and sustained joint experience and an educational platform that enables one to compete for higher-level joint positions. And if the culture stimulates more narrow tactical competence and experience (many want to fly for as long as possible) rather than broad joint experience, there are logically fewer competent candidates for such positions, hence a structural "losing battle" in the joint community, as General Short points out. For the airpower community, it means one risks having less influence and fewer voices in the inner joint circles, which in turn might influence the perception of what airpower can and cannot do in any given context by people with limited knowledge of this particular military tool. Afghanistan might be a case in point.

This factor is closely linked to educational and military organizations being good learning institutions. The failure to adequately involve air planners in a joint venture like Operation Anaconda (2002) might be attributed to failures in pre-Afghanistan basic education. Although other nations were involved, the fact that a similar mistake occurred in Operation Medusa some four years later indicates institutional problems of implementing key lessons into the organization set to plan and conduct joint operations. A huge part of succeeding as a learning organization is related to the formalized education through basic training, military academies/colleges, and established structures *before* the crisis/war surfaces. But it also includes the various military organizations' ability to learn *during* operations—particularly in long-term operations like Afghanistan. Without giving any normative evaluation of the wisdom or influence of FM 3-24, I do think the following paragraph contains a certain element of wisdom: "the most important contribution of the manual is likely to be its role as a catalyst in the process of making the Army and Marine Corps more effectively learning organizations that are better able to adapt to the rapidly changing nature of modern counterinsurgency campaigns."[19] One question the airpower community should address is whether our competence as learning organizations also reflects our cultural preference for the tactical level of war.

The need to adapt and learn how to approach a counterinsurgency operation was a difficult process for the airpower community, which had an influential decade of high-profile conventional wars in Iraq (1991), Bosnia (1995), and Kosovo (1999) preceding the Afghan War. Former secretary of defense Robert M. Gates claims that "all the services regarded the counterinsurgency wars in Iraq and Afghanistan as unwelcome military aberrations. . . . The services all wanted to get back to training and equipping our forces for the kinds of conflicts in the future they had always planned for. . . . For the Air Force, [this meant] high-tech air-to-air combat and strategic bombing against major nation-states."[20] General Hoog argues along similar lines but also emphasizes that the formalized structures for identifying and implementing more-conceptual lessons at the operational and strategic levels are less robust:

> After almost 10 years in Afghanistan, many of our airmen still knew more about taking down an SA-6 than about supporting a ground commander's clear-and-hold mission. As an institution, we had a difficult time learning how to fight the war we were in, and instead relied on the training we had to fight the war we were trained for the decades prior. . . . On balance, however, adaptation was slower than it should have been for all services in both Iraq and Afghanistan. The major rewrite of ground COIN doctrine is a case in point—institutions produced the new doctrine after the hard lessons of the first several years of conflict. At the tactical level, the learning spread quicker between units as they prepared for the next rotation. At the operational and strategic level, several rotations of leaders were required to generate the momentum for change outlined eventually in the 2006 FM 3-24.

Generals Peck and Hoog describe an institutional process of evaluating and implementing procedures and equipment at the tactical level within the US Air Force that is impressive. There seem to be resources, a culture, and an institutionalized structure for identifying lessons, processing them, and implementing technology and procedures that provide important *tactical* contributions to the war effort. Generals Meulman and Holland describe a similar process with regard to JTACs within the ISAF chain of command in 2007. This should be identified and emphasized as an important strength that should be further nurtured and developed. Still, it is the balance between learning, adapting, and improving on all levels of war that in the end might provide the desired political results. General Peck makes an important observation: the bottom-up system for identifying, processing, and implementing lessons learned seemed to be in place in Afghanistan. A conceptual top-down identification and implementation of lessons from the strategic and operational levels was far less visible. Elaborating on this issue, he argues that the bottom-up approach is strong in terms of new tactics, techniques, procedures, and equipment (electronic warfare capabilities, targeting pods for nontraditional ISR, ROVER equipment, precision airdrops, and ISR/kinetic operations integration), while the top-down approach tends to be better resourced and institutionalized (e.g., logistical trail, technical orders, training, education). There is a complementary nature of the bottom-up and top-down approach that perhaps should be nurtured and better balanced in the future.[21]

Strengthening education and becoming a better learning organization on all levels of war is a strategic decision. It involves a fundamental question of how one sees oneself and who one aspires to be. Today, most NATO nations are experiencing reduced budgets and economic hardship. In times like these, some would like to cut down on education. And when pressed for resources, many will rally around the tactical training, where the distance between educational input and tactical output is the most identifiable. But perhaps what Afghanistan has really taught us is the need for understanding the nature of the war one embarks upon and the broader and more overarching competence to analyze how to link ends, ways, and means in a broad and comprehensive manner to meet political objectives in wars none of us are privileged to foresee today. Perhaps the airpower community, in particular, should evaluate its institutional ability to exert influence on all levels of war to ensure that the full potential of airpower—together with all sources of power—is better utilized in the years to come.

Cohesion between Political Goals, Military Strategy, Operational Planning, and the Tactical Execution of Airpower

Evaluating the cohesion among political goals, military strategy, operational planning, and the actual tactical execution of airpower is a complex endeavor. According to the air commanders intimately involved in this process, cohesion was far too limited during most of the first decade. There was little political unity on how to approach the war in Afghanistan before the Obama administration took office in January 2009. There was a general objective of eliminating Taliban/al-Qaeda operatives and helping Afghanistan to become a self-reliant actor on the international stage, but political cohesion appeared not to have advanced much farther than that—if that far. Politically, many nations were comfortable with the PRT construct that allowed each to contribute politically and militarily in a manner that suited its individual needs, even though they knew this compartmentalized approach was neither effects-based, comprehensive in its approach, nor an effective way of organizing the collective effort. The lack of political unity came with a lack of unified military strategy which otherwise could have created more clarity on how to link ends and means. And with the lack of political and strategic unity came a lack of cohesion on the operational level. Looking back on the period from the Bonn Conference and the establishment of ISAF in 2001/2002 until around 2009, the cohesion between political goals, military strategy, and operational planning left a great deal to be desired and created a situation that both militarily and in terms of a broader approach to the situation in Afghanistan was fragmented, insufficient, and inadequate.

This situation gradually improved from 2008 onward, with General McKiernan entering office as COMISAF, the war in Iraq winding down, and, particularly, US resources pouring into the Afghan theater. Once the decision was made to put the Afghans in charge of their own security by the end of 2014, political, strategic, and operational cohesion became clearly identifiable. Mentoring, greater security assistance, and "train, advise, assist" Afghan National Security Forces were broadly the name of the game. As NATO states on its website, "The aim is for Afghan forces to have full responsibility for security across the country by the end of 2014."[22] This timetable may not necessarily reflect the needs of Afghanistan, but it certainly coincided with many nations' desire to end a military mission that had lasted far longer than any had anticipated in 2001/2002. By now, the political patience was largely worn out. It was a strategy to end an operation that was experiencing decreasing political and public support.

There seems to have been greater cohesion at the tactical level. Ground commanders needed to move troops and supplies, they needed close air support, and they needed ISR. The dialogue between SOF, regular ground forces, and air forces produced innovative and creative solutions to surfacing problems. The response time for supporting a TIC was steadily reduced, and, perhaps particularly, the cooperation between SOF and various air assets was combined into a powerful tactical mix of detecting and capturing/killing Taliban and al-Qaeda leaders.

Still, the main challenge of the war in Afghanistan lay, arguably, less in refining the capture/kill chain and more within the realm of linking ends and means in a cohesive manner and at all levels of war to the broad array of problems associated with assisting the government of one of the poorest nations on Earth in getting on its feet and assuming responsibility for its own security. In other words, did the United States and its allies know the nature of the war in which they were engaged? Did they understand the enemy? Did they understand the complex dynamics at play in Afghanistan? Did they have the conceptual and intellectual tools within their military organizations to handle these complex dynamics?

With differing political goals and an inadequate strategy as a formative basis for this endeavor, the airpower community was dealt a poor hand—together with the other services—in handling the Afghan war. Even so, I have yet to hear a strong and influential voice within the airpower community explaining how airpower could have been better utilized to assist the counterinsurgency effort. One answer, of course, might be that airpower, as a supporting service, has been in effect optimized with regard to counterinsurgency operations in Afghanistan—there is little room for improvement. Or rather, it indicates that the airpower community has not devoted enough resources to producing influential strategic thinkers within the domain of counterinsurgency and irregular warfare. Lt Col William E. Pinter, director of the Strategy Division in AFCENT's combined air and space operations center in Qatar (2007–08), makes exactly this argument when evaluating the irregular warfare effort in Iraq and Afghanistan:

> US Air Force doctrine and theater command and control were designed to defeat conventional forces and field armies in MCO. To date, this has resulted in a series of numerous, often ad hoc innovations as Airmen make every effort to adapt. . . . This, for the most part, has been an adaptation out of tactical necessity rather than by operational or strategic design. The current outcome is a system that continually seeks improvement in tactical effectiveness at the margins while ignoring the potential for substantial improvements in tactical and operational effectiveness and even more dramatic improvements in efficiencies that a more comprehensive review could enable.[23]

In broad terms, it seems as if for years the main focus in Afghanistan became refining the system to find ever-improved tactical solutions to tactical problems, and yet again—to quote Dr. John Olsen—to be "brilliant at tactics . . . [but] insisting . . . on technological answers to very complex problems."[24]

How best to apply airpower has been debated for more than a century. Compared to the strategic thinking on how to use land forces or naval forces, that is a relatively short time period. The dominating focus on how to utilize airpower has been how to win high-intensity wars. Two dominating schools of thought have dominated this debate: (1) the *strategic airpower–centric school*, and (2) the *ground-centric school*. The strategic airpower–centric school argues that in contrast to the horrors of the trench warfare of World War I, the airplane offered the ability to reach the enemy heartland without confronting land and naval forces. Advocates of this school of thought argued that airpower should be applied primarily against the enemy's will and industrial capacity to fight and less against its ability to do so at the front. By analyzing the strengths and weaknesses of the enemy society, one could identify critical elements that if struck would reduce its will and/or strategic ability to wage war—be it the will of the people, vital infrastructure, key industrial nodes, or the leadership. This perspective has traditionally focused on airpower's ability to win wars, the ability to do so more quickly and cost-effectively than ground and naval forces, and the need for institutionalized independence for the Air Force. The second school of thought (the ground-centric) has seen the airplane as yet another technological achievement to support the more traditional concepts of land and naval warfare. Airpower should be used primarily against the enemy's fielded forces and thus support the land forces winning the battle on the ground.

The enemy's ability to wage war was eliminated and so was its ability to oppose the attacker's will, contributing to the military victory on the battlefield. This perspective has traditionally been rooted within the Army and Navy, which generally argue that while air superiority is important, closer organizational and doctrinal relationship with the Air Force in a more supporting role is preferable.[25]

One of the leading contemporary voices on military theory, Hew Strachan, argues that the principal contribution of new technology is to enable tactical and operational effects and this has been the key airpower contribution to warfare.[26] Strachan thereby places himself in the second school of thought, and according to the generals contributing to this book, his assessment seems to hold true if one isolates his argument and compares it to airpower's contribution to the war in Afghanistan. Still, Strachan points out that new technology historically—as in World War I or the impact of nuclear weapons—has shaped and determined what strategy to pursue. While classical strategic thought arguably has been shaped by a land-centric view of warfare—from Jomini and Clausewitz to Liddell Hart and Fuller—the invention of manned aircraft and rockets has triumphed over geography and changed the relationship between space and time, thus logically producing geopolitical effects of significance. Professor Strachan holds the RPV to represent the technology with the greatest contemporary capacity to produce strategic effect.[27]

I believe Strachan is right in claiming that classic strategic thinking has been predominantly a land-centric endeavor, and also that the history of warfare has shown that many of the hardline airpower zealots have oversold airpower's ability to unilaterally win wars. To be honest, I find that the debate on whether airpower—or any other service in modern war—can win wars alone contains an unhealthy mix of false premises (in war there is a combination of various sources of power that *might* generate the desired political objectives) and difficult empirical/methodological challenges. When Strachan says airpower's contribution to warfare has been the technology that enables tactical and operational effects, he speaks in past tense. He may well be right in that assertion. My argument is that looking backward for airpower's contribution during the first century of its use is an important but not exclusive methodical approach to analyze what contribution airpower can provide strategic thinking and wars in the future. Afghanistan might, perhaps, be a case in point. Evaluating airpower in Afghanistan might lead to the conclusion that airpower is merely a supporting tactical and operational enabler of effects. But if it is true that strategy in Afghanistan was flawed; that the cohesion of various sources of power was broken (if at all established); that for years airpower was never really invited to discuss the joint approach; that competence on counterinsurgency within ISAF Air and the USAF was almost nonexistent when the war started; that the USAF saw the wars in Iraq and Afghanistan as an unwelcome military aberration away from high-tech, air-to-air combat and strategic bombing against major nation-states; that the culture within the air forces of the world tend to over-focus on tactical competence versus strategic/conceptual thinking; that these air forces' flexibility as learning institutions is far less at the strategic/conceptual level than the tactical one—then the actual role and contribution of airpower in Afghanistan might be a poor indicator of its potential in the future.

The war in Afghanistan might have been unwinnable (acknowledging all the problematic limitations included in the term *winnable/ unwinnable*) regardless of whether a strategy of counterterrorism or counterinsurgency had been chosen from the outset. And instead of debating airpower's unilateral war-winning capacity, I would settle for a debate on how to establish a broad framework that better enables airpower to reach its full potential within the broad spectrum of conflicts and wars. More often than not, this will be in conjunction with other services (in various combinations), and part of a broader effort to exert political influence. Right now, it appears that the US (and NATO) appetite for large ground operations like Iraq and Afghanistan is limited, but history indicates one does not always choose the wars one wants. We might well see operations like Kosovo and Libya in the near future, where airpower is the dominating military component. Or perhaps, a new strategic context surfaces (like the fall of the Berlin Wall or 9/11) that requires new answers to new challenges. The airpower community should spend more time figuring out how its organization, culture, and focus can stimulate innovative and creative thinking on the operational and strategic level to provide these answers. There is an enormous military sphere of influence between the political and the tactical level, and the airpower community should acknowledge that it has not managed to establish structures to sufficiently exert influence within this sphere, and thus it has some soul-searching and important discussions to undertake following the war in Afghanistan. I hope that this book has made a small contribution to this end. In my view, Maj Gen Maury Forsyth illustrates the overarching challenge of the airpower community today, thus providing a suitable ending of this book, when he sums up his perspectives on the use of airpower in Afghanistan:

> Somewhat reluctantly I have to say that in a counterinsurgency fight such as Afghanistan, I believe we have tweaked the system on the margins in terms of accuracy and our ability to use technology for command and control to get coordinates, positions, and the timely information needed to conduct real-time precision engagements. But in terms of affecting the battlespace and the larger objectives of these wars, from an airman's perspective, I believe we have a way to go. We need to improve on the overall cohesion between political goals, military strategy, operational joint planning, and the tactical execution of airpower.

Notes

1. US Army and US Marine Corps, Field Manual 3-24 (Marine Corps Warfighting Publication 3-33.5), *Counterinsurgency*, 15 December 2006, vii, http://armypubs .army.mil/doctrine/DR_pubs/DR_a/pdf/fm3_24.pdf.

2. George W. Bush, *Decision Points* (New York: Crown Publishers, 2010), 194.

3. Ibid., 197.

4. Robert M. Gates, *Duty: Memoirs of a Secretary at War* (New York: Alfred A. Knopf, 2014), 336.

5. Ibid., 569.

6. For additional reading on strategy in Afghanistan, see Peter L. Bergen, *The Longest War: The Enduring Conflict between America and Al-Qaeda* (New York: Free Press, 2011); Jason Burke, *The 9/11 Wars* (New York and London: Allen Lane, Penguin Books, 2011); Sherard Cowper-Coles, *Cables from Kabul: The Inside Story of the West's Afghanistan Campaign* (New York: Harper Press, 2012); C. Christine Fair, "'Clear, Build, Hold, Transfer': Can Obama's Afghan Strategy Work?" *Asian Affairs: An American Review* 37, no. 3 (2010): 113–31; Hew Strachan, *The Direction of War: Contemporary Strategy in Historical Perspective* (Cambridge, UK: Cambridge University Press, 2013); and Bob Woodward, *Obama's Wars* (New York: Simon & Schuster, 2010).

7. Lt Gen Frederik Meulman, interview by author, 3 February 2012.

8. Jouke Eikelboom, e-mail to author, 28 April 2012.

9. Third Viscount Palmerston Henry John Temple, British Secretary of State for Foreign Affairs, 1830–34, 1835–41, and 1846–51.

10. Colin S. Gray, *Airpower for Strategic Effect* (Maxwell AFB, AL: Air University Press, 2012), 247.

11. Hew Strachan, "The Lost Meaning of Strategy," *Survival* 47, no. 3 (2005): 33–54.

12. Ibid., 49.

13. Ibid., 50.

14. This notion was also asserted by former US secretary of defense, Robert M. Gates in *Duty*, 569.

15. Frederik Meulman, e-mail to author, 3 April 2013.

16. Dennis M. Drew, "Air Theory, Air Force, and Low Intensity Conflict: A Short Journey to Confusion," in Phillip S. Meilinger, ed., *The Paths of Heaven: The Evolution of Airpower Theory* (Maxwell AFB, AL: Air University Press, 1997), 321.

17. John A. Olsen, *A History of Air Warfare* (Washington, DC: Potomac Books, 2010), xv–xvi.

18. See Carl H. Builder, *The Icarus Syndrome: The Role of Air Power Theory in the Evolution and Fate of the U.S. Air Force* (New Brunswick, NJ: Transaction Publishers, 1994).

19. US Army and US Marine Corps, Field Manual 3-24.

20. Gates, *Duty*, 118.

21. Allen G. Peck, e-mail to author, 1 May 2013.

22. "Inteqal: Transition to Afghan Lead," NATO homepage, April 2013, http://www.nato.int/cps/en/natolive/topics_87183.htm.

23. William E. Pinter, *Air-Ground Integration in the 21st Century: Improving Air Force Combat Capabilities and Theater Command and Control for Major Combat Operations and Irregular Warfare* (Maxwell AFB, AL: Air War College, Air University, 2009).

24. Olsen, *History of Air Warfare*, xv–xvi.

25. See Phillip S. Meilinger, "Introduction" and "Giulio Douhet and the Origins of Airpower Theory," James S. Corum, "Airpower Thought in Continental Europe between the Wars," and Peter R. Faber, "Interwar US Army Aviation and the Air Corps Tactical School: Incubators of American Airpower," in *Paths of Heaven*; David MacIsaac, "Voices from the Central Blue: The Airpower Theorists," in *Makers of Modern Strategy: From Machiavelli to the Nuclear Age*, ed. Peter Paret (Princeton, NJ: Princeton University Press, 1986), 624–47; Builder, *Icarus Syndrome*, 203–16; Gian P. Gentile, *How Effective Is Strategic Bombing? Lessons Learned from World War II to Kosovo* (New York: New York University Press, 2001), 1–32; Robert A. Pape, *Bombing to Win: Air Power and Coercion in War* (Ithaca, NY: Cornell University Press, 1996), 55–86, 314–31; and John A. Olsen, *Strategic Airpower in Desert Storm* (Portland, OR: Frank Cass, 2003), 65–72.

26. Strachan, *Direction of War*, 190–92.

27. Ibid.

Appendix

ISAF Commanders (COMISAF), 2005-10

Gen Ethem Erdaği, Turkey — February 2005–August 2005
Gen Mauro del Vecchio, Italy — August 2005–May 2006
Gen Sir David J. Richards, UK — May 2006–February 2007
Gen Dan K. McNeill, US — February 2007–June 2008
Gen David D. McKiernan, US — June 2008–June 2009
Gen Stanley A. McChrystal, US — June 2009–June 2010*
Gen David H. Petraeus, US — July 2010–July 2011

* ISAF deputy commander Lt Gen Sir Nick Parker assumed interim command 23 June–4 July 2010 following General McChrystal's resignation until Gen David H. Petraeus assumed command.

ISAF Deputy Commanders–Air (DCOM-Air)/Directors ACE, 2005-10

Maj Gen Jaap Willemse, Netherlands — August 2005–March 2006
Maj Gen Hans-Werner Ahrens, Germany — March 2006–August 2006
Maj Gen Angus Watt, Canada — August 2006–January 2007
Maj Gen Frederik Meulman, Netherlands — January 2007–February 2008
Maj Gen Jouke Eikelboom, Netherlands — February 2008–November 2008
Maj Gen Charles S. Sullivan, Canada — December 2008–November 2009
Maj Gen Jochen Both, Germany — November 2009–July 2010

USCENTCOM Combined Force Air Component Commanders (CFACC)

Lt Gen Walter E. Buchanan III — August 2003–February 2006
Lt Gen Gary L. North — February 2006–August 2009
Lt Gen Gilmary Michael Hostage III — August 2009–August 2011

USCENTCOM Deputy Combined Force Air Component Commanders (DCFACC)

Lt Gen Allen G. Peck — June 2005–June 2006
Lt Gen William L. Holland — June 2006–June 2007
Lt Gen Maurice H. Forsyth — June 2007–June 2008
Lt Gen Douglas L. Raaberg — June 2008–July 2009
Lt Gen Stephen L. Hoog — July 2009–August 2010

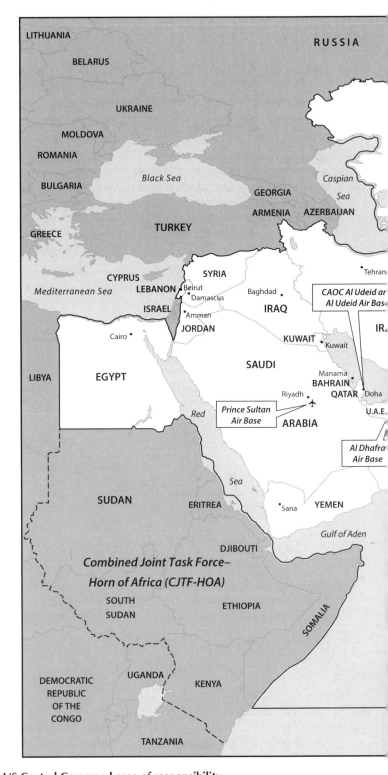

Figure 1. US Central Command area of responsibility
The map also shows the Combined Joint Task Force–Horn of Africa (CJTF-HOA),
which was part of CENTCOM's area of responsibility from 2002 until 2008. On
1 October 2008, the DOD transferred responsibility for Sudan, Eritrea, Ethiopia,

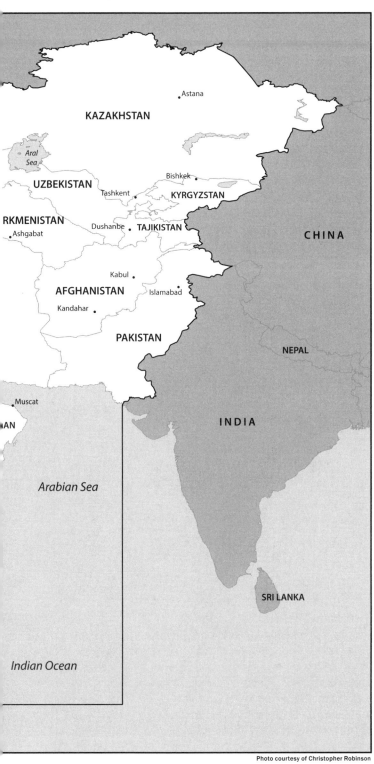

Djibouti, Kenya, and Somalia to the newly established US Africa Command. Egypt, home to Exercise Bright Star, the DOD's largest recurring military exercise, remains in the CENTCOM AOR. (USCENTCOM website, http://www. centcom.mil/area-of-responsibility-countries.)

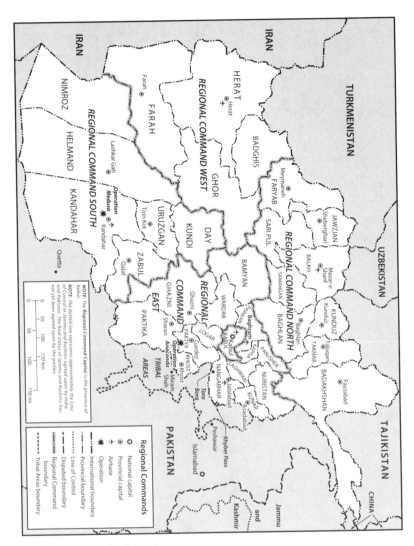

Figure 2. Map of Afghanistan

The map shows ISAF's regional commands and the Federally Administered Tribal Areas (FATA) inside Pakistan. Of particular interest for chapters 1 and 3 are the locations of PRT Maymaneh (Faryab), Operation Medusa (Kandahar), and Operation Anaconda (Paktia). Regional Command Southwest (RC-SW) is not indicated. In 2010, the provinces of Nimroz and Helmand were split off from the rest of RC-South's AOR to form the new RC-SW. RC-SW is omitted so that the map correlates with the situation described in the contributing generals' chapters. (ISAF website, http://www.isaf.nato.int/article/isaf-releases/regional-command-southwest-stands-up-in-afghanistan.html.)

U.S. Close Air Support Sorties 2004–2010

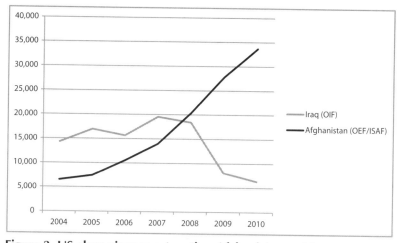

Figure 3. US close air support sorties, Afghanistan and Iraq, 2004–10
A sortie is defined as a flight of a military aircraft on a mission. Figure 3 shows the number of US sorties flown on CAS missions in Afghanistan and Iraq from 2004 to 2010, which for various reasons rose from roughly 7,400 in 2005 to almost 34,000 in 2010. This does not include sorties from other contributing nations. The purpose of providing these statistics is to show the general trend of the use of airpower in Afghanistan and to illustrate the stark increase in CAS and ISR starting in 2006. US airpower used in both OEF and ISAF is included, but non-US airpower in ISAF and OEF is not. This is clearly a limitation; however, unclassified ISAF numbers have proven too difficult to obtain. Still, with the United States providing the overwhelming majority of airpower in theater, the trends in theater should be well portrayed, and including non-US operations would likely increase those trends depicted in these statistics. The statistics provided come from three sources, all who claim their numbers are from USCENTCOM. These statistics are overlapping, as they show numbers from different periods. Some of the overlapping years do not have the same numbers, and the reason(s) for this lack of cohesion is not apparent. Still the differences are small and should prove unimportant in terms of showing the overarching trends in theater. Where diversions occurred, statistics were selected from the most recent source. (Data compiled from Anthony H. Cordesman, *US Airpower in Iraq and Afghanistan: 2004–2007* [Washington, DC: Center for Strategic and International Studies (CSIS), December 2007]; Cordesman and Marrisa Allison, *The U.S. Air War in Iraq, Afghanistan, and Pakistan* [Washington, DC: CSIS October 2010]; and Noam Shachtman, "Afghan Air War Hits 3-Year Low," *Wired.com*, 16 January 2012.)

U.S. Close Air Support Strikes (munitions dropped) 2004–2010

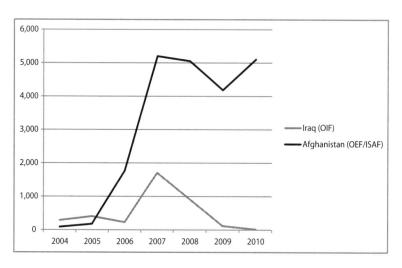

Figure 4. US CAS strike munitions dropped, Afghanistan and Iraq, 2004–10
The figure shows the number of US close air support sorties/missions that dropped munitions in Afghanistan and Iraq from 2004 to 2010, which for various reasons rose from less than 200 strikes in 2005 to around 5,000 from 2007 onward. This figure does not include close air support strikes from other contributing nations. (Data compiled from Cordesman, *US Airpower in Iraq and Afghanistan: 2004–2007*; Cordesman and Allison, *U.S. Air War in Iraq, Afghanistan, and Pakistan;* and Shachtman, "Afghan Air War Hits 3-Year Low.")

U.S. Intelligence, Surveillance, Reconnaissance Sorties 2004–2011

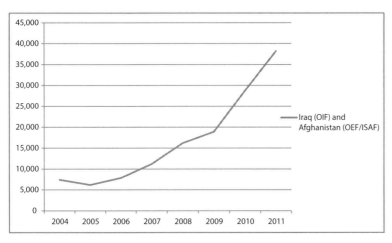

Figure 5. US ISR Sorties, Afghanistan and Iraq, 2004–11
A sortie is defined as a flight of a manned/unmanned military aircraft on a mission. Figure 5 shows the number of US sorties flown on ISR missions in Afghanistan and Iraq from 2004 to 2010, which for various reasons rose from roughly 6,200 in 2005 to more than 38,000 in 2011. This does not include ISR sorties from other contributing nations. With the United States gradually pulling out of Iraq and formally ending its military engagement there in December 2011, the overwhelming preponderance of ISR sorties by the end of this period were in Afghanistan. (Data compiled from Cordesman, *US Airpower in Iraq and Afghanistan: 2004–2007*; Cordesman and Allison, *The U.S. Air War in Iraq, Afghanistan, and Pakistan*; and Shachtman, "Afghan Air War Hits 3-Year Low.")

Bibliography

Air Force Doctrine Document (AFDD) 3-1. *Air Warfare*, 22 January 2000.

Bergen, Peter L. *The Longest War: The Enduring Conflict between America and Al-Qaeda*. New York: Free Press, 2011.

Bonk, David. *St Mihiel 1918: The American Expeditionary Forces' Trial by Fire*. Oxford, UK: Osprey Publishing, 2011.

Boyne, Walter J. "The St. Mihiel Salient." *Air Force Magazine*, February 2000.

Bradley, Rusty, and Kevin Maurer. *Lions of Kandahar*. New York: Bantam Books, 2011.

Builder, Carl H. *The Icarus Syndrome: The Role of Air Power Theory in the Evolution and Fate of the U.S. Air Force*. New Brunswick, NJ: Transaction Publishers, 1994.

Burke, Jason. *The 9/11 Wars*. New York and London: Allen Lane, Penguin Books, 2011.

Bush, George W. *Decision Points*. New York: Crown Publishers, 2010.

Corum, James S. "Airpower Thought in Continental Europe between the Wars." In *The Paths of Heaven*, edited by Phillip S. Meilinger, 151–82.

Cowper-Coles, Sherard. *Cables from Kabul: The Inside Story of the West's Afghanistan Campaign*. New York: Harper Press, 2012.

Day, Adam. "Operation Medusa: The Battle for Panjwai." *Legion Magazine*, 1 September 2007.

Drew, Dennis M. "Air Theory, Air Force, and Low Intensity Conflict: A Short Journey to Confusion." In *The Paths of Heaven*, edited by Phillip S. Meilinger, 321–56.

Faber, Peter R. "Interwar US Army Aviation and the Air Corps Tactical School: Incubators of American Airpower." In *The Paths of Heaven*, edited by Phillip S. Meilinger, 183–228.

Fair, C. Christine. "'Clear, Build, Hold, Transfer': Can Obama's Afghan Strategy Work?" *Asian Affairs: An American Review* 37, no. 3 (2010): 113–31.

Fall, Bernard B. "The Theory and Practice of Insurgency and Counterinsurgency." *Naval War College Review*, Winter 1998. http://www.au.af.mil/au/awc/awcgate/navy/art5-w98.htm.

Gates, Robert M. *Duty: Memoirs of a Secretary at War*. New York: Alfred A. Knopf, 2014.

Gentile, Gian P. *How Effective Is Strategic Bombing? Lessons Learned from World War II to Kosovo*. New York: New York University Press, 2001.

Grau, Lester W., and Dodge Billingsley. *Operation Anaconda: America's First Major Battle in Afghanistan*. Lawrence: University Press of Kansas, 2011.

Gray, Colin S. *Airpower for Strategic Effect*. Maxwell AFB, AL: Air University Press, 2012.

Hallas, James H. *Squandered Victory: The American First Army at St. Mihiel*. Westport, CT: Praeger, 1995.

Hope, Ian. *Dancing with the Dushman*. Kingston: Canadian Defence Academy Press, 2008.

Horn, Bernd. *No Lack of Courage: Operation Medusa, Afghanistan*. Toronto: Dundurn Press, 2010.

Johnson, David E. *Learning Large Lessons: The Evolving Roles of Ground Power and Air Power in the Post–Cold War Era*. Santa Monica, CA: RAND Corp., 2007.

Joint Publication (JP) 1-02. *Department of Defense Dictionary of Military and Associated Terms*, 12 April 2000 (as amended through April 2010).

JP 3-09.3. *Joint Tactics, Techniques, and Procedures for Close Air Support (CAS)*, 3 September 2003. http://www.bits.de/NRANEU/others/jp-doctrine/jp3_09_3(03).pdf.

JP 3-30. *Command and Control for Joint Air Operations*, 12 January 2010.

Kilcullen, David. "Twenty-Eight Articles: Fundamentals of Company-Level Counterinsurgency." *Iosphere*, Summer 2006, 29–35. http://www.au.af.mil/info-ops/iosphere/iosphere_summer06_kilcullen.pdf.

Kugler, Richard L., Michael Baranick, and Hans Binnendijk. *Operation Anaconda: Lessons for Joint Operations*. Washington, DC: Center for Technology and National Security Policy, National Defense University, 2009.

Lauderbaugh, George M. "The Air Battle of St. Mihiel." Air campaign planning process background paper. Maxwell AFB, AL: Airpower Research Institute, n.d.

Lyle, David J. "Operation Anaconda: Lessons Learned, or Lessons Observed?" Master's thesis, Fort Leavenworth, KS, 2009.

MacIsaac, David. "Voices from the Central Blue: The Airpower Theorists." In *Makers of Modern Strategy: From Machiavelli to the Nuclear*

Age, edited by Peter Paret, 624–47. Princeton, NJ: Princeton University Press, 1986.

Meilinger, Phillip S., ed. *The Paths of Heaven: The Evolution of Airpower Theory.* Maxwell AFB, AL: Air University Press, 1997.

Mortenson, Greg, and David Oliver Relin. *Three Cups of Tea: One Man's Mission to Promote Peace . . . One School at a Time.* New York: Penguin Books, 2007.

Olsen, John A. *A History of Air Warfare.* Washington, DC: Potomac Books, 2010.

———. *Strategic Airpower in Desert Storm.* Portland, OR: Frank Cass, 2003.

Pape, Robert A. *Bombing to Win: Air Power and Coercion in War.* Ithaca, NY: Cornell University Press, 1996.

Pinter, William E. *Air-Ground Integration in the 21st Century: Improving Air Force Combat Capabilities and Theater Command and Control for Major Combat Operations and Irregular Warfare.* Maxwell AFB, AL: Air War College, Air University, 2009.

Strachan, Hew. *The Direction of War: Contemporary Strategy in Historical Perspective.* Cambridge, UK: Cambridge University Press, 2013.

Tashner, Michael J. "Examples of Airmindedness from America's First Operational Air Campaign: The St. Mihiel Offensive, 1918." Air Command and Staff College, Maxwell AFB, AL, March 1997.

US Army Field Manual 3-24 (US Marine Corps Warfighting Publication 3-33.5). *Counterinsurgency*, 15 December 2006. http://army pubs.army.mil/doctrine/DR_pubs/DR_a/pdf/fm3_24.pdf.

Woodward, Bob. *Obama's Wars.* New York: Simon & Schuster, 2010.

Index